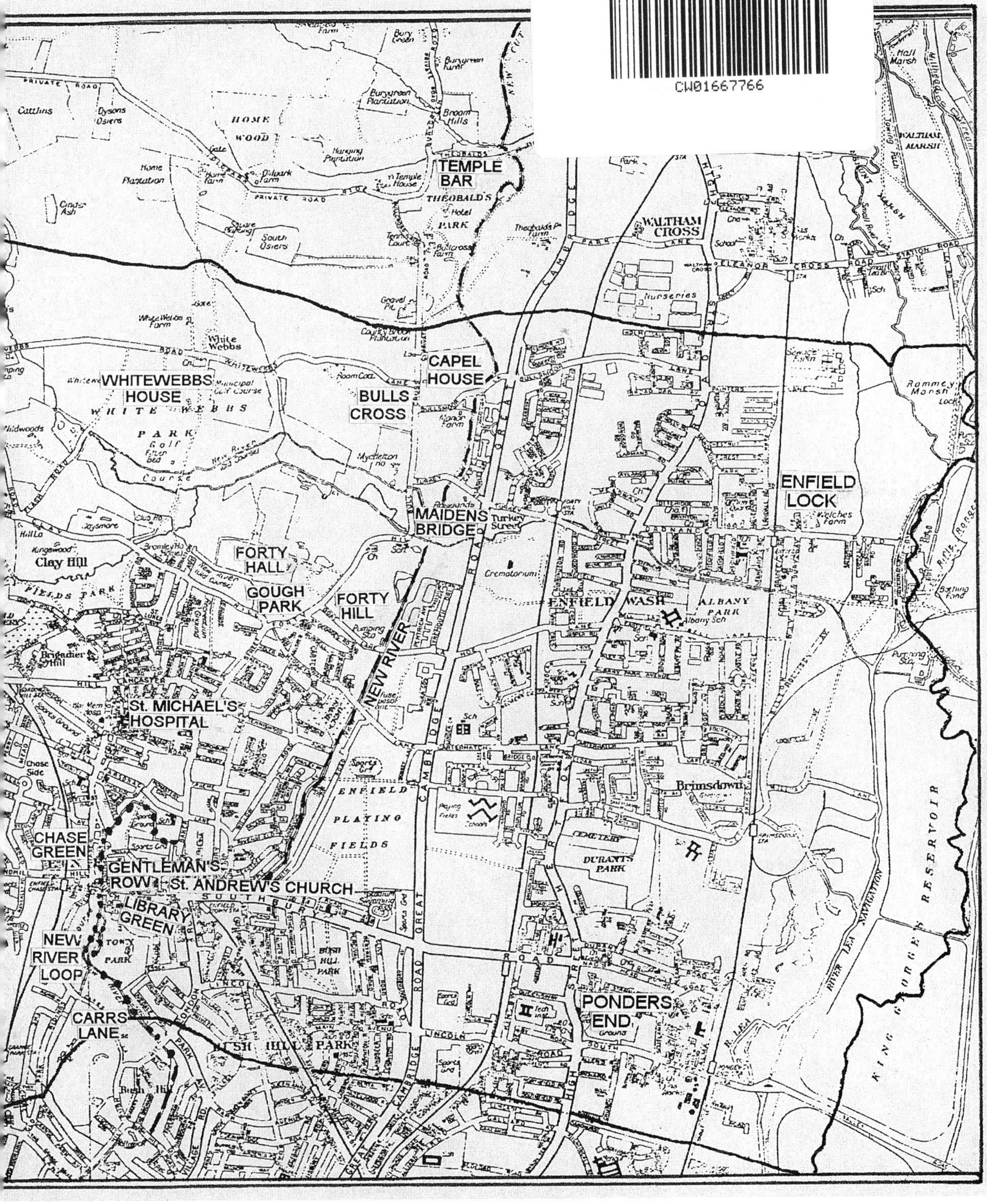
TEMPLE BAR
THEOBALD'S PARK
WALTHAM CROSS
CAPEL HOUSE
WHITEWEBBS HOUSE
BULLS CROSS
WHITE WEBBS PARK
ENFIELD LOCK
MAIDENS BRIDGE
FORTY HALL
Clay Hill
GOUGH PARK
FORTY HILL
ENFIELD WASH
ALBANY PARK
NEW RIVER
St. MICHAEL'S HOSPITAL
Brimsdown
ENFIELD PLAYING FIELDS
CHASE GREEN
GENTLEMAN'S ROW
St. ANDREW'S CHURCH
DURANTS PARK
LIBRARY GREEN
NEW RIVER LOOP
BUSH HILL PARK
CARRS LANE
PONDERS END
KING GEORGE'S RESERVOIR
RIVER LEA NAVIGATION
GREAT CAMBRIDGE ROAD

The Story of Enfield Preservation Society
1936-1996

FIGHTING for the FUTURE

There was a public outcry in August 1937 when Enfield Council decided to sell the Library Green as a site for shops. Following a strong campaign led by the Preservation Society, the sale was dropped. This cartoon appeared in the Enfield Gazette *on 20 August 1937.*

FIGHTING
for the
FUTURE

The Story of Enfield Preservation Society
1936-1996

by
Valerie Carter

Enfield Preservation Society

This book is dedicated to the memory of Irene Smith MBE (1932-1996)
Honorary Secretary of Enfield Preservation Society 1969-1996

ISBN 0 907318 15 0

Published by Enfield Preservation Society Ltd,
107 Parsonage Lane, Enfield, Middlesex EN2 0AB

Registered Charity No 276451

Designed and produced by J. A. Robey, Mayfield Books, Ashbourne, Derbyshire

Printed in the UK by
The Cromwell Press Ltd
Broughton Gifford, Wiltshire

Contents

	Foreword by David Bellamy	6
1.	'Something should be done ...'	7
2.	The Save Enfield Campaign	26
3.	Setting the Pace	41
4.	Keeping Our Character	53
5.	Defending the Green Belt	64
6.	Traffic Takes its Toll	76
7.	The Town in Turmoil	86
8.	Heritage at Risk	100
9.	Attacks From All Quarters	111
10.	Unlocking the Countryside	126
11.	Operation Clean-Up	142
12.	Rescuing the New River	156
13.	Planting & Perseverance	171
14.	The Changing Scene	189
15.	Spreading the Word	204
16.	The Whitewebbs Affair	212
17.	Broomfield & Other Battles	226
18.	Threat of the Superstores	245
19.	As Others See Us	263
	Appendices	
	1. Officers of the Enfield Preservation Society	279
	2. Enfield Preservation Society Publications	281
	Acknowledgements	282
	List of Subscribers	283
	Index	287

Foreword

Sparrows can sing, and this is a song of the triumph of right over wrong. Enfield Preservation Society is sixty years young and its members are still hard at work doing their utmost to preserve their local heritage. This is a truly remarkable account of real people fighting for their patch, all that is left of the heart of a once rural parish, which could have been totally annihilated by the ogre of urban development. Engulfed it may have been by the concrete and tarmacadam of London's suburban sprawl, but its heart still lives on thanks to local people who cared enough, not only to stand up and fight apathy and bureaucracy, but to roll up their sleeves and get down to real hard labour, restoring their past and planting a more hopeful future for their children and grandchildren.

It all started in earnest in 1937 when the Council decided to sell the Library Green as a site ripe for development for shops. Public opinion, orchestrated by the EPS, said 'No' and won the day. What is it about government in all its forms that so often puts power above the good of the people that gave it the franchise? The battle cry is always 'progress', but what really drives the whole process on is the power of money - all too often jargonised as political expediency. More rates mean more money for education and health care, commercial rents are higher, more people are attracted to the town. Cars make things happen faster: roads are widened, down come the trees, horsepower has no need of ponds or rivers. Traffic congestion and polluted air is the result. A ring road is seen as the answer, complete with infill and out of town shopping malls.

All of a sudden the town becomes devoid of the only reason there was for its existence — a close-knit society of people. No wonder the young find their solace in glue, graffiti, vandalism and amusement arcades. The latter certainly never came to fruition in the heart of Enfield, which still beats at a slower pace, giving hope for the future as it has since St Andrew's was built in the fourteenth century.

This is a diamond jubilee of a book, a social history with a difference. It is a celebration of suburban society as it should be and could be, for it is my belief that the green renaissance is at last beginning to happen. More and more ordinary people are questioning the course of so-called progress and the throw-away society. Urban society has begun to come of age, as people from every walk of life stand together on picket lines and demand a new ethic of governance and a place for people in the heritage that links all our pasts with all our futures. This book is a testament to these changing times.

I beg all those faced with similar problems to read and re-read Chapter 18 and find out how local RAGE beat a Rank outsider — so much so that their spokesman said 'We will certainly not be trying to move back into Enfield in the forseeable future'. Then read on and see the problems facing Enfield and every other town in the country as we approach the next millennium. Rejoice in the endeavours of Enfield Preservation Society. Take heart, for you are not alone and there is no need to reinvent the wheel of social protest — every cog has been crafted to perfection in Enfield. Read all about it, then follow suit. Gather your own forces about you to protect your historic heritage and your green belt, and to encourage good design in all new developments that could affect you and your neighbours.

DAVID BELLAMY
Bedburn, October 1969

Chapter 1
'Something should be done ...'

Stand at the centre of Enfield Town, beside the 14th century parish church dedicated to St Andrew, and you could be at the hub of a market town in any prosperous English shire. Leading out of the cobbled square, a passageway alongside the Tudor grammar school joins a network of shaded footpaths that cross the churchyard. They take you towards elegant 17th and 18th century houses, set amid peaceful public gardens and the ancient waters of the New River. Yet remarkably, this tranquil backwater lies only yards from one of the main shopping streets in a busy London suburb. Had it not been for the efforts of Enfield Preservation Society, much of it would have been destroyed long ago. The same fate would have been dealt to the picturesque Library Green nearby, together with historic Chase Green, numerous ancient buildings, fine trees and acres of green belt countryside across the borough. The fact that so much of Enfield's heritage has survived, to be enjoyed by new generations, is silent tribute to years of effort by the Preservation Society's dedicated campaigners.

It was in December 1935 that a group of earnest and well-meaning leaders of the community decided something should be done to protect the ancient buildings and quiet retreats in their home town. The body they formed became so involved in safeguarding the development of the old parish of Enfield that the history of the Preservation Society and that of the Town are inextricably interwoven. Step by step the parish which had grown into a suburb was elevated into a borough, and was then dragooned into amalgamation with neighbouring Edmonton and Southgate. Yet through all these changes the old Enfield for which the Preservation Society claims guardianship has retained its identity, its character and much of its beauty.

In 1935 the Great Cambridge Road, still a single carriageway, formed an effective east/west divide as it sliced through the urban district of Enfield. Most of the local heavy industry was concentrated in eastern Enfield, where the houses were modest in size, public parks were few and far between, and only a handful of the once prolific nursery gardens remained in business. To the west lay spacious semi-detached and detached houses, landscaped parks and rolling acres of farmland, at that time unprotected by green belt legislation. The huge expanse of Trent Park was privately owned, glasshouses covered much of Crews Hill, Bulls Cross remained a peaceful hamlet, only a few houses had been built on the Willow estate. But the whole district was changing fast. Road traffic was increasing, houses were being built at the rate of more than 2,000 a year, and factories for the expanding electrical industry were springing up on the east side of the Cambridge Road.

Between 1921 and1931 the population of Middlesex had increased more rapidly than that of any other county in England and Wales. Throughout the 1930s the growth was

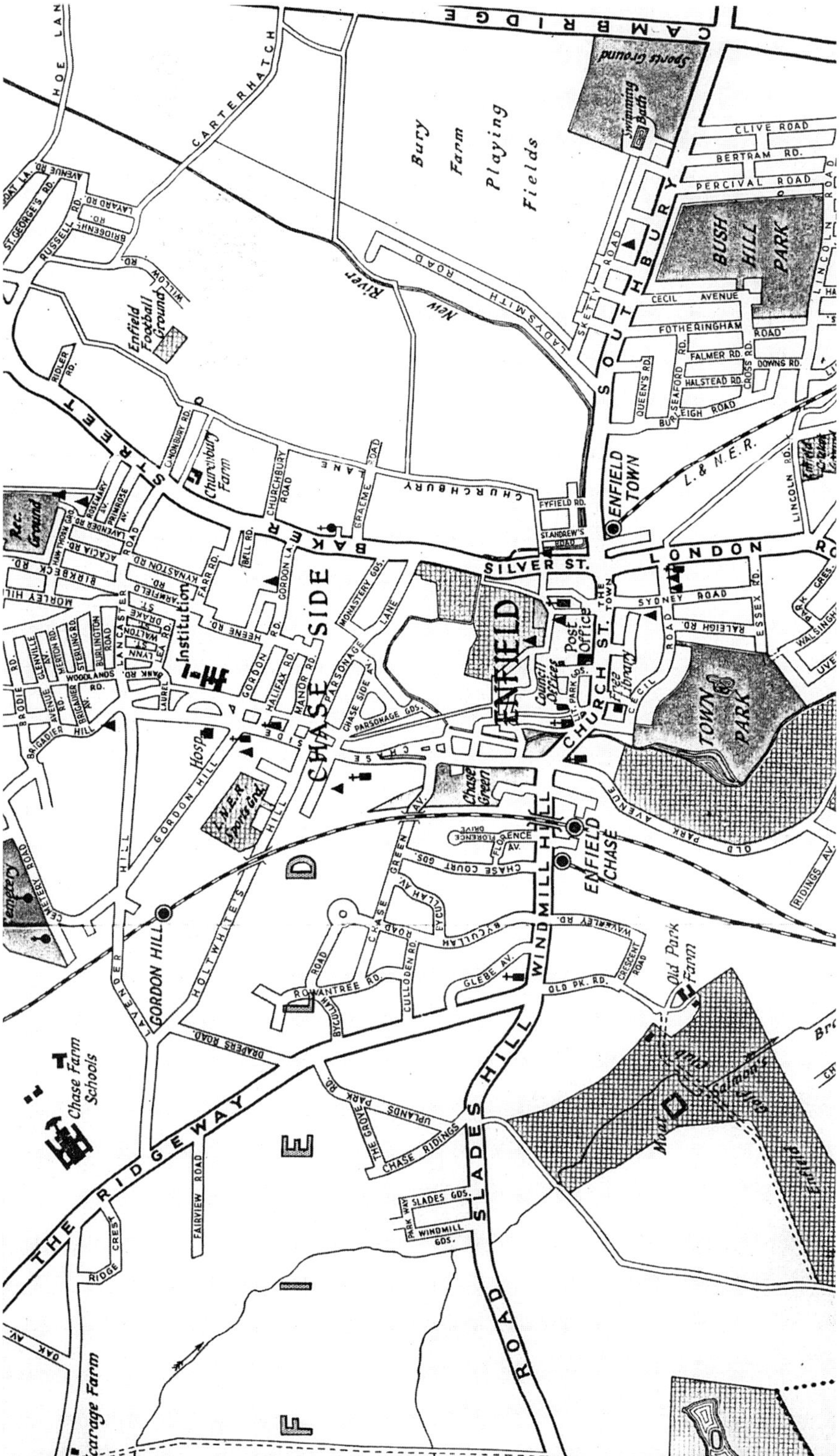

Map showing Enfield Town and the surrounding area in the mid-thirties. None of the respectable estates which now cover the former fiels between Baker Street and the New River had yet been built. Enfield football ground at Cherry Lane and Churchbury Farm are shown.

even greater, with roughly 1,000 people pouring into the county every week. Large tracts of agricultural land became covered by housing and industrial estates, irrevocably altering the face of the countryside. By the mid-1930s many of Enfield's leading citizens had become seriously alarmed as they saw green spaces disappearing, roads being widened, ancient buildings demolished and trees cut down in the onrush of urbanisation. Enfield Urban District Council was preparing an Enfield Town Plan to determine the pattern of future development in the district. It was also seeking a site for a Town Hall. The council had proposed that this should be built on Chase Green, a jealously guarded vestige of Enfield Chase, the ancient royal hunting ground which had come to the parish by the 1803 Inclosure Act when common rights on the Chase were finally abolished. This threat crystallised local fears that Enfield was in danger of losing some of its most cherished features to the tide of supposed progress.

Chase Green provided a pleasing approach to the Town of which Enfield people were justly proud. Even the railway company had been obliged to make special plantings on the embankment across the green and to erect a red brick bridge of fine proportions over Chase Green Avenue. Since 1803 the green had been the popular setting for parish cricket, May Day celebrations and brass band concerts. Now it was under threat.

Early in 1935 posters appeared, inviting the citizens of Enfield to a public meeting in the Oddfellows Hall, Old Park Avenue, to protest against the proposal to erect a Town Hall on 'the people's land'. According to the *Enfield Gazette* of 15 February 1935: 'The champions of Chase Green gathered in force. With Sir Henry Bowles of Forty Hall as their leader and Col. Applin (the Member of Parliament for Enfield) the Revd Geoffrey Daisley (Vicar of Enfield) the Revd Ebenezer Rees (of Christ Church, Chase Side) and Mr Dudley Leggatt of Little Park, Gentleman's Row as able lieutenants, they registered their

1. Brass band concerts were a popular entertainment on Chase Green, 'the people's land', at the turn of the century. The bandstand stood on the site now occupied by the war memorial.

2. Colonel R. V. K. Applin MP, accompanied by Percy Leggatt, inspecting members of the Boys Brigade.

determination to fight to preserve this historic beauty spot'. The meeting was packed to the doors and a number of people had to stand. Col. Applin announced that he had been to see the Minister of Health (whose department had responsibility for local government) and had received a sympathetic hearing about Chase Green. A resolution, adopted 'with tremendous applause' stated: 'This meeting learns with regret that the Urban District Council propose to erect public offices together with a Town Hall on Chase Green, and protests against the general public being deprived of the last remaining portion of the old Enfield Chase'. After the meeting more than 1,000 people signed a petition against the council's proposal. Two months later Mr Daisley voiced his concern at a meeting of Enfield Rotary Club. He suggested a society should be formed on the lines of the Cambridge Preservation Society which had been established for about five years. The aim was not to stop change, but to make sure it did not interfere with the natural beauties and amenities of the district, he said. His fellow Rotarians, who included Ebenezer Rees and Dudley Leggat, were sympathetic. In due course more than 20 local worthies received a letter which began: 'Of recent years the ancient and historic buildings and beauty spots of and around Enfield have been rapidly disappearing and a number of residents have expressed a feeling that ...something should be done in an endeavour to preserve, as far as possible, what is still left.' They were invited to a meeting 'to discuss the possibility of inaugurating an Enfield Preservation Society'.

That meeting took place on 13 December 1935 in the Tudor Room at Little Park,

3. Dudley Leggatt, who played a leading part in the campaign to save Chase Green, lived with his brothers at Little Park, Gentleman's Row. The five Leggatt brothers, who were well-known in the art world, had an extension — the Tudor Room — built onto their house to accommodate an ornate ceiling, fine panelling and a carved overmantel and fireplace taken from the former Enfield 'Palace' when it was demolished to make way for Pearson's department store. Four of the Leggatt brothers remained bachelors and lived in Gentleman's Row all their lives, Dudley (the youngest) surviving until 1952. Standing, Ernest and Martin; sitting, Percy and Dudley.

Gentleman's Row. Those present included T. H. M. Clarke, chairman of Enfield UDC, Stanley Woodfield, president of the Rotary Club, and W. J. Muldoon, chairman of the Chamber of Commerce. A letter of support was read from Col. Sir Henry Bowles of Forty Hall. According to the minutes, Mr Daisley, who was elected chairman of the meeting, 'said he thought sufficient ancient buildings and beauty spots remained to justify the formation of this Society, instancing the oasis round the Parish Church and Market Place, the surroundings of the river near Chase Green, and Forty Hall'. Frank Vanderpump, a local solicitor, explained somewhat optimistically that it would probably cost about £25 to start the Society (he revised his estimate to £40 at the next meeting). Those present agreed to guarantee this sum and 'it was then carried, on the proposal of Mr Woodfield, seconded by Mr Leggatt, that the formation of the Enfield Preservation Society should be proceeded with'. Stanley Adlard was elected honorary secretary and Frank Vanderpump was asked to prepare the Memorandum and Articles of Association. The new organisation was determined to get off to a prestigious start. It was decided to invite the Lord Lieutenant of Middlesex, the chairman of Middlesex County Council (MCC), the chairman of Enfield UDC, the chairman of Enfield education committee, the president of the Rotary Club, and the chairmen of the Chamber of Commerce and the Enfield District Manufacturers' Association to become ex-officio members of the council of management. It was

4. Revd Geoffrey Daisley, Vicar of Enfield and first chairman of Enfield Preservation Society.

also agreed to ask 27 prominent townsfolk to be members of the first council. Those who accepted were E. E. Ashton, Col. Sir Henry Bowles, H. H. Collier, W. B. Cranfield, Revd G. W. Daisley, E. M. Eagles, A. C. Fincken, Revd E. H. A. Koch, Dudley Leggatt, Col. Sydney Medcalfe, Horace Muspratt, R. G. Porter, Dr Proudlock Dunbar, Revd E. Rees, Sir Philip Sassoon, P. W. Smith, Frank Surgey, Kenneth Tansley, Dr B. M. Toop, F. L. Vanderpump, A. R. Wiseman and J. P. Shewring. The only woman invited, Mrs Horace Short, declined to stand, as did E. A. Bowles.

When the council of management met for the first time, on 9 March 1936, Mr Daisley was elected chairman with John Shewring as treasurer and Stanley Adlard as secretary. It was decided to register Enfield Preservation Society as a Limited Company (this was done on 26 March). A committee was appointed to draw up 'an explanatory circular' to recruit members, and to organise a public meeting. Determined that the Society should have the stamp of authority, it was later agreed that six titled gentlemen and the local MP (Bartle Bull) should be invited as speakers, and that this first public meeting, to be held in the Oddfellows Hall on 30 April, should close with the national anthem.

The council of management evidently saw Enfield Preservation Society as an elite organisation. The annual membership subscription was fixed at 10s 6d (equivalent to nearly £15 today) with life membership at £5. The less affluent were assured that associate membership could be 'secured by payment of an annual sum of any amount, large or small, with a minimum of one shilling.' The first membership form quoted one simple aim and object: 'To endeavour to preserve the Historic Buildings and Beauties of Enfield'. An outline of 'the work of the Society' followed. These four principles (with a few amendments) were later adopted as the aims and objects of the Preservation Society.

The work of the Society is to endeavour

1 to preserve for the benefit of the public the amenities of the district of Enfield
2 to protect from dilapidation, disfigurement or destruction any place or building in or

5. *Enfield Town in the early Thirties showing St Andrew's Church, Enfield Grammar School, the Rialto cinema and the Tottenham Gas Company offices facing Barclays Bank at the entrance to the Market Place. The fields in the background were soon to be covered by the Willow estate.*

6. In June 1936 the EPS chairman said Church Street had 'altered out of all recognition in recent years'. In the late Thirties (above) Spikin's jeweller's shop stood on the eastern corner of Palace Gardens, next to the Maypole Dairy. On the western corner was Parkes the chemist, then the Wall-paper Stores, Randall's boots and shoes, Willmott's hairdressing and 'perm shop', the French Cleaning & Dyeing Co. Ltd., and Dorothy Perkins.

near Enfield which is of beauty or historic interest

3 to protect from injury the views of and from Enfield and its neighbourhood

4 to preserve and maintain footpaths, commons and rights of way in and around Enfield.

Over the years there have been criticisms that the Society's name implies an opposition to change. Mr Daisley told the Chamber of Commerce in June 1936: 'We call ourselves the Enfield Preservation Society because our primary aim is to preserve everything that is historically interesting and of natural beauty in Enfield. But we have no intention of stopping progress; on the contrary we aim at taking a hand in creative construction for the future'. The *Enfield Gazette* reported the speech and carried an enthusiastic leading article. 'Despite the fact that the appearance of Enfield's main shopping centres has altered out of all recognition during the past few years and that in other parts peaceful fields and orchards have given place to streets of houses, Enfield still possesses, as the Vicar aptly described, a living soul', it said. 'Enfield Preservation Society has undertaken to try and keep the vital sparks of that soul afire. Enfieldians feel a pride that in the midst of rapid urbanisation the district has not developed into the characterless suburb so frequently found in the environs of London. Posterity will be indebted to Enfield Preservation Society if it succeeds ... the medieval atmosphere and rural aspect should be retained for all time ... they are the district's heirlooms and as such must be treasured and preserved in order that future generations may revel in their beauty and reap full benefit from these amenities.'

Within weeks, the Preservation Society was embroiled in its first campaign. In August

7. The Preservation Society soon established a reputation as a champion of local amenities, as shown by this cartoon which appeared in the Enfield Gazette *in May 1936.*

it was confirmed that Enfield Urban District Council favoured Chase Green as the site for a new Town Hall. The EPS voiced strong opposition and promised to do everything in its power to preserve Chase Green as an open space. Public opinion was mobilised, deputations sent, letters of protest written, and in January 1937 the Society was informed that the council had 'resolved to take no further action in regard to the proposal to use part of Chase Green as a site for a Civic Centre'. However, the battle was not yet won.

Within months, Enfield Council had cast its predatory eyes on the Library Green in Church Street and in August 1937 it took the controversial decision to sell the green as a site for shops. The Library Green, with its fine trees, was once part of the garden of Chase Side House, the home for many years of Phillip Twells, MP for the City of London and a partner in the banking firm which became Barclays Bank. He died in 1880 and on the death of his widow in 1901 the council bought 23 acres of the estate for £13,000 to form Enfield's first park — the Town Park. The following year the Library Green was purchased for £5,200 as a site for the Town Hall, but by 1937 many considered the plot too small for that purpose. The Preservation Society protested against the decision to sell the green, urging that it should be kept as a permanent open space. A letter was written to the Minister of Health and local lobbying was begun. In October a deputation from the EPS was received by the council, which nevertheless decided, by seven votes to six, to apply to the Minister of Health for permission to sell the green. Local opposition intensified, led by the Preservation Society and its chairman Geoffrey Daisley. He was fond of describing the Library Green as a beautiful gateway into the centre of the town and one of the jewels of Enfield. Sixty years on, EPS members will endorse his frequently quoted opinion that 'We demur to the idea that Enfield is in such financial difficulties that it must sell its diamonds'.

As local opposition increased, the Enfield Residents' Association called a public meeting, on the strict understanding that it would not be described as a 'protest' meeting. But after hearing a persuasive speech by the Preservation Society chairman, the association,

8. The Library Green, an oasis in Church Street, now protected as Metropolitan Open Land.

9. Rear view of Silverdale, Silver Street, the house bought by Enfield Council in November 1938 (with the neighbouring Fir Tree House) as a site for the Town Hall. The roof of White Lodge, Silver Street, can be seen on the left.

together with the Chamber of Commerce, agreed to share with the EPS the cost of retaining counsel to oppose Enfield Council at the forthcoming Ministry of Health inquiry. The Preservation Society now began tackling the MCC, suggesting the County Council should take over the site as a permanent open space. The public inquiry was held in January 1938. Enfield Preservation Society's counsel was well briefed and spoke forcefully. His fees left the Society's funds depleted, but the expense was well vindicated when three months later the Minister of Health, Kingsley Wood, announced that 'in view of the strong opposition' he was withholding his consent to the council's proposal to sell the site. Enfield Council was informed that the MCC was willing to make a contribution towards retaining the Library Green as an open space, but it refused to give up, and in May the EPS council of management was shown plans for municipal buildings and a Town Hall on the Library Green. These were firmly rejected and members reiterated the Society's determination that the green should be preserved as a perpetual open space. A few months later Enfield Council tried a different and more devious approach. At the September meeting of the EPS council of management the chairman announced that the Clerk to the Council (S. J. Dabbs) and another council official (Mr Lee) had intended to be present, to inquire whether the Preservation Society would consent to a Town Hall being built on Chase Green by the side of the railway line 'subject to the library site being declared an open space for ever'. In the absence of the two gentlemen, who were unable to attend 'owing to war preparations work' the proposal was firmly rejected. Thanks to the Society's intransigence then, and over the intervening years, both open spaces remain

10. Colonel Sir Henry Bowles, who inherited Forty Hall and its estate from his father. The property later passed to his grandson, Derek Parker Bowles, who sold it to Enfield Council.

intact to this day. Chase Green and the Library Green now have added protection in their designation as Metropolitan Open Land. In 1938 the total membership of the Preservation Society was only 130, but its influence was already considerable. The search for a Town Hall site came to an end in November 1938 when the council decided to buy, by compulsory purchase, two large properties (Fir Tree House and Silverdale) in Silver Street, where the Civic Centre now stands.

The Preservation Society had earlier expressed disquiet at several aspects of the council's town planning scheme. Sir Henry Bowles, the owner of Forty Hall and its estate, complained in a letter to Stanley Adlard that 'Enfield UDC are always altering their proposals' for the scheme (which had already been in preparation for nine years). The Society was particularly concerned to safeguard Forty Hill which it regarded as 'now the one unspoilt tract of the old rural Enfield'. The town planning scheme proposed that land at Forty Hill should be zoned at twelve houses to the acre. Somewhat surprisingly, instead of urging that there should be no development at all in this vulnerable area, a letter was sent to the council in September 1936 stating: 'This Society is of the opinion that the land on both sides of the road at Forty Hill should be zoned at four houses to the acre and is satisfied that two of the principal owners of the frontage lands, viz. Col. Sir Henry Bowles and the Rev. E. Koch [Vicar of Jesus Church, Forty Hill] would be ready to concur in this proposal, provided that the other owner, Mr Hollington [of Clock House] would also agree'. The secretary was instructed to approach Mr Hollington, but whether he did so is not recorded.

A site in Chase Side was also causing concern. Enfield Council was trying to resist a proposal to build 24 three-storied flats on a large plot behind no. 75, where, according to the town planning scheme, development was limited to 12 houses to the acre. The vacant land ran behind Chase Side Place and the Cricketers public house, extending to the New River Loop beside the cottages opposite the Crown & Horseshoes. The EPS strongly supported the council's opposition and the Minister of Health turned down the proposal. Many years later, Parsonage Gardens was extended and two-storey maisonettes were built on this land.

Some months earlier, the Preservation Society had protested that proposals to widen Silver Street from Church Street to Churchbury Lane would involve cutting down mature trees and the probable demolition of the Vicarage and White Lodge. The council reconsidered, and informed the Society in August 1937 that 'the scheme will not affect the Vicarage or White Lodge as the proposed widening is on the east side, ie on the opposite side to that originally intended'. After further lengthy correspondence with Enfield Council and the County Council it was agreed that the belt of trees adjoining the frontage of Enfield Grammar (Lower) School would be preserved, with the road pavement resited behind them.

Files of meticulous, hand-written letters in the EPS archives show that then, as now, it often took months — even years — of dogged perseverance to achieve a result. In June 1937 the Preservation Society asked the council to remove an unsightly advertisement from the railway bridge over Windmill Hill. It was not until June 1940 that the secretary was able to record 'with great satisfaction' that the advertisement had been taken down and the ornamental character of the bridge restored. Blue police telephone boxes (which later found fame as the inspiration for Doctor Who's 'Tardis') were installed in Enfield in 1935, often with little thought for the surroundings. They are now regarded with nostalgia, but in their time they were as unpopular as the modern bottle banks. A police telephone box was deposited without warning in front of St John's Church, Clay Hill, blocking

11. White Lodge, easily the best 18th century weatherboarded house in Enfield, could have been demolished in 1937 to permit the widening of Silver Street, had the Preservation Society not protested. The EPS subsequently chose White Lodge as recipient for its first listed buildings plaque and as the subject for the Society's first local view postcard.

the view of the newly-restored lychgate. It took 18 months of letter-writing by the Preservation Society to get it moved to a less obtrusive position 'in the tea garden of the Fallow Buck'. Taking tea at this rural public house was evidently a popular local outing. In May 1937 Sir Henry Bowles notified the EPS council of management that the Fallow Buck might lose its licence the following year. He suggested the Preservation Society should buy the pub 'and keep it as a Tea House'. The council of management flirted briefly with the idea, but reason prevailed, and it was eventually decided to support Cannon Brewery's application for renewal of the licence, 'provided the weatherboarded building is not replaced by a modern structure'.

This was still a time of great contrast. Enfield's rateable value had doubled in less than ten years and general prosperity was increasing, but a steady stream of between 60 and 70 vagrants could be seen trudging through the district every day. They were mostly young men who had left home to seek work, and who now found shelter each night in casual wards at the workhouse in Bull Lane, Edmonton, adjoining the North Middlesex Hospital. At the Preservation Society's first annual meeting in June 1937 a resolution was passed stating that members were 'greatly disturbed' to learn that Middlesex County Council

12. Parishioners at St John's Church, Clay Hill, were incensed when a police telephone box was installed in front of the new lychgate at the church entrance in 1935. After 18 months of letter writing, the Preservation Society succeeded in getting the police box moved to a less obtrusive position in the garden of the Fallow Buck, just across the road. When this postcard was produced in 1913, the church entrance (behind the lamp-post) was a simple wicket gate.

13. The Fallow Buck, Clay Hill (seen here in the 1920s) had a well-established tea garden in the 1930s.

14. Oak House, Baker Street, built before 1845, was demolished in 1938. Police flats now occupy the site.

intended to build casual wards for 200 vagrants at Enfield House (now St Michael's Hospital) Chase Side, and demanding that everything possible should be done to prevent this. Protests were sent to Enfield Council and the MCC. It is not clear whether any preservation issue was involved, or whether the resolution was prompted by less worthy motives. The MCC intended that the new Enfield wards would replace the accommodation in Bull Lane because the North Middlesex Hospital needed the site for its modernisation programme. The system was that men (the number of women vagrants was negligible) were not admitted to the wards until the late afternoon, so crowds often gathered outside as the day wore on. The men were retained on the following day to carry out various tasks as payment for their board and lodging, and were discharged on the morning of the second day. Enfield Council was also uneasy about the Chase Side accommodation, and following the Preservation Society's resolution representations were made to the MCC and undertakings given. As a result, in December Stanley Adlard was able to reassure local residents, in a letter published in the *Enfield Weekly Herald*, that vagrants would be admitted to the new accommodation at any time of day with no waiting about. He added that as the men would in any case have to pass through Enfield on their journey to Ware (where the next casual ward was situated) it would be an advantage for them to have somewhere to be housed instead of wandering in the district. As it turned out, the Preservation Society's fears were not realised, because preparations for war delayed the work and the accommodation was never built.

Preparations for a possible war became increasingly evident during 1938. Early that year, trenches had been dug across the Library Green, ready for the construction of air-

15. Early in 1939, Enfield Council began digging trenches across the Library Green for use as air raid shelters. Eighteen months later the Preservation Society complained that the trenches had been left open, unfinished and apparently abandoned.

raid shelters. War or no war, the EPS was determined that the green must be protected and in December it protested to the council that the trenches had been left open, unfinished and apparently abandoned. It was not until July 1939, following several more letters, that the Preservation Society received an assurance that the trenches would soon be completed and that every endeavour would be made to improve the appearance of the site. The delay had been caused because Enfield Council had submitted plans for the construction of an underground car park which could also be used as an air-raid shelter. This was rejected, wrote S. J. Dabbs: 'because the Lord Privy Seal is opposed to deep shelters'. His letter continued: 'As, unfortunately, the international situation still imposes the necessity for making provision for the protection of the population, it is considered inadvisable for the trenches to be filled in and the ground restored to its previous condition'. When the international situation deteriorated the trenches were converted into covered shelters, built partly underground, with the excavated soil piled on top.

As war became imminent, Enfield Preservation Society reflected the very real fears of the local population that they would be subjected to devastating bombing raids immediately hostilities were declared. Above all, there was a dread of poison gas attacks. Heroic resolution could not be expected even from the leaders of the community on the EPS council of management. In July 1939 the council of management agreed to protest at the proposal to establish a militia camp on Ridgeway Farm and Vicarage Farm. The minutes list the objections as: '(1) the proximity to Chase Farm Home [now Chase Farm Hospital] which is to be used as a Central Clearing Hospital in time of war, (2) the population of Enfield being over 100,000 and the area including the Royal Small Arms Factory, Gunpowder Factory and many other factories, also the River Lea and large reservoirs, all landmarks for air attack, (3) already "better class" houses exist on all sides of the site except the north-west, and (4) this would extend the danger zone to the whole of Enfield.' It was suggested that a more remote site should be sought.

From the beginning of 1939, meetings of the EPS council of management became less frequent. In July, members had been shocked by the sudden death of the chairman, Geoffrey Daisley, who had inspired the foundation of the Preservation Society. Ebenezer Rees was the automatic and popular choice as successor. Born in Cardiganshire, he had been minister of Christ Church, Chase Side, since 1916 and had formed a deep love for what he described as 'this lovely, little town on the edge of the green belt'. A remarkable preacher-poet, Mr Rees frequently waxed eloquent (in print and from pulpit and platform) about the charms of Enfield and its colourful history, and he had been heavily involved with the Society since its formation.

The destruction which now threatened Enfield from German bombers made the aims of the Preservation Society something of an anachronism and inevitably, support fell away. In 1940, 'owing to the difficulty felt by some of the members in renewing their subscriptions' the annual minimum had to be reduced from 10s.6d to 5s. The following year the council of management agreed 'to invest a further £40 in 3% Defence Bonds, to be purchased in the local War Weapons Week'. Efforts were made to have a monthly news paragraph in the local papers, to keep the public informed of the Preservation Society's activities. However, by 1942 there was little scope for action, although one notable success was achieved. Mrs Hodson, the only woman on the EPS council of management, reported a proposal to remove the decorative Metropolitan Police iron railings round the Old Vestry Offices in Church Street, 'to be used for munitions of war'. The Society sent a vehement letter of protest, demanding that the railings should be retained. They are still in place. Also in 1942, the EPS agreed to affiliate to the Council for the Preservation (now Protection) of Rural England and send a donation of one guinea; locally, subscriptions to the Preservation Society were suspended for the duration of the war. Stanley Adlard, the secretary, resigned on moving away from Enfield. The chairman summed up the situation when he told members at the AGM that 'owing to the continuance of war, there has been little immediate work for the Society to do'. But, he added, 'It must be remembered that the war will not last for ever, so it is vital to keep the Society ready for action when peace returns ... It is hoped that in the replacement of houses and shops demolished by enemy action, the Society may be able to assist the Enfield Urban District Council in securing, as far as possible, that the external appearance of buildings is worthy of Enfield and in keeping with its amenities.'

Nothing more was heard from the Preservation Society until 8 December 1959 when, in the original minute book but written by a different and more flambouyant hand, we read: A meeting of the council of management was held at the offices of Vanderpump & Sykes (by kind permission of Mr Frank Vanderpump) on Tuesday December 8th at 6pm. Present, Revd. E. Rees in the chair, Mr Vanderpump, Mr Shewring, Mr Bennett, Mr Peck, Mr Gowers, Mrs Lane. Apology for absence was received from Dr Toop.' Some of those gentlemen must have had excellent memories, for the minutes blandly continue: 'The chairman read the minutes of the last meeting, which were confirmed ...' The Enfield Preservation Society was in business again.

16. The Lord Mayor of London, Sir Seymour Howard, inspects a guard of honour from the Middlesex Regiment in the flag-decked Market Place on Enfield's Charter Day, 27 September 1955.

17. The Borough of Enfield officially came into being on 23 May 1955 when the newly-elected borough council met for the first time. On 27 September that year, thousands enjoyed a day of pageantry and civic pride when the Lord Mayor visited the borough to present Enfield's first Mayor, Councillor John Cottenham, with the Charter of Incorporation.

To a fanfare of trumpets, the presentation took place on the floodlit stage of the Rialto Cinema in the Market Place, after which civic guests attended a Charter Luncheon in the Grammar School and a service in St Andrew's Church.

In the afternoon, cheering crowds lined the streets to watch the Mayor and Mayoress, in an open carriage, lead a procession of horse-drawn carriages, including the Lord Mayor in his gilded coach, from Enfield Town to Forty Hill. Shown here, the arrival in Forty Hall, where visitors saw an exhibition and watched a display of country dancing by schoolchildren.

Chapter 2
The Save Enfield Campaign

The bold handwriting in the minute book was the work of Carinthia Arbuthnot Lane, who with her husband Clayton (invariably known as Tony) had taken up residence in Gentleman's Row some years after the war. Major and Mrs Lane were to become linchpins of the Enfield Preservation Society throughout its most formative years. In 1959, Mrs Lane noticed white crosses on several of the magnificent trees which towered above the front gardens in Gentleman's Row. On learning that it was proposed to cut down the trees, she organised a protest and wrote a rousing letter to the local press. The trees were saved, and her letter acted as the catalyst that stirred the moribund Preservation Society into action. Ebenezer Rees contacted the surviving members of the council of management, Mrs Lane agreed to become secretary, and since that day the Society has gone from strength to strength.

To consolidate its rebirth, Enfield Preservation Society registered with the Civic Trust, which had been founded two years previously by Duncan Sandys. There was £135 in the funds and it was agreed to spend some of this on advertising, stationery and membership forms. The new membership fee was fixed at 2s 6d, a notice was sent to the *Enfield*

18. Enfield Collegiate School, one of the handsome Victorian houses that once lined London Road, was demolished in the mid-1950s to make way for Salisbury Court flats.

Gazette and the EPS embarked on a recruiting drive. The aims and objects were revised to include the protection of the green belt, which had been established round London in the late 1930s. These aims and objects have remained unchanged:

- to preserve and improve the amenities of Enfield
- defend the green belt from encroachment
- protect any local place or building of beauty and historical interest
- preserve footpaths in and around Enfield
- encourage good design in development in the borough

More than 100 new members were enrolled at a crowded meeting in the Tudor Room in March 1960. Among them were two individuals who almost at once became prominent in the Preservation Society — Don Gresswell, proprietor of a successful bookselling business based in Chase Side, and Donald Potter, a keen-minded insurance actuary living in Gentleman's Row. Before the war the Preservation Society had been top-heavy with local worthies, and when planning the Tudor Room meeting, some members of the council of management had suggested that invitations should be sent to 'local residents of standing'. But times had changed and the minutes state that after some discussion 'it was agreed not to send invitations to local clergymen, etc., who might be interested in the work of the Society'. It was also agreed that the council of management would be elected annually at the AGM, and that the Preservation Society must aim for a wide and representative membership covering the whole of Enfield, which had achieved borough status in 1955. By May 1960 Enfield Preservation Society had nearly 200 members, but Sydney Hills, chairman of the Federation of Enfield Ratepayers' and Residents' Associations, complained at one of his federation meetings that there were no representatives from eastern Enfield on the EPS council of management. A doughty fighter for what he considered to be the deprived part of Enfield, he advised members of FERRA not to join the Preservation Society 'because it was trying to revive a corpse', but to wait and join 'the proposed new amenity society'. On hearing this, the EPS council of management promptly invited Mr Hills to become a co-opted member. He accepted, and remained an active participant for four years. But despite a growing involvement with the eastern part of the borough, the Society for many years had to live with the taunt that it was 'the Enfield Town Preservation Society'.

The 'proposed new amenity society' to which Sydney Hills referred was causing some agitation within the EPS council of management, and the prospect of a rival organisation undoubtedly helped to stiffen the sinews of the growing Preservation Society. Enfield Council had suggested that an amenity society should be formed in the borough to initiate street improvement schemes similar to an innovative project recently carried out in Norwich by the Civic Trust. (The scheme had been inspected by Enfield's Town Clerk, Cyril Platten, who was greatly impressed.) The EPS council of management was dubious. The minutes record that Frank Bennett felt a new amenity society would mean the end of the Enfield Preservation Society, and that 'the word amenity could easily cover such things as expresso bars, rock 'n' roll in the Market Place, a car park on the historic Chase Green, etc., etc.'

Enfield Council's proposals were woolly and unclear, and disagreements about the proposed new organisation rumbled on for well over a year. It was eventually agreed that the body would comprise representatives of local organisations, with no individual membership (a proviso later abandoned) and that it would be called the Enfield Society. It was launched in March 1961, with the Preservation Society as a member. The new body kept going for just over two years. It did its best to initiate face-lift schemes to improve the appearance of neighbourhood shops in parts of Hertford Road and at Forty Hill, but met

19. Sir Seymour Howard, who as Lord Mayor had presented Enfield with its Charter, returned to the borough in 1961 to open the new Civic Centre — still occasionally referred to in the local press as the Town Hall. Here, the mace bearer leads the Mayor (Councillor Ernest Rayment), Sir Seymour, the Town Clerk (Cyril Platten) and other dignitaries to the Civic Centre for the opening ceremony.

20. Enfield's modest Civic Centre in Silver Street, pictured soon after its opening.

with little support from the Chamber of Trade or individual shopkeepers. In October 1963 the *Enfield Weekly Herald* reported that the Enfield Society had written to the Preservation Society, suggesting amalgamation. By that time, the Preservation Society had more than 750 members, whereas the Enfield Society was said to have 82 members, about one-third of whom also belonged to the Preservation Society. The amalgamation was formally approved at a special general meeting of the Preservation Society early in 1964. Robert Dugdale Sykes, chairman of the Enfield Society, was elected a vice-president of Enfield Preservation Society, and local architect William Palmer (a member of the defunct organisation's executive committee) became leader of the EPS architecture and planning group.

Early in 1960, the EPS council of management doggedly resumed its attempts (which had begun in 1936) to receive regular advance copies of Enfield Council's monthly agenda; its persistence was grudgingly rewarded in July 1962 (on payment of one guinea a year). This was a time of great change and development, and the Preservation Society tried without success to obtain a list of 'local preserved buildings and open spaces' so that it could protect vulnerable sites. There had been mixed reactions among townspeople to rumours that the Library Green had been sold to Marks & Spencer. The Society sent letters to the council expressing concern and at the AGM in May 1960 the EPS chairman was able to announce the council's decision to preserve the green as a permanent open space.

Car parking had been a problem in Enfield Town even before the Second World War. In August 1937 the *Enfield Weekly Herald* reported a council plan to slice a strip, 100 feet wide, from the eastern side of the Town Park, for use as a car park. The plan, which involved moving the park gates in Essex Road and felling a considerable number of trees, had caused widespread resentment. It was later dropped, and for the next few years other pressing matters took priority. As Enfield gradually recovered from the effects of the war, more and more vehicles flooded onto local roads and it became clear that something must

21. Trams were still running through Enfield when the Preservation Society was formed. Here, a No.79 drives along Southbury Road en route for Smithfield.

22. In 1938 trolleybuses replaced the tram service through Enfield. The 629, seen here turning from the Town into London Road, went as far as Tottenham Court Road

23. After the Second World War the shortage of parking spaces in Enfield became acute. In 1946 the parking bay outside the George was packed full.

be done, not only to provide more parking space, but to relieve traffic congestion. By 1959, the problem had become urgent. Enfield Town still retained something of the air of a market town, but some new development was obviously needed. Change was in the air and the council found itself faced with an increasing number of planning applications for the redevelopment of properties in the area.

In September 1959 Enfield Council works committee asked the borough engineer to report on the possibility of extending the London Road car park. The following month the council received a petition from the Chamber of Commerce, signed by 30 traders, drawing attention to 'the increasing volume of heavy traffic using Windmill Hill ... which is having an adverse effect on traders in the area'; they also complained about the shortage of car parking spaces in the Town. No action seems to have been taken, and in December 1960 the borough engineer again reported on traffic problems in the town centre. Meanwhile, two major items had surfaced among the routine planning applications — an offer from a developer who wanted to build shops on the Library Green, and a planning application for a large development scheme for the London Road car park and the adjoining land. A master plan for the centre of Enfield had now become essential, and the council instructed the borough engineer, H. Deryck Peake, to prepare a Supplementary Town Map covering an area roughly between Old Park Avenue and Eaton Road (approximately

24. The growing number of family cars added to road congestion and changed shopping habits after the war. Up to 1939 a door-to-door service was provided by individuals like H. A. Hooper, grocer and provision merchant, who from 1929 toured the district with his mobile shop selling a comprehensive range of groceries, cleaning materials and patent medicines. The van is shown outside 34 Halifax Road.

65 acres in total). The plan was produced with more speed than judiciousness. In January 1961, when it was officially launched, it was reported that over 100 maps showing the town centre proposals had already been sold and that an abridged version entitled 'The problems of future development and of car parking in the Enfield Town shopping and commercial centre' was available to the public at 2s 6d. This plan proposed a scheme so destructive of the peace, beauty and history of the ancient village centre of Enfield that the Preservation Society was thrown into consternation and took immediate action.

Mr Peake was invited to explain his scheme at the February meeting of the EPS council of management. He appeared confident that his proposals for a traffic-free shopping precinct would be welcomed, but members' disquiet grew as he produced maps which showed a pedestrianised Church Street encircled by a three-lane highway. To the north, this new road would cut through the ancient graveyard, the grammar school, and the peaceful network of footpaths surrounding St Andrew's parish church, before engulfing Church Lane and part of Churchbury Lane. It would then swing right, along a culverted section of the New River Loop behind St Andrew's Road, go down Genotin Road, and then follow the route of Cecil Road to complete the circle at the junction of Church Street and Little Park Gardens. Mr Peake had scarcely left the room before it was agreed to form a sub-committee to alert the public to the devastating effect the plan would have on the historic heart of the town.

Despite growing public opposition, Enfield Council steamed ahead and announced that alternative plans and suggestions for the Supplementary Town Map must be received

25. 'The Town and cross roads, Enfield' on a postcard published in about 1960. The canopy on Stowell's wine shop (next to Dunn & Co, left) was later demolished in a road accident. Grouts, a long-established ironmonger, was still trading in Southbury Road next to Lloyds Bank. Wendy's dress shop occupied the prominent site on the corner of Southbury Road and London Road.

by the end of June. Enfield Preservation Society decided to call a conference to discuss how to fight the plan. Twenty organisations sent delegates to a meeting in the Gas Showrooms Lecture Hall, Sydney Road. A campaign committee, known at first as the Town Plan Working Party, was elected with Carinthia Arbuthnot Lane as secretary. So began a six-year battle which is described by Lord Kennet in his book *Preservation* as a story which shows 'how a purpose can be achieved through a mass of detailed and time-consuming work'. It was to become the blueprint for all the Preservation Society's major campaigns.

By July 1961 the working party had sent letters (drafted by Donald Potter of Enfield Preservation Society) to MPs, the Minister of Transport, Middlesex County Council (MCC) and Enfield Council. A meeting had been held with county councillors. A fighting fund had been started, and nearly 7,000 Enfield residents had signed a protest petition. Enfield Preservation Society featured the town plan in a strong display at the September Town Show and later at a packed autumn meeting for EPS members. A vigorous correspondence was maintained in the local press. Nevertheless, Enfield Council decided in November to go ahead with the £2m scheme, albeit slightly modified. The council warned that even after approval by the MCC and the minister, it would take up to three years before the scheme could be put into operation. The Preservation Society made it clear that although opposing the ring road, it was in favour of the proposed Palace Gardens shopping precinct. A request for a meeting with the planning committee was refused and the *Enfield Gazette* accused the Labour majority on the council of snapping its fingers at public opinion in its determination to steam-roller the scheme through.

After this flurry of activity the campaigners had to wait more than eighteen months while consultants, engaged by the borough council 'at a fee not in excess of 1,000 guineas', examined the proposals. The plan surfaced again in March 1963, with an exhibition at the Enfield Town Hall which had been opened in Silver Street eighteen months previously. There was an immediate reaction. 'Only this week has the full extent of the plan

MAP SHOWING THE PROPOSED INNER RING ROAD AND AREAS OF REDEVELOPMENT

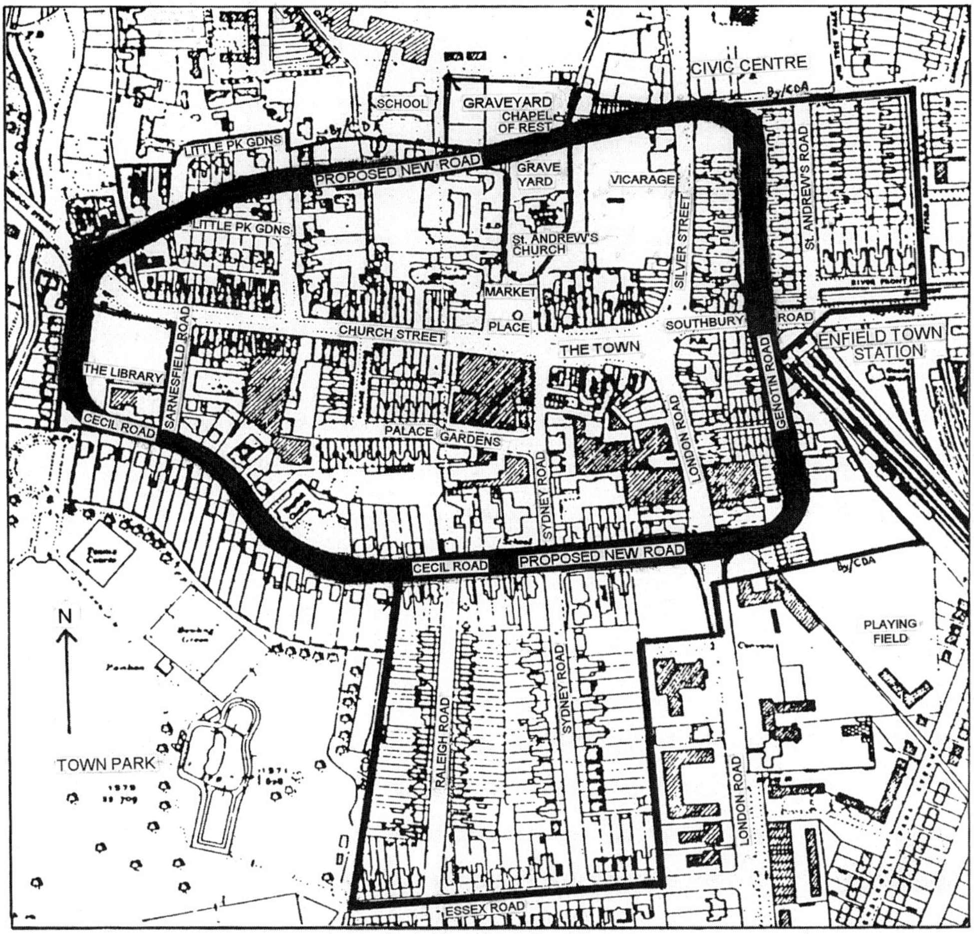

After making a few minor modifications, Enfield Council proposed this inner ring road as a solution to traffic problems in the Town. The intention was that the Town and Church Street (from Southbury Road to the junction with Cecil Road) with Silver Street and London Road (from Churchbury Lane to the eastern end of Cecil Road) would become a pedestrian shopping precinct. Heavy black lines show the extent of the proposed comprehensive redevelopment area covered by the council's master plan.

become apparent', complained the *Enfield Gazette* on 29 March. 'Down will come over 400 houses, scores of shops and offices, two cinemas, at least three public houses — a wholesale extirpation that even the vaunted Luftwaffe could not achieve in the last war.' The town plan working party lost no time in arranging a meeting with Mr Peake together with the area planning officer and the county engineer, to stress the alarm with which the plan was viewed by a large cross-section of Enfield opinion, and the need for that opinion to be heard. They were assured that a public inquiry would be held 'without fail'. Anticipating that a date would soon be announced, meetings of the working party, which had lapsed during the previous year, began again on a monthly basis. Another conference, this

26. Holly Walk, part of the peaceful network of paths behind St Andrew's Church, Enfield Town.

time of twenty-six local societies, was held in April, at which it was decided to engage counsel for the public inquiry (a fee of £500 was mentioned). The campaign began to gather momentum. In June the title Save Enfield Campaign was adopted and the working party was renamed the action committee.Within four months, there was £279 in the fighting fund.

In June 1961 the EPS council of management had given firm support to the growing demand that the so-called D-Ring orbital road round London (now the M25) should be built without delay, as one means of drawing heavy commercial traffic away from the centre of Enfield. This had caused some dissention within the Preservation Society, because a number of members were rigidly opposed to the motorway on the grounds that it would ruin large tracts of green belt land. The action committee now added its voice in support of the orbital road in a letter to the Minister of Transport.

In October 1963 the *Gazette* reported that Enfield Council was considering engaging 'a leading counsel and expert witnesses' in the event of a public inquiry into the Town Plan. The following January, members of the North Middlesex Area Planning Committee, who had been sitting on Enfield's plan for the previous nine months, visited the town centre and inspected the area. In March 1964 the MCC approved the plan and passed it to the Minister of Housing and Local Government. 'If Middlesex County Council is so out of touch with local opinion as to approve a redevelopment plan that has been assailed by residents, ratepayers, shopkeepers, industrialists, churches, women's organisations and the Preservation Society, it is perhaps not a bad thing that it is going to disappear under the local government re-organisation' was the tart comment in the *Enfield Gazette*. For the Preservation Society and the Save Enfield Campaign, the battle now began in earnest. But ironically, H. Deryck Peake, the borough engineer who master-minded the town plan, announced that he was leaving Enfield to take up a similar position with the newly created London Borough of Ealing. No doubt he left with few regrets; on emerging from a particularly stormy public meeting early in the campaign, he had ruefully remarked that his name should have been Daniel instead of Deryck.

Carinthia Arbuthnot Lane, the indefatigable secretary of the action committee, enlisted help from the Preservation Society to stage weekly displays in the Market Place. To illustrate the threat to the town centre, the northern route of the ring road through the churchyard was staked out with white posts. Local people were appalled and the response was overwhelming. By May 1964 more than 9,700 had signed the petition against the town plan. The following month it was announced that David (later Sir David) Napley had been retained as solicitor for the Save Enfield Campaign. He advised that at least £1,000 — £1,500 would be needed to put the campaign's case at the public inquiry. There was just £468 in the fighting fund.

Meanwhile, Enfield Preservation Society had asked William Palmer, the chairman of its architecture and planning committee, to produce an alternative plan to solve the traffic problem in Enfield Town. In essence, his plan envisaged Church Street and Cecil Road as main one-way routes through the town, much as they are today. Unfortunately the plan met with a cool reception from the action committee, perhaps because one of its members

27. Uvedale House, standing between Enfield Grammar School (left) and Uvedale Cottage, at the corner of Holly Walk and Church Walk.

28. The devastating impact of the proposed ring road became clear in 1964 when members of the Save Enfield Campaign erected notices showing where the route would cut through St Andrew's Churchyard. The two markers in the photograph indicate that Holly Walk and its tranquil surroundings would have been obliterated.

(Dr Eric Ridge, representing the North Enfield Ratepayers' Association) lived in Cecil Road and had his own alternative plan. In October the council announced that objections to the Town Plan must be lodged by 25 January 1965. The Preservation Society sent a strongly-worded objection on behalf of its 1,059 members, a striking increase on the March total of 600.

The action committee, which had still not endorsed Mr Palmer's alternative plan, received a curt letter from the Preservation Society reminding them that the EPS had contributed a considerable sum for legal and professional services in the expectation that the committee would mobilise the maximum effort to fight the borough surveyor's plan '... on a positive and vigorous basis by presenting an alternative plan which will achieve all that the Borough Council's plan sets out to do and, at the same time, retain the historic character of Enfield'. The letter complained that for the past six months the alternative plan had been blocked 'by certain of the committee for personal reasons' and continued 'Because this Society sponsored the campaign, it is closely associated with it in the public mind ... if your committee does not wish to present our alternative plan (or an equally good one) at the public enquiry, this Society will be forced to withdraw its support. We shall then publish the alternative plan and be represented at the Inquiry ourselves.' Faced with this ultimatum, the chairman of the action committee resigned. Enfield Preservation Society called another conference which elected a new action committee (strengthened by increased EPS representation) and agreed to present the alternative plan at the inquiry.

Enfield Council was still trying to hustle the plan through. A special meeting of the newly-elected council (still under Labour control) was held in January 1965 to consider 'the advisability of streamlining the statutory procedure' connected with serving compulsory purchase orders. Undeterred, the objectors plodded doggedly on. The Federation of Enfield Ratepayers' Associations, which had opposed the plan from the first, sent an eight-point objection to Richard Crossman, Minister of Housing. Alan Skilton of Enfield Preservation Society built a large and detailed architectural model (later insured for £1,000) showing the Save Enfield Campaign's alternative plan. The campaign had now dragged on for so long that public interest was flagging and in July the campaign treasurer warned that he was seriously perturbed by the lack of response to the most recent appeal letter, especially as legal and specialist fees were mounting. However, Enfield Council was now taking the objectors seriously. The Town Clerk asked for details of the alternative plan 'to save time at the public inquiry'. In December 1965 the model was unveiled at a meeting of the council's town planning committee. Those present included committee chairman Councillor Ted Graham (now Lord Graham of Edmonton), Councillor Ron Daultry (vice-chairman), Norman Stonard (borough architect/planner) and Frank Ladly, the new borough engineer. Councillor Graham, who was leader of the Labour majority, had assumed the main responsibility for putting through the Town Plan. The model had a strong psychological effect on the councillors and it is significant that the council minutes make no mention of the Save Enfield Campaign but refer throughout to 'the Enfield Preserva-

29. Another campaign notice proclaiming 'This is where the proposed ring road will run' (above) showed the route through Church Lane, where Enfield Council had already demolished a row of cottages in anticipation of the development.

tion Society's alternative scheme for the town centre'.

The struggle continued, but as a result of this meeting Enfield Council accepted 'the need to minimise the visual and aural impact of the northern ring road'. In May 1966 it came up with a proposal that the road should be sunk five feet below ground level near St Andrew's Church and Holly Walk. The Preservation Society replied that although this was an improvement, it did not remove the Society's objections to the town plan. The council was told by the borough engineer that of the original 123 objectors, more than 40 had been persuaded to withdraw their objections after discussions with council officers. It was anticipated that at the public inquiry 'the principal objectors are likely to be the Enfield Preservation Society, the church authorities and local associations'.

Nevertheless, the council went ahead and in July the *Enfield Gazette* reported Councillor Ted Graham's announcement that the town centre redevelopment scheme had been approved by the GLC planning committee. A public inquiry was surely imminent. But an unexpected development then occurred which was to relieve both sides of an ultimate confrontation. Ian Nairn, architectural correspondent of the *Daily Telegraph*, had already slated the plan in his column. Now he returned to the attack with an emotive piece in the *Observer Weekend Review*, extolling the individuality of Enfield Town — 'a true town' — where the Market Square 'shades into the leafy churchyard. ... One walk in the huge bosky churchyard is enough to prove that any road here is out of the question' he thundered. This piece made a deep impression, and not only in Enfield. Mr Napley decided to base the inquiry case on the points raised by Ian Nairn — and warned that £2,000 might be needed to finance a lengthy inquiry. With only £641 in the kitty, the action committee desperately scratched around for fund raising ideas and decided to hold a Spring Market early in 1967; the Preservation Society provided the initial finance.

All this time, Enfield's traffic problem had been getting worse. In March 1967 the London *Evening Standard* complained that Church Street was being used by 'a never-ending stream of great goods vehicles pounding to and from the North and the Midlands'. The writer reported that at one stage he had counted 118 lorries moving a few feet at a time eastwards, and asked 'Why should what was once a pleasant country town be assaulted in this way?' The answer was simple. Since the construction of the M1 and M10 and the upgrading of the A1 to motorway standards, Enfield had become one of the main routes to the Thames docks from the Midlands and the North of England.

Meanwhile, officials in the Ministry of Housing and Local Government had become increasingly uneasy about the Enfield plan (maybe they, too, had read Ian Nairn's article). It was not likely to solve Enfield's traffic problem, it would certainly destroy an area of great charm, and it came very low on the capital investment list. A decision was taken. On 19 May 1967 under the banner headline 'Bombshell Decision' the *Enfield Weekly Herald* reported that Anthony Greenwood, Minister of Housing, had rejected the Enfield Town Centre proposals after considering them for over six months, and without waiting for a public inquiry. In his decision letter, which effectively put the ball back into Enfield Council's court, the minister said that any future proposals should bear in mind the need for preserving and enhancing the present character of Enfield, particularly the area north of Church Street.

Enfield Preservation Society and the Save Enfield Campaign found it hard to take in the news. Carinthia Arbuthnot Lane, interviewed by the *Enfield Gazette,* said: 'We were preparing for a terrific fight at the public enquiry — and suddenly, we've won. We are delighted, but at the same time there is a feeling of deflation after all our efforts.' Writing in the same paper to thank the thousands who helped the Save Enfield Campaign, J.

30. Church Lane in 1963.

31. The pleasant Victorian cottages in Church Lane were replaced by a car park.

Waring Sainsbury, first chairman of the action committee, singled out Mrs Lane for the only personal mention. 'But for her enthusiasm, drive and unceasing work ... the campaign might never have been launched, would not have continued so long, and could not have been won' he wrote. 'Future generations will, I believe, have cause to be as grateful to her as we of the action committee are.' The balance of the fighting fund was put into a trust fund to be administered by Enfield Preservation Society. The heart of Enfield had been saved, but as Councillor Ted Graham wearily told the *Gazette:* 'The conditions in Enfield town centre — traffic congestion, deficiency of rear access servicing facilities, adequate shopping expansion, car parking deficiences and safety for the public — were the prime reasons for the council's calling for a comprehensive redevelopment scheme ... The problems remain and other means of solving them will be urgently considered.'

Chapter 3
Setting the Pace

When Enfield Preservation Society sprang back to life in 1959 the local amenity movement was still in its infancy. The Civic Trust has estimated that there were then only 200 local amenity societies in the whole of Britain. However, the movement was rapidly gaining ground; by 1961 the number had increased to over 330 and applications to be placed on the trust's register were being received at the rate of one a fortnight. A similar impetus was stimulating Enfield Preservation Society into vigorous activity. Younger, professional men and women were replacing the 'city fathers' who had been the mainstay of the organisation before the war. At the 1961 annual general meeting the chairman, Revd Ebenezer Rees — by then aged 91 — reluctantly stood aside and allowed himself to be elected the Society's first president. Donald Potter took over the chair, energetic newcomers joined the council of management and the Preservation Society got down to work. A pattern of three members' meetings a year was established.

32. The Reverend Ebenezer Rees, first president of Enfield Preservation Society.

Committees were formed to monitor developments in every part of Enfield, to organise membership subscriptions and to stimulate publicity.

As well as leading the Save Enfield Campaign, the Preservation Society began to speak with new assurance on issues ranging from a threat to replace the Victorian fountain in Enfield Town with a flower-bed (strongly resisted by the EPS council of management) to the relocation of Temple Bar. Tactically, the old council of management had sometimes been unbelievably naive. For example, in September 1960 it had decided that, for the first time, the Preservation Society would be represented at a local planning inquiry. Shell Mex & BP had appealed against Enfield Council's refusal to allow a petrol station to be built in the wooded garden of St James's Vicarage, Enfield Highway. The EPS council of management, which opposed the development, had deputed Sydney Hills to speak in support of Enfield Council at the inquiry. However, on learning that Revd Richie, the vicar of St James's, was in favour of the filling station, the council of management had invited him to address its October meeting. The minutes reveal that the vicar explained his views with some eloquence, 'pointing out the changed character of Enfield Highway, the financial advantage, and that no really fine trees would go'. After a sharp debate the council of management reaffirmed its opposition — but only narrowly, and with five members abstaining. Mr Richie, who had not been asked to withdraw after making his statement, later reported the close voting figures to the public inquiry. The petrol companies lost their appeal but the EPS council of management had learnt a lesson and were not to make this sort of mistake again.

In January 1960 R. Harvey Johns, a member living in Gentleman's Row, wrote to the EPS secretary expressing concern at the neglected state of Temple Bar and suggesting the Preservation Society should mount a campaign to have the monument restored to the City of London. The proposal was taken up with gusto, although the monument stood

33. Temple Bar, a 1902 postcard showing the lodge cottage in use.

just inside the Hertfordshire boundary. Letters were sent to the Legal & General Assurance Society (who used Temple Bar in their crest, and who promised to subscribe if a restoration fund was established) to the Professor of Archaeology at London University (who gave useful advice) and to the Town Clerk of the Corporation of London, who promised to consult the Dean and Chapter of St Paul's on the possibility of a site being provided when the new cathedral precinct was developed. The Ministry of Works, to whom the EPS also complained about recent attacks by vandals, replied with unwarranted optimism that the trustees of the late Sir Hedworth Meux, who owned the monument 'are proposing to erect an unclimbable fence around the structure and it is to be hoped that this will put an end to the trouble'. Built in 1672, possibly to a design by Wren, Temple Bar marked the western boundary of the City of London for more than two hundred years, spanning the road outside the Royal Courts of Justice where Fleet Street becomes The Strand. As City traffic increased, demands grew for the gateway to be removed because, according to critics, it was in the way, was ugly, and was not a piece of antiquity. In the winter of 1878-79 Temple Bar was dismantled. The stones, about 1,000 in all, were carefully numbered and stacked in a builder's yard in Farringdon Street, where they remained for ten years until rescued by a wealthy young brewer, Sir Henry Bruce Meux. He was given permission by the City of London to remove the stones at his own expense and in his own drays, and to re-erect the monument near his mansion in Theobalds Park. The Theobalds estate eventually passed to Admiral Sir Hedworth Meux and, on his death in 1929, to a trust.

The flurry of activity by Enfield Preservation Society stimulated national concern about the deteriorating condition of Temple Bar. It was estimated that it would cost about £60,000 to move it back to London. The EPS continued its campaign to have the monument protected until it could be restored to the City, but vandals, alerted to this easy target, became even more active, defacing the Portland stone with graffiti and stripping away everything portable including the lead roof. Broxbourne Council put up a hideous but ineffective concrete palisade and began its own inquiries into what could be done about this cumbersome historic relic on its doorstep. In September 1967 the London *Evening Standard* reported Enfield Preservation Society's concern that the monument could not be properly supervised, adding that 'high level talks' were to be held between Broxbourne Council, Enfield Preservation Society, the City of London Corporation and the trustees of the estate. Two years later the EPS newsletter welcomed a proposal by Cheshunt Council to restore the monument and create a picnic area in Theobalds Park, with the gateway as the focal point, but nothing came of this. The letter-writing therefore began again, with other organisations chiming in. Enfield Preservation Society tried to involve the Lee Valley Regional Park Authority, but without success. In January 1973 the *Enfield Gazette* reported that as part of its campaign to re-open Forty Hill to through traffic, the Forty Hill Residents' Association had suggested that Temple Bar should be re-erected at the southern entrance to Forty Hill, beside Gough Park. Canvassed for his opinion, Sir John Betjemen was all in favour, saying that he knew Forty Hill and valued it as 'an unexpected piece of rural Middlesex and very important to the district'. Cecil Parkinson, MP for Enfield West, sent a typical politician's reply. If practical from a traffic point of view and if funds were forthcoming, he would support the proposal in any way possible, he promised.

Meanwhile the project to rescue Temple Bar had caught the imagination of a City barrister, Tim Tyndale Daniell. He succeeded in interesting his legal colleagues in restoring the monument, which is widely regarded in most English-speaking countries as an international symbol of the common law. Thanks to his enthusiasm a Temple Bar Trust was set up in January 1977, under the patronage of Sir Hugh Wontner, a former Lord Mayor of London, to raise £500,000 — the sum by then needed to move the gateway back to the City. Mr Daniell set off for the USA to enlist the help of American lawyers, who it was hoped would subscribe half the amount. The trust agreed to buy Temple Bar from the Meux Trust for £1,350, the exact amount paid for the monument when it was built. At the Preservation Society's annual meeting in June 1977, Charles Pluckett, who had recently been responsible for restoring St Paul's Cathedral and was now clerk of works to the Temple Bar Trust, said the top stones of the gateway were becoming so badly eroded that he estimated it would collapse in ten years. He was, however, confident that 'come what may', they would start dismantling and removing the stones on 2 January 1978. Six weeks after that deadline had passed, representatives from Enfield Preservation Society, which had raised £264 for the trust fund, were invited to Theobalds Park College to meet Charles A. Bane of Chicago, chairman of the American Foundation for Temple Bar, responsible for the USA fund-raising appeal. The removal had been delayed for one year, he said, because the organisers were anxious to have £250,000 in the bank before the work started.

Three more years passed before the spring of 1981 saw formal permission being granted for the monument to be re-erected near St Paul's, but the estimated cost of moving it had now soared to £1million. The Temple Bar Trust promised to put a new fence round the monument, but wisely remained silent on the prospects for its removal. Two years later, another complication arose. Several august bodies, including the Society for the Protection of Ancient Buildings (SPAB) were now objecting to the St Paul's site on the grounds that Temple Bar was 'of insufficient quality' and would detract from the cathedral; the objectors preferred a site in Middle Temple Lane. Reporting this development in the EPS newsletter for summer 1983, Len Keeble, leader of the EPS historic buildings group, asked members for their opinions. The outcome was that in January 1984 'after much heartfelt discussion' the Preservation Society lodged an objection at the public inquiry which considered the application from the Meux Trust to move Temple Bar to a site near St Paul's. The EPS now felt that the monument was 'not outstanding and not one of Wren's best works ... would be completely overwhelmed by the bulk of St Paul's, and its poor aesthetic qualities would be very evident'. Instead, the Preservation Society hoped the Department of the Environment would adopt the monument and carry out repairs and maintenance. The inquiry found in favour of the Meux Trust, but nevertheless, it reconvened in December 1984 to consider a proposal from the Historic Buildings and Monuments Commission that Temple Bar should remain in Theobalds Park. Enfield Preservation Society approved this suggestion, provided the monument was restored and public access was assured. However, the minister stuck to his original decision and in 1985 the EPS summer newsletter announced that permission had been given for Temple Bar to be moved to the site near St Paul's Cathedral.

There the matter rested until 1991 when it was announced that after five years of changes of ownership in the new Paternoster Square development, and revised plans for the area, a space adjacent to St Paul's had definitely been reserved for Temple Bar. The *Daily Telegraph* (17 June 1991) reported that the Temple Bar Trust was delighted with the site between two new buildings close to the Chapter House at the entrance to the redesigned square. The trust had asked English Heritage, who were currently restoring the four royal statues which once formed part of the monument, for permission to dismantle and restore the stonework. The operation would take about two years and Sir

34. A 'Save Temple Bar' beer mat was produced in the 1970s during an energetic campaign to raise funds to restore the monument to the City of London.

35. Vandalised and neglected, Temple Bar was a sorry sight in 1989, protected by an inadequate fence of wire mesh.

Hugh Wontner, chairman of the trust, told the newspaper: 'I don't suppose we will get much change out of a million pounds'. In March 1995 Andrew Byrne, recently appointed administrator of the Temple Bar Trust, said the developers aimed to start work on the Paternoster Square site in 1995 or 1996. 'Assuming this occurs we would aim to relocate the Bar in say 1998 or 1999 and will try to get funds from the Millenium Commission amongst others' he said. In yet another effort to protect the monument, the Temple Bar Trust, with the help of a grant from English Heritage, erected new fencing in Theobalds Park in 1994 and carried out security and consolidation works. As a further complication to this interminable saga, a Save Temple Bar Campaign was launched by the Friends of Theobalds in 1991. Its aim was to prevent the monument being removed, on the grounds that dismantling the gateway would ruin the stonework. This campaign was given an unexpected boost in the autumn of 1995 when Theobalds House was sold for use as a conference centre. The new owners announced that they wanted to divert the entrance driveway to the park to skirt Temple Bar and so make the monument a focus of interest. Andrew Byrne told the *Enfield Gazette* in September 1995 that although 'the locals might resist' he was confident the trust would get Temple Bar back to the City. However, this prospect receded still further with the announcement in December that the plans for redeveloping Paternoster Square had been delayed because Mitsubishi, the Japanese multinational and part-owners of the square, wanted a more modern design. By this time the Scheduled Monument Consent for the removal of Temple Bar, given some years previously, had expired, and there were doubts whether English Heritage would grant renewed permission. In March 1996, Andrew Byrne said it was still the strong wish of the Temple Bar Trust to bring the monument back to the City. But in view of all the setbacks, the EPS historic buildings group decided the ideal solution would be to restore Temple Bar *in situ* and make it part of the entrance to Theobalds, where it would be cared for by the new owners and accessible to the public. Fortunately, very few of the Preservation Society's activities have proved as frustrating as the campaign it set in motion to rescue this national monument from neglect and decay.

Speaking at the Preservation Society's first annual dinner, held at the George, Enfield Town in November 1963, the celebrated actor Henry Oscar (an Old Grammarian) said: 'Those of us who love Enfield must bless the Preservation Society for the work it has done and will do'. As well as reporting the function, the *Enfield Gazette* of 9 November carried a leading article which proclaimed: 'Here is a society which scorns bureaucracy and which regards the beauty and heritage of the borough without prejudice or sectional interest'. Mindful of the impending amalgamation of Enfield, Edmonton and Southgate to form the London Borough of Enfield, the article continued: 'If Enfield is to retain its real character, even as part of a larger borough ... it must build on and not sweep away the best of the past. In this we believe the Preservation Society can play an active and vital part'.

As the Save Enfield Campaign gathered momentum, membership of the EPS soared. In September 1963 four active groups were formed to pursue specialised interests. Don Gresswell offered to lead a footpaths group. Christopher Jephcott, a young doctor in general practice in Enfield, eagerly took on a trees group. The first leader of the architecture and planning group, Robert Gowers, was succeeded after six months by William Palmer. The Preservation Society's indefatigable secretary, Carinthia Arbuthnot Lane, agreed to start a historic buildings group in addition to running the publicity committee. Mrs Lane, who was also secretary of the Save Enfield Campaign action committee, had boundless energy and enthusiasm, artistic flair and considerable panache. Before settling in Enfield she had been involved in stage costume design. One of her assignments had been to design elaborate headdresses for the otherwise minimally-clad chorus girls at London's famous Windmill Theatre. For many years she tried to persuade the Preservation Society to let her stage a historical pageant in Enfield, but she failed to enthuse the members of the council of management for this imaginative project. However, Mrs Lane found plenty of other creative outlets. She issued the first EPS newsletter (a duplicated, typewritten sheet) in April 1963 and later that year designed the Preservation Society's first Christmas card, a red and black 'window' which opened to reveal a drawing of the Tiptoft memorial in St Andrew's Church (the cards were priced at five shillings for a packet of six).

A landmark was reached in October 1964 with the enrolment of the 1,000th member — Mr Surety of Ladysmith Road, who was presented with a tree to mark the occasion. In March, membership had been barely 600; by November, when the Preservation Society held its annual dinner, the figure had risen to 1,020. Commenting on this phenomenal increase, Lord Brocket, chairman of the Hertfordshire Society, told the assembly: 'Your Society must have good organisation and great inspiration behind it, to grow so quickly'. With membership still steadily increasing, Enfield Preservation Society boldly embarked on a succession of far-reaching initiatives which established it as one of the country's foremost amenity societies. Don Gresswell began his dogged campaign to establish a network of footpaths in the nearby countryside and also initiated a series of working parties to remove the massive accumulation of dumped rubbish which was disfiguring rural roads and vacant sites in and around Enfield. Dr Jephcott started a programme of tree planting which was to transform the bleak appearance of thousands of neglected areas, especially in eastern Enfield. He also tried, with varying success, to persuade Enfield Council to save scores of mature trees threatened by the housing developments which were changing the character of the Bycullah estate and other established areas. Meetings

36 and 37. In 1964 the Preservation Society sent Enfield Council a list of 40 buildings it considered should be listed. Only two were accepted: St Faith's Cottage, Brigadier Hill (upper) and Little Pipers, an interesting early 19th century house in Clay Hill (lower). Thirty years later, in 1994, the EPS strongly objected to a plan to build six large detached houses in the garden behind Little Pipers. The proposal, which was unpopular with local residents and opposed by the council, was rejected after a planning inquiry.

organised by the Society and publicity put out by the Save Enfield Campaign had stimulated a thirst (largely unsatisfied) for local history, and in December 1964 the EPS launched the first of its many successful publishing ventures. It was decided to reprint Cuthbert Whitaker's *History of Enfield*, originally published in 1911, but long since out of print. The neccessary permissions and estimates having been obtained, the only remaining problem was to raise £500, the cost of reprinting 500 copies. Some members of the EPS council of management thought the outlay too great and the outcome too speculative to go ahead, but Don Gresswell generously offered a loan to cover the initial expense. His trust was amply justified when the book, which went on sale the following July at £1 12s 6d a copy, sold out in less than two months. Further successful reprints followed in 1969 and 1975, by which time the selling price had risen to £4 50.

To consolidate the formation of the EPS historic buildings group in September 1963, the Preservation Society affiliated to the Society for the Protection of Ancient Buildings. The group's immediate aim was to compile a list of local buildings worthy of preservation and make sure none were demolished without proper consideration. The first all-England survey to ascertain which buildings should be listed for their architectural or historic merit

38. Using the Enfield Beast as her inspiration, local artist Mahala Hill designed the EPS bronze plaque which is now displayed on scores of Enfield's most interesting listed buildings.

39. Rupert Jarvis (secretary of the London and Middlesex Archaelogical Society) and Tony Lane (Enfield Preservation Society chairman) fix the first EPS listed building plaque to White Lodge, Silver Street in August 1966, while the Mayor holds the ladder steady.

was well under way, but when completed in 1969, after 20 years work, it ignored most Victorian buildings. Although unscrupulous owners continued to neglect the historic buildings in their care (nationally, hundreds of listed buildings were being lost each year — some 400 went in 1966 alone) listing gave the best protection then available against damaging alterations or demolition. When the borough's schedule of 26 listed buildings was published in 1964, the Preservation Society considered it to be woefully incomplete and sent Enfield Council the names of 40 additional buildings that should have merited inclusion. Only two — Little Pipers, Clay Hill and St Faith's Cottage, Brigadier Hill — were accepted. In the *Enfield Weekly Herald* of 12 June 1964, Rupert Jarvis, secretary of the London and Middlesex Archaeological Society, condemned the council's rejection of so so many worthy buildings as 'outrageous'. The local schedule of listed buildings has been gradually expanded over the years, often at the suggestion of the Preservation Society, but despite persistent attempts there have been repeated refusals to list a handful of excellent buildings including Barclays Bank in Enfield Town and Whitewebbs House.

In 1964 the general public had no means of knowing which buildings were listed, so to stimulate interest in the borough's rich architectural heritage, the EPS historic buildings group suggested that a small identification plaque should be presented to the owner of every listed building. Mahala Hill, a local artist, produced a design based on the Enfield, the mythical beast from the old Borough of Enfield coat of arms, which was later adopted as the symbol for the new London Borough of Enfield. Chase Non-Ferrous Metals in Genotin Road agreed to cast 28 plaques in bronze alloy at a cost of £3.6s.1d each. In August 1966 Rupert Jarvis and Tony Lane (the EPS chairman) gingerly climbed ladders to fix the first plaque to the weatherboards of White Lodge, Silver Street, watched by an admiring crowd that included the Mayor, Councillor Charles Wright, who held the ladders steady. Some time later Franklin Englemann interviewed Mrs Lane when the BBC's *Down your way* programme visited Enfield. She mentioned the listed building plaque while chatting about the Preservation Society's activities and received letters from amenity societies all over the country asking for details.

From the early 1960s, applications from land-hungry developers anxious to build housing estates began to threaten the large swathes of green belt which were zoned as nursery gardens in and around Enfield. Anticipating a fat profit, many owners were anxious to sell, pleading dereliction and played-out land. Both the Preservation Society and FERRA had forseen this danger and had jointly sponsored a meeting in October 1962 to express concern. The first major challenge came the following year with a plan to build a housing estate and shopping centre at Crews Hill. Enfield Council refused permission and the developers lodged an appeal, which was rejected after a public inquiry in January 1964. The proceedings lasted nearly two days — not as long as many inquiries subsequently attended by the EPS, but long enough to deter members of the public whose evidence (following the established procedure) was not heard until the main protagonists had put their case. Don Gresswell, who represented the Preservation Society, complained to the *Enfield Gazette*: 'Not until lunch-time on the second day were members of the public invited to speak. Of 24 interested persons who attended at the start, only twelve survived until the second day. How can Mr Everyman state his case if it means taking days off work to speak for two or three minutes?' Despite frequent complaints from national and local amenity societies (including Enfield Preservation Society) that the local inquiry system was weighted against ordinary members of the public, it was over 20 years before the procedure was made more flexible by the introduction of written representations to determine minor appeals, and the use of more relaxed, informal hearings as an alternative to the original confrontational procedure.

An ominous setback to the local green belt occurred in June 1964. Enfield Council's refusal to allow the eight-acre Rochford nursery site on part of the Dell, off Turkey Street, to be used for housing, was overturned by the Minister of Housing and Local Government, Sir Keith Joseph. He said that any decision about Rochford's should be taken in conjunction with the future use of other nursery sites in the borough. He considered 'it would be right to release for housing such small parts of the metropolitan Green Belt as appeared to have little value for that purpose'. This did not bode well for the future of the remaining nursery sites in the district. Three nurseries were still in production (Bullsmoor Lane nursery, Cairo nursery and Forty Hill nursery close by Turkey Street station). Bridgefield nursery, by the Bullsmoor Lane bridge, had already been demolished and was covered in grass. On 5 June 1964 the *Enfield Weekly Herald* reported that following the minister's decision the EPS council of management had reaffirmed its policy of defending the green belt from further encroachment. Don Gresswell, interviewed as spokesman for the Preservation Society, quoted a recent government report (*The South East Study 1961-*

40. Still in business in the mid-1960s, Fidler's Nursery, on the south side of Turkey Street, east of the Cambridge Road, was one of many local nurseries that were developed for housing during 1965-1970.

1981) which called for green belt land land to be used in a positive and effective way 'so that opportunities for recreation, which are increasingly in demand, can be fully exploited'. Don Gresswell said the policy needed immediate application in north-east Enfield, where there was already a shortage of open space between the A10 and Hertford Road. The population of Enfield was increasing. According to council records, there were currently over 1,000 dwellings, council and private, under construction, which could mean accommodation for a further three or four thousand people, he said. Planning applications showed that the process was continuous, 'one house goes and six maisonettes take its place'. Every acre lost meant that more people were sharing less open space. The remedy was to use the green belt nursery sites for positive recreation. For example, said Mr Gresswell, by damming the Turkey Brook, the Rochford site and part of the Dell could be transformed into a lake large enough for sailing, boating and water sports, providing a valuable amenity on the fringe of the built-up area. Nothing came of this visionary suggestion.

Throughout 1965 and much of 1966 the Preservation Society led a campaign, widely reported in *The Times*, the *Guardian* and the *Evening News*, against the compulsory purchase by Enfield Council of four of the remaining nurseries, but to no avail. Sydney Hills, secretary of FERRA, told the *Enfield Gazette* in October 1965 that the minister's decision on the Rochford site had been the green light for a change of policy not only by the government but by the GLC and Enfield Council: 'No more do we hear them talk of preserving the green belt, but of how many houses they can build on this newly discovered land in the Lea Valley', he said. All the remaining nurseries in eastern Enfield, including Fidler's (adjoining Rochfords) and Smith's in Gilbert Street, went for development. However, Enfield Council eventually spared a total of 17 acres for open space on the Smith's site and at Bridgefield nursery in Bullsmoor Lane, which was laid out as a public recreation ground. More green belt sites were engulfed in Hertfordshire just north of the borough boundary. The EPS newsletter for September 1966 reported the result of a

41. Portcullis Lodge, Baker Street, a large house set back from the road behind the New River Loop, was demolished by Enfield Council in 1968.

week-long public inquiry concerning 275 acres at Cheshunt. The Preservation Society's representative had given evidence on the threat to encircle Enfield with housing. The Inspector recommended that the entire application be rejected, but the minister, Richard Crossman, had overruled the recommendation and had 'justified an exception in this instance' for 220 acres, which meant that a township of 11,000 would be built at Flamstead End.

Development was also threatening other aspects of the green belt in the mid-1960s. In the spring of 1965 Enfield Council announced plans to build four 16-storey tower blocks near the top of Lavender Hill. The EPS joined the chorus of protest at an unsuitable scheme which it considered would drastically change the character of a pleasant area close to the green belt. The height was reduced to 14 storeys, but even the most vehement opponents of the flats had not anticipated the full horror of their impact, which was glaringly evident when the tower blocks were in place, starkly intruding into views over a wide area of countryside. These monstrosities on the skyline became, for travellers from the north, their first glimpse of Enfield. Wise after the event, the Preservation Society thereafter viewed planning applications on the edge of the green belt with an even more critical eye. The green belt fringe was under constant pressure from in-fill development. Among the planning applications refused by Enfield Council in 1964 was a scheme to demolish Clock House and Waltham Cottage on Forty Hill and build 20 terraced houses, with a new road giving access to nearly five acres of backland on the site. The proposal caused widespread alarm because, as local resident Valerie Carter told the *Enfield Weekly Herald*: 'For most people in Enfield, the countryside begins at Forty Hill'. Mrs Carter presented a petition with over 540 signatures at the packed public inquiry at the Civic Centre in February 1965. The Preservation Society led other organisations in protesting that the development would create a dangerous precedent and would open the door to new green belt applications which would be difficult to refuse. The appeal was rejected and Valerie Carter was invited to join the EPS and edit its newsletter.

Events were already taking shape which would bring another activist into the Preservation Society. In August 1964 Enfield Council bought Portcullis Lodge, a sizeable house with a large garden adjacent to Enfield (Lower) Grammar School in Baker Street. The house once belonged to Sir Alfred Somerset, the master of the Enfield Chase pack of staghounds, who lived at Enfield Court, now the school. Portcullis Lodge was so named because a portcullis was the badge of his family. The council's stated intention to use site for additional school playing fields seemed innocent enough, but the Preservation Society remained uneasy about the future of this important open space close to the heart of the town. Its suspicions grew when, in 1968, the council announced that it was about to clear the ground and cut down numerous trees, ostensibly to enlarge a football pitch. In May, the Preservation Society sent a strong protest to Enfield Council 'because it suspected that the real idea was to provide a car park'. Others were equally alarmed. Irene Smith, a resident in Parsonage Lane, organised a petition to save the trees and was persuaded to join the EPS. Within months, she was making herself indispensible as acting secretary, and at the AGM in 1969 she was elected, with acclaim, as honorary secretary of the Preservation Society.

It is fashionable to decry the powerful 'nimby' (not in my back yard) syndrome. One wonders why? Individuals who do not want to see their own corner spoiled have every right to say so and to make their objections heard. Many successful campaigns have been inspired by one person's determination to protect a favourite tree, walk, building or view. A so-called selfish protest is often the only way to alert a wider public and make people aware of threats in the locality and the need to defend its cherished features. It is significant that some of the Preservation Society's most prominent activists were first motivated by environmental threats on their own doorstep.

Chapter 4
Keeping Our Character

A milestone in the amenity movement came in 1967 with the passing of the Civic Amenities Act, which had been introduced in 1966 as a Private Member's Bill by Duncan Sandys MP, then president of the Civic Trust. The basic aim of the Act was to improve the appearance of both town and countryside by introducing new legislation on three widely differing subjects (including many issues which Enfield Preservation Society had tried to promote locally). Local authorities were required to provide proper facilities for the collection of derelict cars and other unwanted articles and thus tackle the problem of indiscriminate dumping which was disfiguring the scene. Tree preservation orders were made more effective and duties were placed on planning authorities to protect existing trees on development sites, or to have new trees planted. Laws on the preservation of historic buildings were strengthened. Most important of all, the Act made provision, for the first time, for the protection of areas as distinct from individual buildings. Planning authorities were required to identify local areas, whether whole town centres or smaller groups of buildings, that were 'of special architectural or historic interest, the character or appearance of which it is desirable to preserve or enhance' and to designate them as conservation areas. This was an important shift of emphasis from negative control to creative planning for preservation. Additional controls were placed on development within conservation areas, to help preserve their character. The Act also urged authorities to enlist public support and to collaborate with local civic societies to raise the environmental quality of conservation areas — a welcome tribute to the growing power of the amenity movement.

Enfield had anticipated the provisions of the Civic Amenities Act. In December 1966 the EPS council of management gave wholehearted support to an Enfield Council report suggesting improvements to enhance the unique character of one the borough's historic gems. This was Gentleman's Row, where 11 of the handsome 18th and 19th century houses had been listed. In March the following year the *Enfield Weekly Herald* reported that a study group had been set up, at the suggestion of Enfield Preservation Society, to look into the treatment of Gentleman's Row and the surrounding area. Enfield Council, which was described as 'enthusiastic' about the idea, authorised officers from the architect's, town planning, engineer's and parks departments to participate in the study group.

Godfrey Groves, a member of the EPS council of management, was elected chairman of the Gentleman's Row Study Group, which sent letters of invitation to all residents in the area and held its first meeting on 27 April 1967. A master plan was agreed, and work began on the first phase, a face-lift for River View and the Crown & Horseshoes. Close-boarded fencing on the footbridge was removed to open up a view of the riverside houses,

42 and 43. A successful improvement scheme for the area near the Crown & Horseshoes won a Civic Trust award for Enfield Preservation Society in 1967. Above: for years, decaying wooden fencing hid the view of the New River Loop and masked the public house. Below: the scene transformed, with graceful iron railings on the bridge and a lower fence in front of the pub. To complete the face-lift, the brewery painted the Crown & Horseshoes to an agreed colour scheme and residents brightened their gardens, making this a corner in which to look and linger, not to hurry past.

whose owners responded by brightening their gardens. The bridge and the public house were repainted. The *Enfield Gazette* reported delightedly on 16 June 1967: 'It was a scruffy spot in a charming backwater of old Enfield. Now it has been transformed. With a few simple improvements, the Crown & Horseshoes and the New River Loop have been given a dramatic face-lift'. The scheme won a commendation for Enfield Preservation Society in the Civic Trust awards for 1967. The citation for 'this modest and successful scheme' notes that: '... the cleaning up and repair of the river, footpath and bridges, and general removal of clutter has been well conceived and carried out in the best tradition of a civic "rescue" operation, to help give back to this part of Enfield a delightful, unique, unsuburban setting'. Gentleman's Row and the surrounding area was designated a conservation area in October 1968. It was later to be considerably enlarged and renamed the Enfield Town Conservation Area.

In June 1968, when Enfield Council organised a Borough Arts Festival, the Preservation Society participated by conducting a walk to introduce the public to some of the interesting but often overlooked features of the area around Enfield Town. An illustrated guide, *A walk around Enfield Town* was published to give details of the route and its historic background. Nearly 300 turned up for the walk and despite torrential rain more than 100 hardy souls gathered for a repeat performance the following week. An annual conducted walk round Enfield Town was to become a popular feature of the Preservation Society's calendar; the illustrated guide, enlarged and revised, has been reprinted several times. The growing enthusiasm for the terms 'conservation' and 'amenity' prompted William Palmer, an EPS vice-president, to propose at the 1968 annual meeting that because preservation was only one aspect of its work, Enfield Preservation Society should change its name. Enfield Civic Society or Enfield Amenity Society were suggested, but

44. It might have been Enfield in the 1820s — but this picture was taken in June 1968 when 'Charles and Mary Lamb', recreated by Derrick Stone and Jane Twitchett, left Clarendon Cottage, Gentleman's Row (one of the local houses occupied by the Lambs) to lead the first EPS guided walk round Enfield Town.

45. Standing in front of the magnificent carved stone overmantel, David Pam points out some of the treasures in the Tudor Room, Gentleman's Row, to a group on an EPS guided walk round Enfield Town in July 1983. The inaugural meeting of the Preservation Society was held in this room, which for many years was the inspiring setting for monthly meetings of the EPS council of management.

objections from the floor were so fierce that, after a lengthy discussion, it was decided it was safer to make no change 'for the time being'. Following a report of this debate in the local press, the EPS secretary received various suggestions from members, one being that Enfield Preservation Society should be renamed Enfield Lovers Society. Not surprisingly, this well-meaning idea was turned down on the grounds of ambiguity.

The Gentleman's Row Conservation Area area was enlarged to become the Enfield Town Conservation Area in 1972. The new area took in most of the town centre, Chase Green and Chase Side and the study group was renamed the Enfield Town Study Group. The boundaries were later extended still further with the inclusion of Sydney Road, Essex Road and Raleigh Road. The Preservation Society invited residents in the enlarged area to join the study group, which was subsequently relaunched as an independent body, comprising local residents with two EPS representatives.

The Preservation Society has been a prime mover in stimulating Enfield Council to designate more conservation areas and in helping residents to organise local study groups. When Forty Hill Conservation Area was designated in October 1968, covering Forty Hall park and the old villages of Forty Hill and Bulls Cross, the EPS organised a meeting in the parish hall at Maidens Bridge. More than 150 people turned up to hear Norman Stonard, the borough planning officer, talk about practical conservation, and enough volunteers were forthcoming to form the flourishing and independent Forty Hill & Bulls Cross Study Group. The same procedure was followed, with less success, for Clay Hill. The Preservation Society first urged Enfield Council in 1968 to designate a Clay Hill Conservation Area, partly because it felt that the large properties, many of them listed and with extensive gardens touching the green belt, were vulnerable to developments which could destroy the attractive rural character of the district. In 1983 the council finally acquiesced to renewed appeals from the Society, and the stretch from Stratton Avenue to St John's Church was designated a conservation area. Scores of invitations were sent out by the EPS, but a public meeting in St John's Church Hall attracted only 36 people. A study group was formed but attempts to sustain it were abandoned by the Preservation Society after some months, owing to the apathy of residents. It was agreed that the Forty Hill & Bulls Cross Study Group would look after the interests of Clay Hill.

46. Part of the Old Bakery, Forty Hill, was used as a greengrocer's shop in the 1960s. In 1967 the Preservation Society vainly tried to stop the house being pulled down. Although it was on the supplementary list of buildings worthy of conservation, and despite opposition from Enfield Council, the weatherboarded house and the outbuildings were demolished in 1968 and replaced by a terrace of six houses. A few months later, the Old Bakery would have had additional protection following the designation of Forty Hill Conservation Area.

47 and 48. The Rose & Crown, Clay Hill, in the early 1960s. By 1964 the little shop selling wines and spirits had become a grocer's and sweet-shop. The abundance of advertising signs did not appeal to Don Gresswell, who took the photograph below as an example of undesirable street clutter. The shop was closed long before the Rose & Crown was included in the Clay Hill Conservation Area in 1983.

There was an immediate, positive response from the authorities when the Preservation Society requested, in April 1973, that Trent Park should become a conservation area. Following the rapid expansion of Trent Park College, several damaging alterations to the park had taken place in 1970; a new road had been cut through a famous garden reputedly designed by Humphry Repton and a large number of trees had been felled. Three

49. Aerial view of Trent Park, taken when the house was occupied by Sir Philip Sassoon.

50. The forecourt of the mansion was cluttered with parked cars for many years after Trent Park (now part of Middlesex University) had become a teacher training college. Enfield Preservation Society led a successful campaign to ban parking in front of the handsome building.

years later, there were fears that further extensions to the college buildings and facilities could seriously affect the surroundings, which the GLC was about to open as a countryside park. The Preservation Society proposed that the whole of Trent Park should be made a conservation area 'to help ensure that future changes will not detract from the splendour of the George III mansion and Humphry Repton landscape'. The proposal was accepted and Trent Park Conservation Area was designated in September 1973. A college conservation group, which had been set up in 1972 at the suggestion of the EPS, accepted the wider remit of monitoring the conservation area. The group also agreed to pursue the suggestion, originally made by the Preservation Society in 1970, that car parking in the mansion forecourt should be forbidden. The college authorities stubbornly refused to take action. However, in 1979 resurfacing work necessitated a two-month ban on parking in front of the mansion. Its appearance was transformed, and the management, appreciating at last why the Preservation Society had insisted that the clutter of vehicles should be removed, prohibited forecourt parking immediately.

In the 1970s and early '80s the Preservation Society became increasingly worried at changes in parts of Bush Hill Park, where many of the substantial houses were being extended and converted into residential homes, or demolished to make way for blocks of flats and slabs of town houses. This piecemeal development was destroying the distinctive character of the gracious, tree-lined roads of handsome Victorian villas which had been laid out with such care. Similar developments had already disrupted most of the Bycullah estate, of which little now survives, and the EPS was anxious that the best remaining part

51. The Anchorage, a finely detailed listed building at the corner of Village Road and Private Road, Bush Hill Park. The Preservation Society persuaded Enfield Council to designate part of Bush Hill Park as a conservation area in 1987. Thanks to persistent efforts by the EPS, the conservation area was extended in January 1994 to include Private Road so that its special character could be protected.

52. Wright's Flour Mill, Wharf Road, Ponders End, was the first conservation area in eastern Enfield. A mill was recorded on this site in 1086; the present flour mill has been run by the Wright family for five generations.

of Bush Hill Park should be made a conservation area before that also disappeared. An official request was made to Enfield Council and the Bush Hill Park Conservation Area was designated in July 1987. Martin Jewell, the borough planning officer, agreed to speak at a public meeting. The Preservation Society booked a local school hall and asked Enfield Council to print leaflets to inform local residents about the meeting. The council refused to help, so the EPS paid for the leaflets, which were distributed by members of the Bush Hill Park Ratepayers' Association. Nearly 100 residents attended the meeting, and the study group formed as a result has been vigilant in monitoring planning applications and trying to improve the area.

The first conservation area in eastern Enfield was designated in July 1970 to protect the last remaining early 19th century industrial building still in use in this part of the Lea Valley — Wright's Flour Mill, standing in ancient water meadows at Ponders End. A second picturesque remnant of eastern Enfield's rural past was given conservation area status in November 1972 when a group of old buildings flanking the Turkey public house, together with two ancient cottages on the other side of the brook in Turkey Street, were designated as the Turkey Street Conservation Area. Once again, the initiative came from the Preservation Society, following an application to demolish one of the weatherboarded cottages and build 15 flats. An Eastern Enfield Study Group, set up jointly by the EPS and FERAA in 1975 to look after these two small areas, was welcomed by local residents' associations. This study group also assumed responsibility for the Enfield Lock Conservation Area (comprising the lock, lock-keeper's house and cottage, cottages in Government Row, etc) when it was designated in November 1976.

53. Tucked away behind the Turkey public house, these charming old cottages in Turkey Street are at the centre of a group of houses fronting the north bank of the Turkey Brook, situated between two footbridges giving access to the road. In 1972, following an application to demolish the right-hand cottage for the erection of 15 flats, the Preservation Society successfully proposed that the public house and cottages should be protected as a conservation area.

54. The lock-keeper's house and cottages at Enfield Lock.

After the Civic Amenities Act, more acts to strengthen conservation powers followed. In 1974, with 3,065 areas designated nationally, the Town and Country Amenities Act brought added protection for trees and made it an offence to demolish any building within a conservation area without the consent of the local authority. The Act also imposed a statutory requirement on local planning authorities to produce enhancement schemes for their conservation areas and to submit the proposals to a public meeting. There was no time limit on this duty and most of Enfield's conservation areas are still waiting for their enhancement schemes. However, numerous minor improvements have been carried out, in co-operation with local conservation area study groups. Up to the spring of 1996, despite manpower shortages, Enfield Council did its best to make sure that officers from the planning department attended meetings of the study groups to consult and to seek opinions on planning applications, thus making good use of a fund of local knowledge and experience. Comments were reported to the Conservation Advisory Group (CAG), which was set up by Enfield Council in 1969 on the initiative of Norman Stonard, the borough planning officer, following advice in a circular from the Ministry of Housing. Enfield Preservation Society is a member of the group, together with FERAA, Southgate Civic Trust, study group representatives, specialist bodies such as the Society for the Protection of Ancient Buildings and Edmonton Hundred Historical Society, councillors and council officers. Recommendations from the CAG are made to relevant council committees (usually, the planning sub-committee) with varying degrees of success.

One hopes this admirable system will continue to operate, but early in 1996 there were indications that a minority of councillors, who had made no secret of their antipathy to conservation areas, were becoming more vocal in their demands that expenditure on them should be reduced. For the same reason it appears unlikely that further conservation areas will be designated in Enfield in the forseeable future. In 1991, when the borough planning officer carried out a review of conservation areas, Enfield Preservation Society suggested that several new areas should be considered. These included Bush Hill and the environs of the New River, where redevelopment of the Halliwick School site (now almost complete) was still anticipated; Grovelands Park, which could benefit from a management scheme to restore its historic aspect; and part of Grange Park, where the stylish and distinctive Edwardian architecture is still surprisingly intact. Regrettably, no action was taken on these proposals or on similar suggestions from other organisations.

Chapter 5
Defending the Green Belt

'The Ridgeway loveliness saved!' was the headline in the *Enfield Gazette* on 7 August 1936 when it was announced that Middlesex County Council had agreed to buy 2,005 acres on both sides of The Ridgeway as part of London's green belt. These rolling fields, mostly owned by the Duchy of Lancaster, were the last remaining portion of the ancient Enfield Chase still held by the Crown. Bought for £315,000 plus legal fees, it was the largest single purchase of land the MCC had undertaken. The following year the MCC asked Enfield Urban District Council to contribute towards the £150,000 needed to buy 586 acres near The Ridgeway north of Hadley Road, which were owned by Trinity College Cambridge; this land included seven farms and Crews Hill

55. Part of Enfield Chase, the borough's splendid green belt countryside, seen from Cuckolds Hill on The Ridgeway, looking south-west across the valley of Salmons Brook towards Hadley Road.

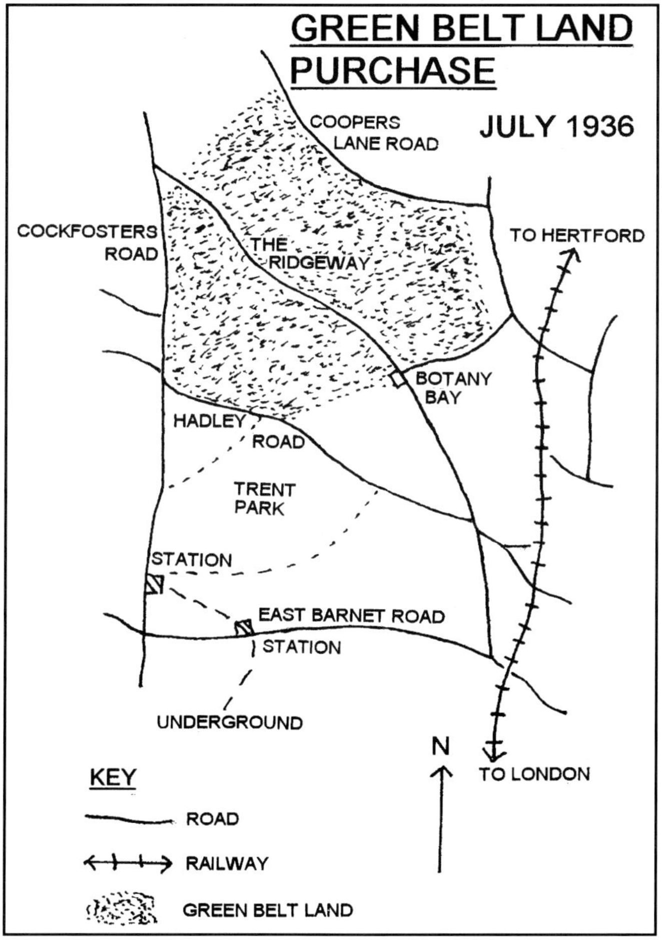

golf course. To the disgust of Sir Henry Bowles (an Enfield representative on the MCC) Enfield Council refused. Sir Henry complained to Stanley Adlard, secretary of Enfield Preservation Society: 'I hear today at the County Council that Enfield UD Council will not join in the idea of giving only one-tenth towards buying that beautiful site at the back of Enfield Ridgeway belonging to Trinity College, which the College is willing to sell at a very modest price and the County would find the other nine-tenths. I cannot understand the UDC.' The Preservation Society immediately wrote to Enfield Council urging it to make the money available. The Town Clerk replied that 'in view of their financial position and the fact that with the acquisition of the Duchy lands one-fifth of Enfield will consist of permanent open spaces, and that it is necessary to consider the production of rateable value, the Council did not see their way to agree.' Enfield Council did agree to buy the 130 acres of Crews Hill golf course, but its refusal to participate in the main purchase was a very serious matter. The Preservation Society was not alone in deploring that a body as far removed as Trinity College Cambridge should be willing to make a contribution to Enfield's future, by selling its land at a low price, while the local authority quibbled and demurred, endangering the completion of the green belt. It was not until the MCC had persuaded Trinity College to remove restrictions and allow 95 acres to be re-sold for

56. Forty Hall in 1963 — a delightful view now ruined by the clumsy seats which clutter the grass in front of the mansion.

housing, '... providing the protection of amenities is borne in mind, particularly keeping open the frontage to The Ridgeway and the preservation of Crews Hill golf course ...' that Enfield Council agreed to join in buying the land, thus completing one of the finest expanses of green belt countryside in the London area.

The future peace of the woods and green belt parkland at Forty Hall, Whitewebbs and Hilly Fields hung in the balance at the start of 1970. The previous year, unbeknown to the Preservation Society, Enfield Council had decided to review some of the borough's parks to see whether they should be developed to encourage more public use. Councillor Barry Lewis had subsequently visited De Efteling, a recreation centre in an extensive natural park near Tilburg in Holland. He was entranced by the facilities: boating ponds, 'full action playground' and children's pleasure garden, fairytale forest with music and recorded fairy tales, miniature railway, zoo, playing fields, pony trekking, boating lakes, etc. He was also impressed that this profitable enterprise was attracting roughly 1,300,000 visitors a year. His colleagues caught his enthusiasm, and in July 1969 Enfield Council approved, in principle, the idea of developing Forty Hall, Whitewebbs and Hilly Fields as a similar type of Family Park, but on a smaller scale. Council officers were instructed to prepare a feasibility study.

57. Turkey Brook, Forty Hall, in 1970. Thanks to Enfield Preservation Society this woodland area has retained much of its informal charm.

The public reacted with fury. The thought of background music and imitation toadstools broadcasting recorded fairy stories in Forty Hall woods was too much to stomach. Tony Lane, the Preservation Society's chairman, was inundated with correspondence after sending a letter to the *Enfield Gazette* seeking the views of EPS members. All were dismayed at this threat to the natural beauty and tranquility of the parks, insisting they should be kept for informal recreation. Councillor Lewis was invited to address members of EPS council of management and the Forty Hill Study Group. They were not impressed and the Preservation Society wrote to the council insisting (as it has done on several subsequent occasions) that these parks were the wrong location for 'improved' or commercial leisure facilities. 'No recreational development should be allowed in Hilly Fields, Forty Hall or Whitewebbs Parks which would in any way impair their appeal to the simple walkers, picnicers [sic], bird watchers, etc.' said the Society's letter. In face of this forceful opposition, the family parks proposal was quietly shelved. In July 1970 the *Gazette* reported that the council's new civic amenities committee had decided to drop the whole idea.

Other features in the green belt were also in jeopardy. In November 1969, John Hannah, leader of the EPS trees group, received an anonymous telephone call reporting that during the past year 80 mature trees had been cut down on two green belt farms on Enfield Chase, and that more trees were to be felled on all the farms along The Ridgeway.

58. This mature oak was spared in the orgy of felling carried out by GLC tenants on farms along The Ridgeway between 1969 and 1979. All the hedge in the picture was later ripped out, including at least six trees 20-30ft tall.

59. A fallen giant, typical of the hundreds of sound, mature oak trees cut down on the GLC Ridgeway farms in the 1970s, despite strenuous protests by Enfield Preservation Society.

Investigations revealed that approval had been given by the GLC (the landlords) and the Ministry of Agriculture. Immediate protests, with demands for replacement planting, were sent to the GLC, Enfield Council and the borough's three GLC councillors, but the destruction continued. Late in 1970 the anonymous caller telephoned again, alleging that roughly 110 mature trees had been destroyed that year. In the EPS newsletter for December, John Hannah lamented that the stump of a 150-year-old oak, five feet in diameter and apparently in perfect condition, could be seen on a farm off The Ridgeway. This, he said, was one of 23 majestic oaks felled in recent weeks. Protests to the GLC met with the reply that some of the trees 'had been dying' and others had to be felled 'for drainage schemes'. The Society enlisted the help of the *Enfield Gazette,* which in a lengthy article reported 'the strenuous protests by Enfield Preservation Society to stop this official vandalism'. After renewed complaints, the EPS was invited to inspect some of the felling sites with GLC officials. The Society asked that the borough planning officer, Norman Stonard, should be present; after the meeting, the GLC promised that no further fellings would take place without consultation with Enfield Council.

The promise was short-lived. In less than three years the Preservation Society was again writing letters to MPs, the GLC and others to protest at drastic tree felling, hedge clearance and the wholesale destruction of a spinney, all of which had been authorised by the GLC. The protests were ignored, and the Society watched with increasing frustration as more important landscape features were destroyed. In February 1979 it wrote again, urging the GLC to stop giving blanket approval to farmers to remove trees and grub out hedges. Within the previous ten years, complained the Preservation Society, drastic hedge clearance, out of all proportion to normal agricultural practice, had begun to give the once rural green belt landscape a semi-urban appearance. Each time a new tenant farmer took over, one of his first actions was to uproot or decimate a hedge line. Two blatant examples had prompted the letter: the removal of a substantial hedge near Chase Farm Hospital, and damage to a footpath with the slaughter of highway trees and the destruction of a long stretch of hedge in East Lodge Lane, which had been left devoid of much of its former charm. A complacent reply was received from the GLC expressing satisfaction with its own management policies. This reply, with the Preservation Society's letter, was forwarded to Enfield Council (which added its own protest) and to the district auditor, with the suggestion that the cost of reinstating the path and the trees should be recovered from the GLC, who had not followed any of the agreed consultation procedures. The upshot was that in April, Stuart Mills (EPS footpaths group leader) was able to report that he had held a satisfactory site meeting with the farmer and the GLC senior land agent. The GLC had agreed to plant 300 quickthorns along East Lodge Lane to replace the hedge, the farmer had ordered saplings to screen new farm buildings near the path, and an agreement had been reached on hedge trimming. This incident, which had involved yet another serious loss of hedgerows (some of them probably dating back to the inclosure of the Chase in 1777) with the resulting loss of wildlife habitat, prompted the Preservation Society to ask once again for representation on Enfield Council's green belt committee. This comprised only farmers, sports council representatives and LBE officials. To the Society's chagrin, it was many years before this request was granted, although the input of the Preservation Society on green belt matters was considerable. When the council, as part of the preparations for the Borough Development Plan, issued a report of studies on the green belt, the EPS made a thoughtful 10-page response. In July 1976 the *Enfield Gazette* featured points from this document, including the Preservation Society's warning that if inappropriate recreation facilities were expanded there would be a risk of diluting the rural character of Whitewebbs, Forty Hall and Trent Park, which was of particular value so close to the metropolis. By then, the EPS had successfully led a crucial campaign to save a vital part of Enfield's green belt from development.

On 22 September 1972 the *Enfield Gazette* reported that Wates, a powerful firm of developers, wanted to build 405 houses on 40 acres of nursery land on both sides of Cattlegate Road, Crews Hill. Five shops with flats above were also proposed on the new estate, which would extend from the railway line almost up to Burnt Farm Ride (excluding Woldens Nursery and the Plough public house) with its southern boundary against the back gardens of properties in Beech Hill and Rosewood Drive. Because of its scale, the

60. When Enfield Preservation Society was formed, the Plough, Crews Hill, was situated in a house still standing at the corner of Theobalds Park Road and Cattlegate Road. The old pub , pictured here in 1910 when the licensee was J. T. Firmin, closed in 1937 when the new Plough was opened 100 yards away in Cattlegate Road.

council invited comments from Enfield Preservation Society, the Federation of Enfield Residents' and Allied Associations (FERAA), Crews Hill Residents' Association and North Enfield Ratepayers' Association before the plan was formally considered. Opposition to the scheme was unanimous. On 26 January 1973 the *Gazette* announced that Enfield Council had rejected the proposals after the borough planning officer, Norman Stonard, had warned that a 'yes' to Wates could open the floodgates for building on the surrounding land.

As expected, Wates appealed against the decision. Local apprehension about the firm's chance of success was heightened by a bombshell from the government: the Environment Secretary, Geoffrey Rippon, published a White Paper proposing that 2,000 acres of the London green belt should be released for housing. No areas were specified, thus putting the entire green belt at risk. In May 1973 Enfield Preservation Society wrote to 23 organisations, inviting them to join an action committee to co-ordinate local opposition to any attempt to encroach into the green belt, with an assurance that the EPS intended to fight the Wates appeal 'and would resist any similar applications'. Even before the replies were received, came another shock: Haringey Council, with a housing waiting list of over 10,000, announced it was considering making a compulsory purchase order on the Crews Hill nursery land, and also intended to build houses on a 10-acre site owned by Haringey on the A10, opposite the crematorium and forming part of the Dell, Forty Hill. The Preservation Society immediately asked the borough's MPs to consider sponsoring a government bill to prevent one local authority making a compulsory purchase order in another's territory.

In September, 24 organisations from all over northern and eastern Enfield sent del-

61. The poster used in the 1973 Defend Enfield's Green Belt campaign was featured by Alan Skilton (seen here) in the Forty Hall exhibition he designed to mark the Preservation Society's 50th anniversary. The shaded area on the display map shows that Enfield's green belt covers roughly one-third of the borough.

egates to a public meeting called by the EPS in St John's Church Hall, Clay Hill. A campaign committee was elected with Tony Lane (EPS) as chairman, John Hook (Crews Hill Residents) secretary, Trudy Maunder (EPS) treasurer, and representatives from participating organisations. It was agreed that the first task was to concentrate on the Crews Hill public inquiry, which was seen as a test case: if the minister allowed the disputed 42 acres to go for housing, an additional 65 acres of green belt nursery land in Crews Hill would immediately be at risk. Wates would undoubtedly employ counsel for the inquiry, so the campaign committee decided it must raise £1,000 for its own legal representation and general publicity. To demonstrate public opinion, a petition was launched — 10,000 local signatures was the aim. Enfield Preservation Society lent money to finance publicity material and soon lurid, green posters and car stickers with the campaign slogan — Defend Enfield's Green Belt — appeared all over the borough. Leaflets were printed and distributed. A stall was set up in Enfield market on successive Saturdays and later taken to Edmonton Green to raise money by selling Defend Enfield's Green Belt posters, key rings and other items, and to collect signatures for the petition. In October, public support increased following widespread consternation at a decision by the Department of the Environment to release more than five acres of green belt land off The Ridgeway for housing, without even a public inquiry. But money for the Defend Enfield's Green Belt campaign was only coming in slowly. In December, with the Crews Hill inquiry announced for February 1974, the customary illustration was dropped from the front page of the EPS newsletter to make room for an urgent appeal for funds. The Preservation Society promised to match the first £100 raised, pound for pound, with a £100 donation. Before

62. View across the green belt from the top of one of the Lavender Hill tower blocks, 1974. Part of Lavender Hill Cemetery is on the right, with Rendlesham Viaduct, popularly known as Fourteen Arches, in the middle distance.

the fund closed, individual EPS members had donated £276, the Society had added £100 as promised, and contributions from Crews Hill and other residents' associations, Women's Institutes, the RSPB and general fund raising had achieved a total of £703. A few days before the inquiry, Tony Lane chaired what the *Enfield Gazette* described as an 'eve of battle' meeting in St John's Church Hall, supported by leading members of all three political parties and an audience of over 200.

More than 150 people turned out to attend the week-long inquiry at the Civic Centre. David Trustram Eve QC, appearing for Wates, said the developers had secured options on all 13 separate nurseries on the site, most of them covered with pre-war glasshouses which could not be adapted for modern production.He submitted that the land served no green belt purpose. 'It is not open country. It has buildings on it. It is not attractive visually and if left it could not be expected to improve. Indeed, the reverse could happen' he said. Seven recent appeal decisions to allow development on green belt nursery land were cited, including sites at Turnford and Waltham Cross. Opposing the application, Enfield's planning officer, Norman Stonard, would not accept Wates' contention that the site did not perform a green belt function. 'One of the fundamental reasons for the Metropolitan Green Belt is to stop the outward spread of development and this quasi-agricultural transition (the glasshouses) fulfils this function' he said. 'What Wates appear to be advocating is a commuters' village centred on Crews Hill Station and unrelated to the rest of the borough.' Speaking on behalf of the Defend Enfield's Green Belt Campaign, Christopher Jephcott said that if the green belt was to remain viable countryside, rural activities such as farming and market gardening must be permitted and even encouraged, and it must be accepted that some of these uses would be unsightly. Once the principle was established that marred sections of the green belt could be built on, it would act as a positive incentive to spoil and neglect the land. When Dr Jephcott presented the campaign's petition, signed by 6,176 residents of the borough and 1,314 people living outside, Mr Eve poured scorn on the document, pointing out that the signatures had been collected over the previous three months, yet represented only a small minority of the residents of the borough.

It cannot be denied that although the overwhelming majority of local people wanted to see the green belt remain intact, many had no scruples in admitting that they intended to be first in the queue to buy houses at Crews Hill if Wates won their appeal.

The Inspector deputed to preside at the inquiry preferred the arguments put by the borough council and the Defend Enfield's Green Belt Campaign. Recommending that Wates' appeal be rejected, he said: 'I am in no doubt that this proposal, if allowed, would generate strong pressures, extremely difficult to resist, for the release of more nursery land, particularly immediately to the south of the Rosewood Estate, which would tend to change the character of this mainly rural locality and lead to coalescence of Crews Hill with Enfield.' However, this by no means settled the problem of the Crews Hill nurseries, as the *Enfield Weekly Herald* warned (with more accuracy than elegance) on 5 July 1974: 'The attempt to bust Enfield's green belt by building houses on nursery land at Crews Hill has been given the thumbs-down by Environment Secretary Anthony Crosland. But a question mark still hangs over the future of the 41 acres of land and their run-down glasshouses, as nursery owners fear that rising costs will force them to quit.' The report went on to quote the bitter reaction of Trevor Borgman, a leading nurseryman and rose grower in Crews Hill since 1926, who complained that most of the nurseries were uneconomic and that the decision was 'an absolute disaster'. Following the minister's refusal to allow the appeal by Wates, Haringey Council abandoned its plan to issue a compulsory purchase order on the Crews Hill nurseries.

63. The Ridgeway, Enfield, 1969.

By the early 1970s, housing developments of various sizes fronted the western side of The Ridgeway from Dunraven Drive to Hadley Road, extending unevenly into the green belt fields behind. Many of the larger houses had spacious gardens and local developers (notably Fairview Estates and A. C. Nicholas) had acquired garden plots and other holdings, hoping the land would one day be released for housing. In June 1972 Fairview applied to Enfield Council for planning permission to build on 5.7 acres at the rear of Crofton Way, off The Ridgeway. When no decision had been announced within two months — the statutory time limit — Fairview appealed to the Secretary of State for the Environment, Geoffrey Rippon. The council's decision to oppose the development was announced a month later; the volume of planning applications coupled with shortage of staff was blamed for the delay. No public inquiry was held, although objections to the application had been made by Enfield Preservation Society, FERAA, and numerous local residents. Instead, the parties involved were invited to submit written representations. On 19 October 1973 headlines in the *Enfield Gazette* proclaimed: 'Shock for Council as Minister sanctions housing in Green Belt... A decision by the Secretary of State to release 5.7 acres of green belt land off The Ridgeway has astounded everybody involved — Enfield Council, the objectors and the developers.' The Preservation Society protested vigorously to the council and to Geoffrey Rippon. Deploring this 'most iniquitous' decision, the letter to Mr Rippon said: 'The inhabitants of Enfield greatly value their fine green belt heritage, which can still be enjoyed by them all, and indeed by anyone from Greater London, as a result of enlightened planning policies since the war. We are determined to do everything in our power to prevent it from being taken from us. Land of such amenity value should not be touched until every derelict acre in the country has been used.' Enfield Council

64. Rural peace on one of Enfield's green belt farms, only a mile or two from the town centre. This winter scene shows Bay Farm, off The Ridgeway (opposite East Lodge Lane) in 1991.

appealed to the High Court but lost and had to pay the costs of the hearing (£1,200).

One of the most surprising aspects of the decision was that just a year beforehand, the Secretary of State had refused Fairview permission to build on half an acre of adjacent green belt at 58 The Ridgeway. In January 1974, despite two previous refusals, Enfield Council agreed to let Fairview build on this half-acre site, which had become completely enclosed. Happily, the following year another part of this good green belt overlooking Trent Park was saved from development. When A. C. Nicholas applied to erect houses on the thickly-wooded 2.5-acre site at the rear of Farmlands and Fairview Road, the EPS protested vehemently. Enfield Council refused planning permission and at the subsequent planning inquiry the Preservation Society voiced its strong objection to the destruction of trees on the site. In rejecting Nicholas's appeal, the Inspector agreed that the trees made a significant contribution to the rural character of the area to the west of The Ridgeway. He recommended that the council should endeavour to preserve the woodland feature, because it enhanced the rural outskirts of Enfield.

From its inception, the Preservation Society unwaveringly opposed building developments which might spoil the special character of Forty Hill, and supported Enfield Council's determination to keep the Dell, Maidens Bridge and the adjoining land as open space. In January 1974 the council rejected for the second time an application by Haringey Council to develop its 10-acre site adjacent to the Dell. Claiming to have the worst housing problem of any London borough, Haringey wanted to build more than 200 homes on land which fronted the A10. The site had been acquired for cemetery purposes but was now cut off from the crematorium by a dual carriageway with central barrier. The Preservation Society and others joined Enfield Council in strongly resisting the application and gave evidence at the subsequent inquiry. The Inspector refused to allow the development and commented in his report (in January 1975) that the 'very vulnerable' site was an important stretch of open land linking the Great Cambridge Road with the green belt areas of Forty Hill. 'The preservation of this open wedge is more important than the erection of 200 houses on the site, which would only spoil the amenity and character of the locality. There are no exceptional circumstances which would justify this loss to the green belt,' he said. When the result was announced the borough planning officer told the *Enfield Weekly Herald* that the most important thing to come out of the inquiry was that, despite the housing need, the government's green belt policy had not changed. In the years that followed, applications to use the land as a golf driving range and a pets' cemetery were successfully resisted, but how long the Dell will remain undeveloped, remains to be seen.

Chapter 6

Traffic Takes Its Toll

In an attempt to ease the congestion as lorries and heavy traffic thundered through Enfield *en route* for the docks, a one-way gyratory system came into force in Enfield Town on 31 August 1969. Following the lines drawn up by William Palmer in 1964, it worked smoothly from the start and has remained virtually unchanged. However, in the EPS newsletter for December 1969 Christopher Jephcott said the Preservation Society was disappointed that the scheme, though successful, had been achieved only at the cost of much damage to the atmosphere and appearance of the Town. He suggested that the use of architectural design could have made an immense difference, for example by intro-

65. A forest of traffic signs sprang up in Enfield Town in August 1969 to guide drivers through the complexities of the new one-way gyratory system. This was the scene in Church Street at the pedestrian crossing to Cecil Road and the Library Green. EPS representatives later toured the area with the borough engineer and suggested various improvements.

ducing attractive paving with varied patterns and textures. (This improvement was eventually made some 20 years later.) Soon after the one-way system began operating, EPS representatives toured the area with the borough engineer, Frank Ladly, and made numerous suggestions for reducing clutter and rationalising the proliferation of confusing road signs. Many of the suggestions were acted on, with good results, but the relentless increase in traffic was also threatening other aspects of the Town.

In autumn 1970 the EPS newsletter complained: 'Changes brought about by the one-way traffic system have left only two approaches to Enfield Town with any vestige of charm. Both of these are now threatened by road "improvement" schemes which are being resisted by the Society'. On the northern approach there was a suggestion (later dropped) that the listed brick wall at the end of the Vicarage garden in Silver Street should be demolished and the road widened. At the western end of the Town, traffic lights were to be installed by Enfield Council (acting for the GLC) at the junction of Windmill Hill with Church Street, Chase Side and Old Park Avenue. This was a necessary improvement, but the Preservation Society feared that the council's plan to set the kerb line back several feet would almost certainly kill the magnificent trees bordering Chase Green Gardens beside the New River Loop in Enfield Town Conservation Area. The GLC, most of whose members and officials had never set foot in Enfield, was adamant that the scheme must go ahead; possible alternatives were ruled out because they would cost more. The Preservation Society's demand for a public inquiry was refused on the grounds that no development was involved. The Society persisted in its opposition and Sir Graham Rowlandson (one of Enfield's GLC members, and an EPS vice-president) persuaded GLC representatives to meet a Preservation Society delegation at the site. In February 1971 the *Enfield Gazette,* reporting this meeting, commented that the GLC 'appears to accept the Preservation Society's arguments and certainly appreciates the devastating effect on this lovely approach to Enfield Town if the trees and shrubs were to disappear'. Following the meeting it was intimated that more money would be made available. Enfield Council, as agents for the GLC, put forward three different schemes, all protecting the trees, and all approved by the Preservation Society. The traffic lights came into use in May 1975 and the trees still enhance this entrance to Church Street.

Disputes over new road schemes frequently caused friction between the Preservation Society and Enfield Council in the 1970s. Engineers, anxious to push ahead with their plans, grudged the delay caused by consulting with residents or local organisations, and often resented the Preservation Society's comments, regarding them as a slur on their professional judgement. On 15 December 1972 the *Enfield Gazette* reported a pointed rebuke from the EPS chairman, Donald Potter. Speaking at the Society's annual dinner, he said the Preservation Society tried to be precise and careful in its judgements, and hoped those who had dealings with it would also be precise and careful. 'I sometimes think that worthy people, because they believe it to be their job, often use methods which they would scorn to use for their own personal gain,' he said. He gave as examples the use of 'experimental' to describe a traffic scheme on which so much money had been spent that it could not possibly be reversed, and the proposal to take 'a small piece of green' for road works, without mentioning that there were five forest trees standing on it.

Sometimes, however, the engineers were justified in thinking they knew best. As part of its attempt to speed the flow of traffic through the heart of Enfield, the GLC decided in 1974 that a mini-roundabout would ease congestion at the busy Windmill Hill/Slades Hill/Ridgeway junction. The EPS and FERRA condemned the £173,000 scheme as a waste of money and sent a joint deputation to County Hall to express concern. Fortu-

66. The magnificent trees bordering Chase Green Gardens were threatened when the GLC decided to install traffic lights at the junction of Windmill Hill with Church Street, Chase Side and Old Park Avenue. Thanks to intervention by the Preservation Society, money was made available for a more sensitive scheme which spared the trees.

nately the GLC took no notice of this short-sighted attitude and installed the roundabout, thus eliminating a dangerous bottleneck.

Heavy industrial traffic had been causing problems in Enfield since the early Sixties. Quiet residential streets and country lanes had become lorry routes almost overnight as drivers adopted them as short cuts. In his 1964 report the borough engineer, Deryck Peake, said Enfield's country roads would have to undergo complete reconstruction to cope with the heavy vehicles which used them as alternatives to congested routes. He quoted Whitewebbs Lane and Whitewebbs Road as typical examples of roads which must be 'improved'. His attitude, widely held by officials at that time, was not shared by the Preservation Society. In a letter to the *Enfield Gazette* (10 July 1964) Don Gresswell called for heavy lorries to be banned from using Whitewebbs Lane and asked 'We have waited so long for the "D" ring road [now the M25], why destroy our last few country lanes as a temporary expedient for heavy goods vehicles?' The proposed route for the new trunk road was published four years later, in 1969. A letter to the Minister of Transport from Enfield Preservation Society in May 1969 stated that although the road would run through green belt farmland 'of very high amenity and landscape value' the EPS would

67. There was no car parking problem in Trinity Street when this card was posted in 1945. Trinity Street School (left) now Chase Side School, was built in 1901.

raise no objection 'because it forms part of the overall road network planned for London and because of the need to take the heavy through traffic out of Enfield'. The letter stressed the importance of fitting the road into its beautiful surroundings by keeping the embankments as low as possible and using adequate landscaping. The Preservation Society lodged a formal objection to one aspect of the scheme — the proposal to build a high embankment to carry Bulls Cross Ride over the ring road — and suggested an alternative. EPS representatives later gave evidence at the public inquiry which heard objections to the proposed route, and a compromise solution was reached.

In 1969 the EPS was one of more than 300 local amenity societies that responded to a transport questionnaire from the Civic Trust. The resulting report *Heavy Lorries* (1970) which was described by the trust as 'a daunting indictment of damage and disruption', made 30 recommendations for government action. Some, such as the establishment of lorry parks and the prohibition of overnight street parking by lorries, were put into operation, although not until 1975/6. But the Department of the Environment jibbed at the proposal that it should designate a network of lorry routes and it asked local authorities to work out their own plans. Three years later the Civic Trust Newsletter reported 'the heavy lorry is still running riot'.

This was a national problem but Enfield was suffering more than most districts. On 19 January 1973 the *Enfield Weekly Herald* reported 'another lorry driver seriously injured on The Ridgeway' and commented that in 1972 there had been 32 serious accidents on this road, and that two (one of them fatal) had already occurred in the current year. A few weeks later Christopher Jephcott spoke on BBC Radio London giving the Preservation Society's objections to a proposal by the European Commission to allow larger and heavier lorries on UK roads. The EPS had been campaigning vigorously on this and other transport matters and had already sent written protests to the Ministry of Transport and the EEC Traffic Commissioner. The Road Haulage Association was meanwhile holding meetings all over the country as part of strenuous efforts to improve the image of road transport and counter the rising demand for designated lorry routes. In May 1973 Enfield residents crowded into the George Inn, Enfield Town, for a heated debate with members of the association. Representing the EPS, Valerie Carter said heavy lorries had become the greatest threat to local amenities and were making life intolerable when they drove along narrow, residential roads. Enfield Preservation Society was pressing for a comprehensive transport policy and for designated lorry routes to include the A10 and the North Circular Road, but not The Ridgeway, she said.

When the GLC at last issued proposals for lorry routes through London in 1975, they came as a bombshell. Juggernaut lorries were to be directed along The Ridgeway, down Windmill Hill, through the Church Street one-way system, and along Southbury Road and Nags Head Road to the Lee Valley Road. The Preservation Society — and most of Enfield — did not approve. The reaction to the proposals was described by the *Enfield Gazette* as 'one of the biggest demonstrations of public anger ever seen in the borough'. In August 1975, giving details of the GLC consultation, the *Gazette* stated that of the 12,040 letters of protest sent to the GLC by individuals, 9,500 had come from Enfield. In addition there had been 234 letters from local societies and groups in Enfield, and 34 petitions. In May 1977, before any decision had been made, the Tories (who captured all three of Enfield's GLC seats) took over at County Hall and the matter was back in the political melting pot. The Tories eventually proposed a ban on lorries over seven-and-a-half tons in the area west of the A10, but this in turn was deferred when Labour swept back into power in 1981. The new administration shelved the scheme and decided to carry out yet another traffic survey, while local streets continued to suffer a constant battering from heavy lorries on their way between the M1 and the docks.

Protesting yet again to the Secretary of State against the EEC proposal to increase the length and weight of articulated vehicles, Christopher Jephcott wrote that 'the anti-social effects of heavy lorries generates more emotion and hostility among members of Enfield Preservation Society than any other topic'. A considerable amount of emotion and hostility was also generated among EPS members by the choice of guest speaker at the Society's annual dinner in 1976. John Tyme, well known as a campaigner for an integrated transport policy, had recently made national news following his disruptive tactics at the Aire Valley and Archway Road motorway inquiries. In a scathing speech at the dinner he accused the government of 'wrecking our rail system by neglect just as they have wrecked our waterway system'. He also asserted that the country's transport system was being systematically dismantled to serve the financial interests of the road lobby. At this time the anti-motorway lobby was vocal but non-violent. The protesters were already threatening to become more militant, but none of the audience realised how soon Mr Tyme's predictions would come true. He went on to warn that as public anger grew over new motorway schemes 'people will end their present passive resistance and take the law into their own hands by going onto building sites and using physical means to stop the bulldozers'. Although not instigating the new campaign of tough tactics, Mr Tyme made it clear he would support it, and he added: 'Something is very wrong and we have a right to do something about it.' These remarks did not go down well with the law-abiding members of the Presesrvation Society, several of whom sent letters complaining about the choice of speaker.

In 1980 Enfield and Barnet councils made a joint approach to the GLC asking for a ban on heavy goods vehicles in the area; it was estimated that 80% of lorry movements along The Ridgeway, Southbury Road and its continuation east of the A10 had no business calls locally. The EPS newsletter for autumn 1981 complained: 'The new regime at County Hall refused to implement the ban and has set up an inquiry, the age-old excuse for official inaction. The Society has protested twice to the local GLC councillor (McBreaty) who does not even reply.'

Construction of the M25 from Potters Bar to Enfield started in autumn 1977 and was completed in July 1981 at a cost of £4million a mile. In January 1982 the *Enfield Gazette* reported that a 12-hour vehicle count, carried out before and after the M25 opened, showed 'a dramatic change in local traffic patterns'. There was a 70% drop in the number of lorries cutting along The Ridgeway and down through Enfield Town, but Bullsmoor Lane was now suffering a 30% increase in heavy lorry traffic. The Preservation Society urged that the M25 should be continued beyond the A10 as speedily as possible. It also gave active support to local demands that the so-called North/South Road should be directly linked to the M25. This eight-mile road was designed to carry industrial traffic from Bullsmoor Lane to Tottenham Hale, linking up with the North Circular Road and thus improving access to industrial areas on the west side of the River Lea and relieving congestion on the Hertford Road. Vigorous campaigning to get a junction on the M25 giving direct access to the North/South Road began in 1977 but the Ministry of Transport refused to approve the link, saying it would be too close to the M25/A10 junction. The route of the North/South Road, when finally approved by the GLC in February 1983, dismayed Enfield Preservation Society and the residents of Enfield Lock because it cut right across one of the few remaining open spaces in eastern Enfield; they suggested a realignment to the east. Wally Woodfield spoke on behalf of the EPS at the public inquiry to decide the matter, but after more than fourteen days of evidence the GLC route was

68. Situated close to the road, the picturesque nineteenth century cottages at Maidens Bridge, Forty Hill, have suffered from the increasingly heavy traffic flooding through Forty Hill Conservation Area.

69. Ansells Green, Forty Hill, in the 1960s. In 1971 Myddelton Avenue (in background) was extended across the green in an attempt to divert through traffic away from the narrow road through Forty Hill and Bulls Cross. Twenty years later, despite the diversion, traffic levels in the conservation area exceeded those of 1971.

confirmed. Work began in August 1985 and the £7.5 million section linking Bullsmoor Lane with Ordnance Road was opened in June 1989. The final section of the North/South Road, which is made up of Mollison Avenue and Meridian Way, was opened in December 1990. It is estimated that the road cost £100 million. Efforts to have it linked directly to the M25 have continued to this day.

Traffic was also causing difficulties in Forty Hill throughout the 1980s. This was not a new problem. In April 1938 the *Enfield Gazette* noted that, in response to a council proposal that Maidens Bridge should be widened 'the Enfield Preservation Society feel this little corner should be left alone in its sylvan beauty'. Plans to widen the bridge were dropped but the rural peace was gradually destroyed as the narrow, winding road through Forty Hill and Bulls Cross became a popular rat-run for the commuter traffic and commercial vehicles that streamed in and out of Enfield along Baker Street. By 1962 heavy lorries and even car-transporters were adding to the danger as they manoeuvered their way over Maidens Bridge. In 1968 a lorry crashed into the ancient bridge, damaging it so severely that the upper part had to be rebuilt. One-way traffic lights were installed at the bridge but heavy traffic continued to pour through the area, shaking the foundations of cottages and listed buildings along the route. The problem became so acute that Enfield Council decided the only solution was to close Forty Hill at its junction with Clay Hill, extend Myddelton Avenue across Ansells Green, and thus divert through traffic to the A10 via Myddelton Avenue and Carterhatch Lane. The Preservation Society, though regretting the destruction of Ansells Green, gave its reluctant approval. When the diversion came into effect on 24 September 1971 the *Enfield Gazette* printed a picture of cars nose to tail, over the caption: 'Traffic jams and chaos as cars block Hallside Road, trying to find a short cut round the blocked section of Forty Hill'. Most of the confusion was caused by poor signposting, but the North Enfield Ratepayers' Association and others who had opposed the diversion from the start, stepped up their acrimonious campaign to have Forty Hill re-opened. The EPS remained unmoved. At the annual dinner in December the chairman, Tony Lane, admitted there had initially been traffic chaos but stated: 'We have not changed our minds on this. The closure is for the good of the old villages of Forty Hill and Bulls Cross and we stand firm.'

However, the closure was undoubtedly making life unpleasant for residents in roads off Carterhatch Lane, which were blocked with commuter traffic during the morning and evening rush hours. The Preservation Society urged the GLC to improve the roundabouts (now changed to traffic lights) on the A10, because congestion between Bullsmoor Lane and Carterhatch Lane was forcing traffic to seek an alternative route through Forty Hill. In April 1972 a joint meeting of the Preservation Society, Forty Hill Study Group, North Enfield Ratepayers' Association and the Willow Residents' Association called on Enfield Council to produce an integrated traffic plan for the whole of the Forty Hill/Willow Road area. The outcome, after nearly three years of deliberation, was a suggestion from the GLC that Maidens Bridge should be closed to vehicles. Enfield Council consulted the EPS and other organisations and found the plan was unpopular in every quarter. The *Enfield Weekly Herald* reported in February 1975 that the Preservation Society was not in favour of closing Maidens Bridge 'because of the hardship to residents in Turkey Street

70. The Goat green and village shops, Forty Hill, in 1968. When Baker Street was closed at the junction with Clay Hill, buses from Enfield Town were diverted down Carterhatch Lane. In 1968 a police telephone box and 14 items of 'street furniture', including three litter bins and a wartime air raid siren, still clutter the green. On the right, next to The Hermitage, houses are being built on the site of the recently demolished Old Bakery.

and the Capel estate' but had proposed a barrier in Bulls Cross just north of Turkey Street. Taking the easy option, Enfield Council then announced it proposed to shelve a decision because there was no money to implement any scheme, even if one was approved.

The M25, although taking heavy commercial traffic away from Enfield Town, was proving a mixed blessing. After the motorway was completed in 1986 there was a significant increase — 4.5% over a 24-hour period — in traffic flows throughout Enfield. The borough planning officer's report for 1987 said initial monitoring suggested that the motorway may have contributed to these increased traffic levels. There was no doubt that the M25 was adding to the problems in Forty Hill and Bulls Cross. In 1985, the borough planning officer had noted that ever since the M25 had been completed between the A10 and the M11, traffic flows on the whole length of the A10 had increased because it was feeding vehicles to and from the motorway, and that as a consequence there had been an increase in traffic through Forty Hill. The situation grew steadily worse and in 1993 Enfield Council sent leaflets to 3,000 households in the Forty Hill area asking for comments on a proposal that Maidens Bridge should be closed for a trial period. This would have been an ideal opportunity to assess the merits and disadvantages of permanent closure, but unfortunately the questionnaire did not include proposals for protecting adjoining areas from the likely increase in traffic flow if the bridge was closed. Less than 30% of the households canvassed bothered to reply but 80% of those who did were against, so the plan was abandoned. The Preservation Society, as before, felt unable to support the bridge closure because of the effect it would have on neighbouring roads. There had been suggestions that the southern end of Forty Hill should be reopened. The EPS was not in favour and Christopher Jephcott wrote to Enfield Council reviving the proposal that the wrought iron gates to Gough Park should be repositioned across the closed road. A traffic management plan for the whole Forty Hill area was demanded yet again, but although several piecemeal schemes were produced by council engineers in 1995 none were implented, owing to a brutal reduction in the budget for traffic calming measures.

71. (opposite) The upper part of Maidens Bridge, Forty Hill, was carefully rebuilt by Enfield Council after being extensively damaged by a lorry in 1968.

Chapter 7
The Town in Turmoil

The Seventies were a time of upheaval in and around Enfield Town. For ten years, following the amalgamation of Enfield, Edmonton and Southgate in April 1965, the London Borough of Enfield was administered from the council offices of the three former boroughs. By 1975 Enfield's new £5 million Civic Centre, its 12 storeys incongruously clad in shining stainless steel, had risen in Silver Street alongside the Town Hall to tower above some of Enfield Town's oldest buildings . The Civic Centre was opened by the Queen Mother in May 1975 amid widespread criticism about its design and cost. In an interview published in the *Enfield Gazette* on 1 May, Alan Young, the

72. Fir Tree House in Silver Street, bought by Enfield Council in 1938 as part of a site for the Town Hall. After the original Civic Centre (just visible on left) was built, the borough's education department moved into Fir Tree House. In 1974, when the house was about to be demolished to make way for the new high-rise Civic Centre, Enfield Preservation Society suggested that the decorative iron gate and railings should be used to form an entrance to St Andrew's Churchyard from Church Lane.

73. Some of the splendid trees from the garden of Fir Tree House soften the view of Enfield Civic Centre on this EPS postcard.

council leader, assured ratepayers that Southgate Town Hall would eventually be sold 'for an estimated £2 million'. At Edmonton, he said, Enfield Council had decided to keep the Town Hall and preserve the façade, but it expected to sell the large area of land at the back. Today (1996) Southgate Town Hall is still occupied by council departments (though some of the land at the back has been sold for housing) while Edmonton Town Hall was razed to the ground in 1988 despite a valiant struggle to preserve the ornate Victorian facade, led by Councillor Fred Jarvis and supported by Enfield Preservation Society and numerous other organisations.

Eight months before the opening of the Civic Centre the borough engineer, Donald Treweek, produced a 12-page report stating that at peak shopping and business hours Enfield Town was short of more than 900 parking places. That serious situation, he warned, would become even more critical when about 1,200 council staff, most of them car drivers, moved into the Civic Centre from offices in other parts of the borough. The two-storey car park in the new building would hold 482 vehicles, which meant that on every working day at least 490 drivers would have no parking space. The implication was that hundreds of cars would swamp the already inadequate shoppers' car parks. Confirming the Preservation Society's fears, Mr Treweek proposed that as an immediate 'first aid' solution the temporary car park at the Portcullis Lodge site should be extended from the present 65 spaces to about 370. According to the *Enfield Gazette* (17 October 1974) Councillor Leslie Merrion was the only member to echo the Preservation Society's long-held opinion that the site should not be used. 'Once cars are allowed on Portcullis Lodge they will be there for at least ten years' he said. 'Once you take this, it has gone for ever — a beautiful open space in the middle of the conservation area.' Councillor Rita Smythe,

74. Portcullis Lodge car park, seen from Enfield Grammar School playing fields and the New River Loop. It was many years before the vehicles were hidden by a planted screen. In the foreground, rubbish dredged out of the river has been left on the bank ready to be collected — or to be pushed back into the water by vandals.

voicing the popular opinion, maintained that shops in Enfield Town were losing trade because people were fed up with not being able to park. The Preservation Society protested that Portcullis Lodge was a focal point in a valuable open space close to the centre of the Town, forming one of the chief attractions of Enfield Town Conservation Area. It angrily accused the council of acting as judge and jury in its own case, and wrote to the Secretary of State asking him to call in the application. Bryan Davies, the newly elected Labour MP for Enfield North, gave his strong support in a letter to the EPS but the minister refused to intervene. In February 1975 a modified scheme to accommodate 200 cars was given approval for four years, with promises that the site would be adequately screened by new planting. For fourteen years, despite persistent requests from the Preservation Society, Enfield Council made little attempt to minimise the impact of the car park. The EPS newsletter for winter 1989 commented bitterly: 'Following several extensions of temporary permission for an overspill staff car park, with broken promises about planting an adequate screen, Enfield Council is applying for a permanent car park, with no landscaping, but with widening of the access road. The EPS cannot agree.' After further efforts by the Society the access road was made less obtrusive and a landscaping programme was at last provided and implemented.

Throughout the Seventies, traffic was also taking its toll on one of the most unusual listed buildings in Gentleman's Row. Built in 1756, Archway House, now a privately owned dwelling, had been used as a public house towards the end of the nineteenth century. The house incorporates an arch over a short passage giving access to Chapel

75. The arch and walls of Archway House, Gentleman's Row, were damaged by vehicles on 17 occasions before Enfield Preservation Society succeeded in getting the opening closed to traffic. This picture, taken from Chapel Street in 1965, shows the archway before closure.

76. Archway House, with bollards in place, seen from Gentleman's Row.

Street. Originally the arch spanned a muddy track, but in the early 1960s following the erection of several houses in Chapel Street, the road was made up and vehicles of all sizes began trying to scrape through Archway House. Beginning with a coal lorry, which took a side wall with it when it blundered through the arch in 1963, the building was battered by dustcarts, more lorries and even a Harrods delivery van until in 1971 the householder's insurers refused to renew the policy covering the arch. The Preservation Society suggested the arch should be closed to vehicles and after an insistent campaign Enfield Council agreed. The council granted a temporary closure order in 1976 and provided alternative access to Chapel Street through Little Park Gardens. The following year the GLC refused to renew the closure order and decreed that public consultations must take place. The archway was reopened, only to suffer damage from another accident (the seventeenth in fourteen years). The Preservation Society sent a deputation to the GLC and a letter to the Secretary of State for Transport supporting Enfield Council's demand for permanent closure, and this was duly granted. It remained a source of irritation to the Preservation Society that although Archway House was (and still is) a listed building in the borough's prime conservation area, the traffic barrier installed by the council consisted of ugly pipes filled with concrete. However, in 1984, encouraged by a financial contribution from the Preservation Society, the council replaced the pipes with good quality metal bollards. A happy outcome followed: Enfield Council decided to discontinue using concrete bollards and to instal metal ones throughout the borough for new schemes and replacements.

The seemingly insoluble problems of too much traffic and not enough car parking spaces in Enfield Town also bedevilled the council's plans for the Palace Gardens shopping precinct. Alderman John Lindsay, chairman of the town planning committee, described the proposals at the Preservation Society's AGM in 1972. A capacity audience at Foresters Hall, Chase Side, heard him outline an ambitious £4 million scheme which included a public meeting hall, and a central tower block of 60 flats. On the site behind Woolworth's, a multi-storey car park was to be linked to the main precinct by an underground shopping arcade beneath Sydney Road. The Preservation Society was unhappy with some details of the plan, particularly the siting of the multi-storey car park which it feared would dominate Church Street, but it welcomed the scheme in principle. However, the GLC did not approve. It suggested Enfield Council should revive and seek public comments on an earlier plan which had included proposals for closing Church Street to traffic and converting Cecil Road into a massive two-way through route. 'The proposal to widen Cecil Road and build a relief road between London Road and Southbury Road, dubbed the "slip road", were dominant issues at the recent GLC elections in Enfield' reported the *Gazette* in July 1973. The Preservation Society considered the slip road (which was to resurface 20 years later as the Genotin Road link) would only encourage more traffic to pass through the centre of Enfield, and suggested the money would be better spent on improving the Great Cambridge Road, or on the early construction of Ringway 3 (now the M25) so that heavy traffic could pass through the borough without using roads needed for local traffic.

At the public inquiry on the precinct proposals in May 1974, the Preservation Society stressed the need for quick action to halt the decline in Enfield Town as a major shopping centre. The precinct scheme, which had been at the planning stage for 15 years, was approved soon after the inquiry. With construction costs rising rapidly and the Town declining month by month, Enfield people waited impatiently for building to begin. It was to be a long wait. In January 1975, in an attempt to stop Enfield Town from dying as a shopping centre, the council put a total ban on the conversion of any more shops in the

77. In 1975, in an attempt to brighten the gloom pervading the shopping centre, the council installed concrete planters round the fountain island in Enfield Town.

Town, Church Street and part of Southbury Road into non-retail use. By the end of 1976, with still no action, it was clear that the scheme had hit a major snag. In December the *Enfield Weekly Herald* reported a speech at the Preservation Society's annual dinner by Peter Perryman (a member of the EPS council of management) hinting that the delay was due to a demand by the developers that the flats should be removed from the scheme. 'The return on capital from residential accommodation cannot possibly match the cost of borrowing money to build the precinct' he pointed out. His speculation proved correct, although at the time Wilfrid Day, Enfield Council's chief executive and town clerk, admitted only that 'discussions were taking place' with the Norwich Union Insurance Group and Legal & General Insurance Society (the joint developers).

In January 1977 Tesco moved out of London Road and the shopping streets in the Town took on a new look of dereliction. On 13 January the *Enfield Gazette* reported that a panel of councillors had been appointed 'to try to stop Enfield becoming a ghost town'. In the past ten years, said the report, Enfield Council's town centre account had chalked up a loss of more than £400,000. At the current level of rates, every further year of delay was costing £100,000. 'A blighted town' was the paper's verdict. The cover of the EPS newsletter for March 1977 showed a desolate view of the empty seven-and-a-half-acre site behind Pearsons and carried a vigorous editorial encapsulating public opinion: 'Given the government go-ahead more than a year ago, the multi-million pound scheme has still not been finally agreed between Enfield Council and the two insurance companies who are providing the money. Meanwhile, in Enfield Town trade slumps, shops stand empty, building societies and offices replace the dwindling number of retail shops ... the continued failure of the developers to submit detailed plans and the lack of any firm starting date, must be a cause for increasing concern.' Following the expansion of shopping centres at

78. The EPS newsletter for March 1977 carried this desolate view. The seven-and-a-half-acre site behind Pearsons had been cleared for the new shopping precinct, which had become bogged down by financial problems.

Edmonton Green, Wood Green and Waltham Cross, would the Palace Gardens precinct be out of date and unviable even before work started? To take a fresh look at all the possibilities, the EPS set up a new group 'to prepare a statement of objectives for Enfield Town Centre and consider possible actions'.

In June Enfield Council's policy was called into question when the Halifax Building Society appealed against the refusal to allow it to open an office at 61 Church Street. Concern about the dwindling shopping choice in the Town had become so great that when Enfield Preservation Society announced it would give evidence in support of the council, 15 women's organisations in and around Enfield asked the EPS to represent them at the public inquiry. The town slid further into decline and by August, according to a survey carried out by the *Enfield Gazette,* there were ten empty shops in Church Street and The Town. The remaining retail outlets included one department store, seven food shops (including bakers), six shoe shops, eight shops selling ladies clothing and eleven selling men's clothing.

Later that year, in November 1977, a revised £13 million plan for the shopping precinct was published and comments were invited from the public. Enfield Council had agreed to pump in £2million for the land and the provision of public services. The meeting hall, flats and subway under Sydney Road had been dropped from the scheme because of rising costs, and the multi-storey car park had been moved to its present position in Sarnesfield Road. Christopher Jephcott reported in the EPS newsletter for spring 1978 that the Preservation Society generally welcomed the new plan, which he described in some detail. With the EPS architecture & planning group he later made numerous imaginative suggestions for improving details relating to the design, materials and other aspects of the scheme, many of which were incorporated into the final specifications.

In March 1978, at the invitation of Enfield Council, Sir Colin Buchanan conducted a public meeting at the Civic Centre to investigate the merits of the revised scheme. A large number of individuals and organisations had registered objections to specific proposals, many of them concerning the multi-storey car park and traffic in Cecil Road, and the proceedings were spread over several days. When Christopher Jephcott stated that Enfield Preservation Society supported the council's outline proposals, including the new site for the car park, there was a furious reaction from Sydney Hills, secretary of FERAA. To the astonishment of those present, he launched a vituperative attack on the EPS, accusing it of supporting the desecration of the Library Green. Mr Hills wound up his tirade by calling

79. These old cottages were part of the Laings Garage site on the north side of Cecil Road, demolished in 1979 as part of the clearance for the Palace Gardens precinct. Picture shows James and Emma Griggs outside the cottages in 1912.

80. The old-established family printing business of J. W. Hatch & Son, at the corner of Palace Gardens and Palace Mews, which ran behind the Church Street shops. When these properties were demolished in 1979 to make way for the shopping precinct, Hatch closed his business. In the mews behind J. W. Hatch was another printing concern, Pika Print, which transferred to new premises in Genotin Road. Apart from the first duplicated sheet, Pika Print produced every issue of the EPS newsletter until the death of its founder and proprietor, Dusan Plenicar, in 1992. The firm was subsequently acquired by Chipperfield Press, which still prints the newsletter.

for the Preservation Society to convene a special general meeting to discuss the siting of the car park. In his report to Enfield Council Sir Colin recommended that the scheme should go ahead, but commented: '... a large project of this kind is bound to hurt someone ... the function of the public authority is to weigh all the hurts and benefits and see where the public advantage lies.' Sir Colin continued: 'The only person to put this point unequivocally at the meeting was Dr Jephcott on behalf of the Enfield Preservation Society and his view, subject to some detailed reservations, was that ... the new scheme was better than the old ... It is certainly a view which accords with my own.' The outline plan was subsequently approved by Enfield Council.

In due course the EPS secretary was presented with a written request for an extraordinary general meeting signed by Sydney Hills and seven individuals, not all of whom were paid-up members of the Preservation Society. This fell far short of the one-tenth of the membership (approximately 180 signatures) required under company law, but so that his criticism could be publicly debated by the EPS membership Mr Hills was invited to table a resolution at the 1978 AGM. This he did. The resolution 'regretted' that the evidence presented at the inquiry on behalf of Enfield Preservation Society 'had enabled Sir Colin Buchanan to recommend approval of a multi-storey car park in Sarnesfield Road' and added: 'Such a scheme, in the opinion of this meeting, will be detrimental to the environment of the Library Green'. It was a difficult meeting. The EPS council of management considered that if the resolution was carried it would be as good as a vote of no confidence in the Preservation Society's administration. In a unique departure from the usual easy-going procedure, voting cards were issued to members on arrival, to make sure that outsiders did not distort the result. Adding to the tension, the proceedings began on a solemn note with the announcement of the sudden death of Godfrey Groves, the EPS president. Proposing his resolution, Sydney Hills said that at the Civic Centre hearing 30

81. Sydney Road in August 1978, looking towards Barclays Bank in The Town. On the left by the 'No Parking' sign are the fine Eastern Gas showrooms and offices. On the right is the Duke of Abercorn public house, the two old Enfield Gas Company offices (1897 and 1906) and the National Westminster Bank.

people had objected to the new siting of the car park while only four supported it. He had been shocked to hear the Preservation Society support a proposal which would cause traffic chaos and spoil the view from the Library Green. Seconding the proposal another ratepayers' representative, Dennis Keighley, was concerned that the scheme would have a major impact on Cecil Road. After a tense debate, the resolution was defeated by 53 votes to 40. The local press pounced gleefully on this rare example of controversy at a Preservation Society AGM. 'Car park plan splits society' shouted headlines in the *Enfield Gazette* on 29 June, followed in the *Enfield Weekly Herald* a week later by 'Split over backing for multi-storey car park'. However, there was no adverse reaction from the membership at large, most of whom appeared to agree with Dr Jephcott's statement. The vehement opposition to the siting of the multi-storey car park may not have been unconnected with the fact that one of the most prominent activists in the ratepayers' movement lived in Cecil Road.

In December 1978 Sir Colin Buchanan was guest speaker at the EPS annual dinner. He recalled that he had presided at a 'rather curious meeting' at the Civic Centre in April. 'And how pleasant it was' he said 'to have a Preservation Society who managed to express an unequivocal view, and what is more, to come out in favour of change.' He thought some of the objectors were quite misconceived in their views and hoped that time would show their fears were partly true, but partly exaggerated. Palace Gardens shopping precinct was inaugurated early in December 1982 when Boots opened its doors to customers, followed by Marks & Spencer shortly before Christmas. On 31 July 1986, in a special feature to mark the Preservation Society's 50th anniversary, the *Enfield Gazette* commented: 'In 1977-78 Enfield Preservation Society stood alone among local amenity and residents' organisations in supporting proposals for the Palace Gardens shopping precinct development. To the EPS, preservation has never meant stagnation, and the Society's conviction that the precinct was the way forward for a prosperous, lively town has been well justified.'

One of the Preservation Society's main preoccupations — how to ensure that new developments in Enfield Town did not destroy its historic features and special character — was put to the test in 1977 when Enfield Town was defined as an Action Area in the Greater London Development Plan. The Palace Gardens precinct, at the time still in

82. Sir Colin Buchanan (left) with Alan Skilton at the EPS annual dinner, December 1978.

83. Palace Gardens shopping precinct, looking towards Church Street from Sydney Road, a view featured on an EPS postcard.

limbo, was regarded as only the first phase in Enfield Town's development and council officials began preparing a local plan to adapt the town centre to meet future needs for more shops, adequate car parking, and smooth passage for local and through traffic. In November the borough planning officer, Norman Stonard, invited the EPS to become directly involved with forming proposals and policies on the conservation aspects of the Action Area Plan before it reached the formal consultation stage. This was a gratifying acknowledgement of the reputation the Preservation Society had built up for constructive and far-sighted comments on planning matters. Between January 1978 and May 1979 a small committee, chaired by Christopher Jephcott and attended by EPS representatives and Enfield Council officers, held 13 meetings. Detailed recommendations were made about traffic patterns, shopping, recreation, education and the visual aspects of theTown. The result was a report, seen by every council committee, which tried to identify and foster the features that give Enfield Town its special character — described in the report as 'still some of the ambience of a small market town'.

While it was helping to formulate these long-term plans the Preservation Society was engaged in a spirited struggle to preserve one of Enfield's most historic features which it had fought so hard to save in the Sixties — St Andrew's Churchyard. For years, as a result of minimal upkeep by the church authorities, graves in the northern section of the churchyard had become engulfed by a creamy froth of cow parsley every summer, a rural sight that pleased some townspeople more than others. Following the Save Enfield Campaign, the Preservation Society had taken a protective interest in the churchyard. Since 1963, EPS volunteers had organised occasional working parties to clear brambles and undergrowth and help tidy up the churchyard. An attempt had also been made to record inscriptions on the gravestones, many of which had become damaged. In 1974, shortly before Fir Tree House was demolished to make way for extensions to the Civic Centre, the EPS suggested that the decorative iron gateway and railings from the Edwardian

84. The gate and railings from Fir Tree House make a dramatic improvement to what was a rather dismal corner of the churchyard.

house should be moved across the road and re-erected between Church Lane and the churchyard; the result was a dramatic improvement to what had been an undistinguished corner. On learning that the Parochial Church Council (PCC) was trying to persuade Enfield Council to take over the maintenance of the churchyard, the Preservation Society wrote to the PCC and the Town Clerk early in 1975 offering to help clear up and plan the area. The offer was not taken up. The following year the PCC announced its intention to remove most of the tombs from the northern section of the churchyard, which (with the help of £18,000 from the Hundred Acres Charity) was to be laid out as a public garden and maintained by the borough council. As well as getting rid of nearly one hundred tombs, the scheme involved lopping lower branches from several yew trees, reducing the height of the ancient yew hedge and clearing the ground for four seating areas. The EPS, which had condemned the plan as 'ruthless', was invited to participate in discussions.

A St Andrew's Churchyard committee was set up under the chairmanship of the vicar, Revd Peter Morgan, with representatives from the PCC, Enfield Council parks department and the Hundred Acres Charity. Enfield Preservation Society was represented on the committee by Irene Smith and Valerie Carter, who urged that far fewer gravestones should be moved so that the essential character of the churchyard was preserved. The vicar countered that no stones would be removed from the churchyard; they would be resited or placed against a wall. He remained unmoved when the EPS representatives quoted from *The Churchyards Handbook,* a Church of England publication, which states: 'Tombstones should never be laid beside or stacked against a churchyard wall like a pack of cards. If you are unfortunate to have inherited a churchyard where this has happened, consideration should be given to restoring them to their rightful place'. (This was unpalatable advice, because the old southern part of St Andrew's Churchyard had long since been ruined by ignorant 'improvers' who had lined ancient gravestones round the perimeter like soldiers waiting to be shot.) After fierce arguments, a few minor alterations were conceded and it was agreed to hold a site meeting. The PCC called in reinforcements from the ecclesiastic heirarchy and the gloom of a February day in 1977 was briefly lifted for EPS representatives by the spectacle of an archdeacon, resplendent in swirling cape and green wellington boots, stomping round the disputed graves with members of the

Diocesan Advisory Committee. Unfortunately these worthies proved as insensitive to the historic value of the churchyard as was the PCC. The Preservation Society once again pleaded for the retention of more gravestones, especially the unusual 'body-stones', horizontal monuments shaped to resemble mummified bodies. *The Churchyards Handbook* cautions: 'These body-stones are of historical value and generally they should not be removed or destroyed'. But with a disdainful wave of the hand, the examples in Enfield's parish churchyard were dismissed by a St Andrew's churchwarden as 'macabre'. Several acrimonious exchanges took place at the subsequent meeting of the churchyard committee. The minutes record that Irene Smith 'referred to the meeting on site and made adverse comments on some of the representatives from the Diocesan Advisory Committee which the chairman ruled out of order and asked to be removed from the minutes'. Detailed arguments put forward by the EPS representatives in a last effort to save more monuments met with no success. The PCC was determined that the church should shed its responsibility for maintaining the churchyard. However, Enfield Council had agreed to take over the upkeep only if all the preparatory work was done beforehand, at no expense to the council. The Hundred Acres Charity was willing to finance this work 'subject to its approval of the plans for the churchyard as a public amenity'. This was largely a matter of personal interpretation, but most of the committee were unsympathetic to the Preservation Society's view. They agreed with a PCC representative when he suggested it was unlikely that people would want to sit and eat their lunchtime sandwiches 'surrounded by tombs'. By a majority vote the committee approved a plan which retained only 29% of the tombs and made extensive alterations to the layout of the churchyard.

In the EPS newsletter for autumn 1977 Christopher Jephcott complained: 'Although the planned removal of three-quarters of the tombstones and monuments is contrary to the advice given in both the Church of England's handbook and the guidance from the Secretary of State for the Environment on churchyards in conservation areas, there has been almost no modification of the original plan to suburbanise this last vestige of Enfield as an old market town. The EPS originally welcomed the proposal to tidy up the graveyard and offered to provide voluntary labour, but this insensitive scheme is one to which we could never lend our support.' The Preservation Society wrote in protest to the Diocesan Advisory Committee and sent Enfield Council a list of the graves it thought should be saved. Assurances were given that the proposals would be reconsidered, but in August 1978 the *Enfield Weekly Herald* reported that the council had approved the original scheme 'on the nod'. This meant that of the 137 existing tombs between Church Lane and the garden of rest, only 39 would be left *in situ*; some of these were table tombs with brick vaults, which would be lowered to ground level. The Preservation Society withdrew its offer of voluntary help. When a statutory notice of the clearance was pinned up in the church porch early in 1979, the EPS council of management decided to send formal objection to the Consistory Court against the grant of a faculty (without which the work could not be carried out). The Chancellor of the Diocese replied that the Preservation Society could not be a Party Opponent, but that two or three EPS members who were parishioners of St Andrew's could enter an appearance in opposition. Two volunteers were found without difficulty. They entered five grounds for objection and it was agreed the EPS would indemnify them against costs. However, in September that year a paper given by the Chancellor of the Diocese of London at the annual conference of the Diocesan Advisory Committee clearly indicated that the objectors would lose their case. In view of the high costs likely to be awarded, the Preservation Society asked them to withdraw and the faculty was granted without a court hearing.

85. Some of the fine tombs and monuments still standing near the entrance to St Andrew's Church, Enfield Town.

A year later, when the clearance was in full swing, Irene Smith received reports that a body-stone had been smashed to pieces. On investigation, she found that despite written assurances from the PCC, the work sheets being used on site did not give protection to the few body-stones still *in situ*. Following urgent discussions an Enfield Council officer visited the site and gave instructions that the agreed conditions must be observed. An irreplaceable part of Enfield's historic past was lost with the clearance of this section of the churchyard. In trying to save it, the Preservation Society had found itself battling against the short-sighted intentions of those who should have been its most ardent protectors. The public open space which future generations will inherit still suffers, as did the old churchyard, from litter, vandalism, and inadequate maintenance.

Relations between Enfield Preservation Society and St Andrew's Church were frosty for some time after the churchyard controversy. The EPS, which had moved its main meetings from Foresters Hall, Chase Side, to St Andrew's Parish Centre, found it was unable to obtain forward bookings in the new hall, ostensibly because no dates were available. EPS working parties to tidy the churchyard were suspended, breaking a tradition which had begun in 1964. As time passed, a gradual thaw set in, and during recent years volunteers from the Preservation Society have spent many hours clearing litter and planting bulbs in efforts to improve the appearance of this historic enclave in the heart of Enfield Town.

Chapter 8
Heritage at Risk

To mark the United Kingdom's entry into the EEC in 1973, the Civic Trust began planning a European Architectural Heritage Year. This was to be celebrated in 1975 and the trust appealed to its 1,100 registered amenity societies to organise events to stimulate an interest in 'purposeful, creative conservation'. Enfield Preservation Society responded with alacrity. By happy chance a new schedule of listed buildings in

86. Brooklyn, one of two elegant houses built next door to each other in Private Road in 1883. They were designed by A. H. Mackmurdo, the Edmonton pioneer who was a key figure in the development of modern architecture, for himself and his brother. Halcyon, the second house, was pulled down in 1967 before Enfield Preservation Society could intervene, but the EPS stepped in to save Brooklyn when it was threatened with demolition in 1970.

Enfield had been published by the Department of the Environment early in 1973 and the Society decided to make a second issue of EPS listed building plaques. Although still omitting a number of buildings the Preservation Society considered worthy of protection (most of which were added in subsequent years) the revised DoE list clearly showed the wide range of interesting structures surviving locally. New listings ranged from oddities such as the one-room Victorian school at Maidens Bridge to the 18th century St Andrew's Vicarage in Silver Street. Also included, to the delight of the Preservation Society, was Brooklyn, an unusual house in Private Road which was designed in about 1883 by A. H. Mackmurdo, a pioneer of art nouveau. Thanks to a tip-off from a member, the EPS had been able to save Brooklyn in 1970 when it had been threatened with demolition to make way for five three-storey houses.

Chase Non-Ferrous Metals quoted a price of £6.50 plus 8%VAT for each EPS plaque and it was agreed to offer them to owners of listed buildings at £7.50 each. There was an enthusiastic response and by the end of the year 56 plaques had been fixed to every imaginable type of property — cottages, mansions, family homes, schools, public houses, a flour mill, almshouses — calling attention to Enfield's rich architectural heritage. Unfortunately Enfield Council refused to buy plaques for the listed buildings owned by the borough, but local branches of the Women's Institute came to the rescue by offering to sponsor six plaques as a European Architectural Heritage Year project. These are now displayed on Forty Hall, Capel House, Bramley House and The Firs in Clay Hill, Redlingtons in Silver Street (all owned by the council) and the Forty Hill schoolroom, now part of a private dwelling but then owned by the 20th Enfield (Jesus Church) scouts.

Another, more ambitious project was also planned by the EPS to mark European Architectural Heritage Year: a major exhibition in Forty Hall. Five years previously, in the

87. Built in 1848, the single-classroom village school at Maidens Bridge, Forty Hill, was financed entirely by the Meyer family then living in Forty Hall. The school closed in 1894 when James Meyer died. Subsequent owners included the 20th Enfield (Jesus Church) Scouts. The school, now part of the adjacent cottage, bears one of the six EPS listed building plaques which were sponsored by local branches of the Women's Institute to mark European Architectural Heritage Year.

88. Irene Smith (honorary secretary) cuts the cake made by EPS member Elsie Hart at the reception to mark the Preservation Society's 40th anniversary. With her (left to right) are 'Spot' Ashton, a founder member of the council of management, Valerie Carter (chairman) and Stuart Mills, at that time the newest recruit to the council of management.

spring of 1970, the Preservation Society together with Enfield Camera Club and Enfield Archaeological Society had staged *Enfield's Heritage in Pictures* in the gallery at Forty Hall. More than 7,000 had flocked to see it, which was then a record attendance for a local exhibition at Forty Hall. The Preservation Society decided to mount an even larger exhibition in 1975 but found to its dismay that the gallery was fully booked. With considerable ingenuity the Society turned this setback to advantage. The following year, 1976, would mark the 40th anniversary of the formation of the Preservation Society. The gallery was reserved for the whole of August 1976 to present an exhibition, *Looking at Buildings*, brilliantly designed by Alan Skilton. It was opened by the Mayor (Alderman Peter Elvidge) at a reception to celebrate the Preservation Society's 40th anniversary. On this occasion Enfield Preservation Society looked beyond its usual territory. *Looking at Buildings* displayed photographs of more than 200 buildings then existing in the London Borough of Enfield, arranged in chronological order alongside panels listing national architectural milestones. The result was a fascinating local record of the development of English architecture over the past four centuries. Some of the superb black and white photographs had been used in the earlier EPS exhibition, but more than 150 were specially taken by members of Enfield Camera Club, Southgate Photographic Society and Edmonton Camera Club. The exhibition was outstandingly successful and was seen by nearly 15,000 people. One hundred of the pictures were later used to illustrate *Enfield's Architectural Heritage*, a book published by the Preservation Society to show the rich diversity of buildings contained within a single London borough. As a token of thanks to the photographers, the EPS presented the Heritage Challenge Trophy for annual competition among local camera clubs. The silver salver is awarded to the club or society submitting the best panel depicting some aspect of the environmental heritage within the London Borough of Enfield.

As well as trying to increase public appreciation of the local built heritage, the Preservation Society continued urging Enfield Council to demand higher standards of design

89. Thanks to the Civic Trust and organisations like the EPS, the 1970s saw a new appreciation of domestic architecture. In 1968 Cottage Place, Forty Hill (above), was spoilt by a rash of porches, trellis and fencing.

90. By 1979, a sensitive new owner had removed the porch from No.3, replaced the windows to match his neighbours and taken down an ugly gate, revealing the pleasing symmetry of these 1833 artisan cottages.

for new developments and to employ more staff in the planning department. Street clutter and obtrusive advertising had been frequent targets for the Society's criticism from the early 1960s. The EPS newsletter for autumn 1972 complained that no action had been taken to prohibit garish illuminated signs reported to the council three years before. 'If lack of staff is the problem, this should be remedied. Penny-pinching in this vital department, whose decisions affect our environment for years to come, is one economy the borough cannot afford' wrote Christopher Jephcott. As leader of the EPS architecture & planning group, he personally examined most of the planning applications submitted to Enfield Council, making specific suggestions whenever necessary. It was a daunting and often depressing task. In 1975 he viewed 250 applications at the Civic Centre and wrote more than 50 detailed letters. Typical comments taken at random from this correspondence, include: ... 'this proposal would appear to introduce a rather unsatisfactory form of piecemeal development into the area '... 'the high, narrow side dormer would constitute an undue intrusion in the street scene and we consider it should be modified or omitted' ... 'the design is marred by the flat roof of the proposed extension' ... 'the future of the whole of this backland needs to be considered comprehensively' ... 'this development is out of scale for a residential road' ... 'the design of the new extension is totally unrelated to the vigorous Edwardian styling of the original house and detracts from it considerably'. Frequently his suggestions were acted on, but many went unheeded. As the number of planning applications rose and council staff came under increasing pressure, many unsatisfactory schemes slipped through. Planning applications reached a peak of 2,160 in 1979. In the June 1979 EPS newsletter, following the completion of Colonel's Walk ... 'an unrelieved expanse of neo-Georgian on The Ridgeway' ... Dr Jephcott asked: 'Why has so much private housing built in the borough during the last 20 years been so mediocre, with so few good schemes?' Many neighbouring authorities did better, he said, because

91. Cottage Place (right) stood next to a row of old cottages in Forty Hill which were pulled down to make way for a block of old people's flats. The roof of the new building is clearly visible in this picture, which was taken in 1960 shortly before the cottages were demolished.

92. Enfield Preservation Society struggled for five years to save Gate Lodge Cottage in Carrs Lane, at the entrance to Bush Hill Park golf club. On learning in 1971 that the golf club wanted to demolish the small thatched cottage, the EPS urged that it be restored. Three years later Enfield Council refused the club permission to pull down the cottage and build a modern house. At the subsequent planning appeal the Inspector found in favour of the golf club, but his decision was overturned by the Secretary of State, who ruled that the building was capable of being sympathetically extended and rehabilitated. The golf club duly submitted a planning application for a two-storey extension, but no work was begun and in 1976, shortly before the cottage was due to be listed, it was mysteriously destroyed by fire.

they issued design guides (which Enfield Council had refused to produce) to encourage better layout and materials. It was not until 1984, following another strong recommendation by Dr Jephcott, that the council changed its policy and began publishing a series of design guides, a step welcomed by the Preservation Society.

Enfield Preservation Society became a registered charity in 1978. At the close of the 1970s, with nearly 1,700 members, its reputation and influence was considerable. In a series entitled London's Villages in the *Illustrated London News*, the author Tony Aldous wrote in February 1978: 'Enfield Town is a lively and attractive place, and much of the credit for it must go to its Preservation Society. Without their efforts many of the buildings which the townsfolk today admire and enjoy would have vanished; green belt landscapes would have been built over and footpaths would have vanished ... much else which council and citizens alike now value would have fallen either in the path of road-building or redevelopment. Some councillors, like Eric Ridge, argue that the preservationists sometimes go too far, demanding retention of buildings too badly decayed and too expensive to renovate. But a decade or two of steady propaganda has won over most of the critics, and on most issues Dr Ridge is now with the conservationists.'

Then, as now, the Preservation Society's activities and membership were concentrated mainly within the boundaries of the old borough. At the Society's annual dinner in 1972 the Mayor, Councillor Lionel Genn, expressed surprise that 'Enfield' in the Preservation

93. Eastern Enfield lost one of its few buildings of character in 1974 when Enfield Council allowed this Victorian lock-keeper's cottage at Rammey Marsh to be pulled down. On learning that British Waterways intended to demolish and rebuild the cottage, the EPS suggested it should be upgraded rather than replaced, but these protests, together with those from other organisations, went unheeded.

Society's name applied only to the old Borough of Enfield. He urged the EPS to 'look outwards and pay attention to the whole borough', forgetting perhaps that the Southgate Civic Trust was well established in his own former borough.

Occasional squabbles over territorial boundaries and spheres of influence, which had caused friction among local amenity societies and residents' organisations from time to time, were exacerbated by the creation of the London Borough of Enfield in 1965. The Federation of Enfield Ratepayers' and Residents' Association (FERRA) had built up a strong organisation within the former Borough of Enfield. On the amalgamation of Enfield, Edmonton and Southgate it was logical that ratepayers' and residents' organisations from the three boroughs should band together and a federation was formed covering the entire London Borough of Enfield. Sydney Hills saw this as the perfect opportunity to entice Enfield Preservation Society and Southgate Civic Society (now Southgate District Civic Trust) to become affiliated to the new federation, of which he was secretary. Perhaps with this end in mind the organisation had been named the Federation of Ratepayers' and Civic Associations of the London Borough of Enfield. Both amenity societies decided not to affiliate and their respective committees became increasingly irritated by the public assumption that they were part of the ratepayers' umbrella body. In November 1965 the EPS council of management agreed to ask the federation to drop the word 'civic' from its title, but the request was unanswered. Six months later, in May 1966, the *Enfield Gazette* published a letter from Carinthia Arbuthnot Lane (EPS secretary) and Audrey Lennox (Southgate Civic Society secretary). This effectively called Sydney Hills's bluff by challenging him to publish a list of affiliated organisations. No list was forthcoming, but Mr

94. Another building lost in the 1970s was the Emmanuel Baptist Chapel in Baker Street. The Preservation Society would have liked to have seen the imposing facade incorporated into a new development. The old shops on the bend were pulled down when the road was widened.

Hills responded the following week with a letter claiming that all the federation's affiliated bodies were in fact civic associations, because they were concerned with civic affairs. 'We have co-operated and will continue to co-operate with the Enfield Preservation Society and with our rival federation, FERRA' he wrote. 'Surely the fact that we are all concerned to encourage Enfield people to take an active interest in civic affairs is of much greater importance than the constitutional niceties that divide us'. Some time later the word 'civic' was quietly dropped, but Sydney Hills was not a man to give up without a struggle. He desperately wanted to add the strength of the Preservation Society to his lobbying power and in 1977 he once again urged the EPS to affiliate to the federation. This had now been mysteriously renamed the Federation of Enfield Ratepayers' and Amenity Associations (FERAA) but whether any *bona fide* amenity organisations were involved is doubtful. The overture was firmly rejected by the EPS council of management, but it was agreed to send a Preservation Society representative to FERAA meetings as a visitor/observer if invited. No invitation was received, and the relationship between the two organisations continued to be one of guarded cordiality. 'Amenity' later disappeared from the name of the federation, which for many years has been called the Federation of Enfield Residents' and Allied Associations (FERAA).

Enfield Preservation Society lost two of its outstanding personalities in the 1970s. Tony Lane, a driving force in the EPS since the early Sixties, died in 1975 aged 72. Born in India, the son and grandson of officers in the Indian Army, his hopes of an Army career were dashed by bad eyesight, though long service in the Territorial Army earned him the Territorial Decoration, and he served in the Royal Engineers and REME during the Second World War. Genial and hospitable, he was also a stickler for correct procedure. His

95. Godfrey Groves, EPS president (centre) presented an antique silver cream jug to Tony and Carinthia Arbuthnot Lane in 1972 as a token of members' appreciation of their outstanding service to the Preservation Society.

96. Carinthia Arbuthnot Lane opens the memorial gate linking St Andrew's Churchyard with the Parish Centre. The simple but strong pattern of the ironwork, designed by EPS member Ron Paxton, echoes the shape of the gables on the new centre. The brickwork, built up to match an older gateway a few yards away, bears a stone tablet which reads: 'This gateway was erected by the Enfield Preservation Society in memory of Clayton Arbuthnot Lane TD, 1903-1975'. With Mrs Lane is Revd Peter Morgan, vicar of Enfield.

military training was deeply ingrained and his punctilious attention to detail, though often frustrating to his more impetuous colleagues (including his wife) helped build the Preservation Society on sound foundations. Before the annual Town Show or similar events he would prepare a plan of action under headings such as 'Information, Intention, Execution' with every detail planned in advance. It was Major Lane who organised the system, still in use, for distributing the EPS newsletter by a network of volunteers. Once set on a course of action, he refused to compromise or be deflected and was never intimidated by officials, however highly placed. He played a crucial part in fund-raising for the Save Enfield Campaign, held numerous offices within the EPS and was chairman of the Defend Enfield's Green Belt committee. Reporting his death, the *Enfield Gazette* described him as 'A champion of Enfield ... with an unsurpassed record of conservation work in Enfield over two decades'. Alderman Bill Cook, a former Mayor of Enfield, said that without the efforts of Major and Mrs Lane, Enfield would have been a very different place. In recognition of Tony Lane's long service to St Andrew's Church as well as to the Preservation Society, the EPS provided a gateway to link the church with the Parish Centre in Silver Street.

Godfrey Groves, who had been elected president of the Preservation Society in succession to Ebenezer Rees, died while on holiday in Malta in 1978. Quietly spoken and unassuming in manner, he exerted considerable influence as a local property owner, as president of the Enfield-Southgate Conservative Association and (for a few years) as a member of Enfield Council. Although his personal interests sometimes conflicted with

97. Godfrey Groves in the front garden of Little Park, his home in Gentleman's Row. On the right, surmounted by a weather-vane, is the annexe built by the Leggatt brothers to contain the Tudor Room.

EPS policy, these differences of opinion never affected his loyalty to the Society. He allowed the the council of management to meet in the magnificent Tudor Room attached to Little Park, his home in Gentleman's Row, and he encouraged the Preservation Society to hold functions there and show its treasures to parties of visitors. A keen local historian (he was born in Tottenham) Godfrey Groves was an avid collector of prints, documents and pictures. He did not make a will, reportedly because he wanted to give as many people as possible the opportunity to buy items from his collection. This kind thought was largely thwarted when his property was sold at an auction held in a packed marquee erected in Gentleman's Row. According to the *Enfield Weekly Herald* (6 November 1980) the high prices surprised even the auctioneers (Phillips of London). 'A portrait of Queen Elizabeth I, which had hung in the original palace of Enfield, estimated at £5,000, fetched £12,500', said the report. 'The high prices disappointed Enfield Preservation Society who, supported by a personal gift of £500 from Don Gresswell, had hoped to buy a souvenir of their late president.' After several unsuccessful bids, the Preservation Society secured two wash drawings by John Chessel Buckler, one of Westwood Cottage, Chase Side and the other of Tottenham Church, which were given on permanent loan to Forty Hall Museum and Bruce Castle Museum respectively. Godfrey Groves was a director of Tottenham Hotspur Football Club and in 1979 representatives from Spurs and Enfield Preservation Society planted 22 trees in the Town Park, Enfield, in his memory.

Chapter 9
Attacks From All Quarters

The painstaking process of planning the future shape of Enfield took a step forward in 1980 with the publication in October of the draft Borough Development Plan (BDP). This set out Enfield Council's policies on matters affecting the use of land and buildings. It was based on a series of twelve reports of studies which had been issued at intervals since 1975 on specific topics such as the green belt, housing, transportation, environment, shopping, recreation and leisure. The Preservation Society had submitted detailed comments on most of the reports. The Society was now concerned that because the public consultation period included the Christmas break, many organisations and individuals would find it difficult to register their views on this long and complex document. One assumes this example of bad timing was accidental, but despite protests it was unfortunately repeated on several subsequent occasions when consultation periods on important council proposals were effectively curtailed by the Christmas holiday. In the EPS newsletter for December 1980 Christopher Jephcott confirmed that the Preservation Society would be submitting its reactions and urged members to study the copy of the UDP displayed in the Civic Centre foyer. But he cautioned: 'The time, energy and expertise which so many people put into creating this plan will only have been worthwhile if the result is acted upon, and not merely regarded as a pious statement of good intent. Already there are signs that this could happen'. The BDP was approved by the council in June 1981. Objections were heard at a public inquiry in March 1982 and after some modifications the plan was formally adopted in September 1983.

The first indications of the catastrophe that was to overtake Enfield's industrial base came in the early Eighties. In October 1982 the *Enfield Weekly Herald* reported: '...6,000 jobs have gone in the last three years and local businessmen can see little sign of an end to the slump. Since 1979 almost twice as many jobs have been lost in Enfield as in neighbouring boroughs'. Despite the slump, car ownership continued to rise. By 1981, 64.6% of households in the borough had access to a car compared with only 56% ten years earlier. Traffic on most local roads was steadily increasing, a dramatic exception being The Ridgeway, where the number of vehicles had halved following the extension of the M25 from Potters Bar to the A10 in July 1981. This reduction had slightly eased the traffic congestion in Enfield Town, but a startling proposal by the GLC in autumn 1982 brought fears that the relief would be short-lived. The GLC announced that it intended to introduce a contra-flow bus lane through Enfield. Buses would run from Southbury Road, against the direction of the one-way traffic in Church Street, to a mini-roundabout by the Library Green. Although the bus lane would cut through the Enfield Town Conservation Area, the GLC was not obliged to consult the local authority and there were fears that the

London bureaucrats would use their statutory powers to implement the scheme, despite the overwhelming and unanimous local opposition. The EPS autumn newsletter, under the heading 'Stop this crazy bus lane plan' denounced the scheme as 'a grave and long-term threat to the free movement of pedestrians as well as traffic in the town centre'. It pointed out that among other changes, three metres would be sliced off the fountain island and many more guard rails would be installed in Church Street, thus narrowing the already congested pavements.

Within weeks 1,400 had signed a protest petition hastily organised by the Preservation Society. Thousands more would no doubt have added their names if the petition had been kept open, but Enfield Council asked for its early delivery to strengthen its negotiations with the GLC. The petition was accepted by Councillor John Bowyer, chairman of Enfield Council's environment and land committee, at the beginning of November. The absurdity of the proposal became evident when the *Enfield Independent* reported on 10 November 1982: 'The GLC believe the scheme will speed up local buses with estimated savings of between 43 seconds and two minutes 36 seconds per journey'. This, said the Preservation Society, was a marginal benefit when set against the damage to the Town's environment, the probable cost of £112,000 and the disruption and inconvenience to pedestrians and other road users. Enfield Council and local organisations continued to voice their implacable opposition to the bus lane at meetings, in letters to the GLC and through the local press. In September 1984 the GLC finally abandoned the plan. Sadly, one voice that had often been raised in support of local causes fell silent during the campaign — 7 April 1983 saw the final edition of the *Enfield Weekly Herald*, which ruefully announced that it had been forced out of business after 122 years 'by economic circumstances'.

While the bus lane controversy was raging, the government announced its intention to abolish the GLC, which under the chairmanship of Ken Livingstone had become a *bete noire* to the Prime Minister and her colleagues. Enfield Preservation Society, in common with amenity organisations all over London, viewed the abolition with alarm, and did not hesitate to say so. Though remaining, as always, scrupulously aloof from political controversy, the EPS followed its usual practice of speaking out firmly on matters that could affect the local environment. At the Society's annual dinner in December 1983, Alan Skilton (EPS chairman) said: 'In spite of some of the strange quirks of the GLC, most of us see the need for a single, elected, over-ruling authority for the strategic planning of Greater London'. He listed the Preservation Society's misgivings in the February 1984 EPS newsletter, explaining that the Society had written to the Secretary of State for the Environment 'in quite strong terms' urging that if the GLC was abolished, arrangements should be made to compensate for the loss of existing services. It was feared that the GLC Historic Buildings Division, with its specialist skills and resources, would be dismantled, leaving historic buildings more vulnerable. The green belt could suffer if protection was left to individual boroughs without the GLC's overall planning strategy. The continuation of the GLC's efforts to revitalize derelict inner city land was still essential to relieve pressure on outer boroughs such as Enfield. 'Enfield Preservation Society has had notable disagreements with the present GLC, in particular with regard to the proposed contraflow bus lane in Enfield Town' wrote Alan Skilton. 'But such incidents seem hardly sufficient, in my view, to support the excessive measures of removing altogether the accountable GLC for an unknown central authority.' There were furious objections from a handful of members who apparently wanted to see the back of the GLC at any price. One even wrote to the Secretary of State making it clear that he disagreed with the Preservation

98. Peacock Cottage, one of Enfield's few weatherboarded buildings, stood on The Ridgeway almost opposite Chase Farm Hospital until it was demolished in 1986. The Preservation Society made several unsuccessful attempts to have this charming cottage listed.

Society's attitude. It was decided that the chairman, who had the full support of the council of management, would make an explanatory statement at the EPS spring meeting.

Despite the protection of the GLC (which was not finally abolished until 31 March 1986) the Preservation Society was becoming increasingly despondent at the deterioration of many of Enfield's historic buildings. In the summer of 1980 the EPS newsletter complained that for the second year running, Enfield Council had decided not to make any repair grants to owners of listed buildings, many of whom were finding it difficult to fulfill their legal obligation to keep their property in good repair. There was no improvement in the financial situation in the years that followed and grants from the council dried up completely. The situation was made even more difficult by the imposition of VAT on all building repairs. Len Keeble, who had become leader of the EPS historic buildings group in 1978, told the *Enfield Gazette* in June 1984 that he feared, because of rising repair costs, that owners would be tempted to knock down their buildings instead of putting them in good order. The demise of the GLC, the only source of grants for repair, would put listed buildings under increased pressure, he said. The historic buildings group favoured a law requiring permission before any listed building was demolished and it was actively campaigning, with national organisations, for repairs to listed buildings to be exempt from VAT. Meanwhile, the Preservation Society protested locally against proposals to convert three of Enfield's historic buildings into offices.

The most important of these buildings was Grovelands House, one of only two Grade I listed buildings in the borough. Because of its local significance Enfield Preservation Society stepped outside its traditional boundaries and became actively involved in the efforts to save Grovelands, a magnificent classical villa with extensive grounds in The

99. One of only two Grade I listed buildings in the borough, Grovelands House, built by John Nash in 1797, stood empty and rotting for twelve years until it began a new life as Grovelands Priory Hospital in 1987.

Bourne, Southgate. Built by John Nash in 1797 Grovelands House was used as an annexe to the Edmonton Military Hospital during the First World War; it subsequently remained in use as a hospital until it closed in 1977. Enfield Council granted permission for the conversion of the house in 1980. Since that date there had been an ambitious plan, originated by Southgate Civic Trust, to use the house as a community and arts centre. Although supported by Enfield Preservation Society and other organisations, the plan was turned down by the council which instead chose Millfield House in Edmonton. A proposal to convert Grovelands into offices, which was strongly opposed by the Preservation Society, fell through and the house, inhabited only by security guards, continued to deteriorate until 1985, when Enfield Council approved an application to use the building as a private psychiatric hospital. By then, after years standing empty, the building was gradually succumbing to dry rot. However, many of the fine internal features remained intact, including the famous Birdcage Room, an elegant octagonal parlour in which the walls and umbrella vaulted ceiling were covered with *trompe l'oeil* paintings to represent an idyllic landscape seen from inside a birdcage. The new owners of Grovelands proved unusually sensitive to the demands of the historic building and the EPS newsletter for winter 1988 announced with satisfaction that the company had been awarded a national Civic Trust Commendation for the careful restoration of the house. Four years later the Preservation Society was dismayed to learn that Enfield Health Authority had put in a planning application to build 53 houses, a community care unit and a bowling centre in Grovelands Park, very close to the mansion. The EPS joined other organisations in opposing the application which was eventually turned down, thus safeguarding the setting of the finely proportioned building. Now known as Grovelands Priory Hospital, the exterior of Grovelands House, still set in historic parkland, looks much as it did when it was first built.

In other parts of Enfield, the Preservation Society's efforts to save distinguished and historic buildings met with with only limited success at this time. In October 1981 the *Enfield Gazette* reported that the EPS was leading the fight against the demolition of the old Police Station at the corner of London Road and Cecil Road, Enfield Town. Built in 1873, this was one of the few late Victorian police stations surviving in north London but it had been empty since 1966 when the police moved to Silver Street. The Preservation Society urged that the facade, at least, should be preserved but to no avail. The building was destroyed and a four-storey office block built on the site.

There were bitter debates in 1984 about the fate of Ingleborough, a large property in Cavell Drive, which until the spring of that year was in use as a residential home run by Enfield Council. On 5 July, the *Enfield Gazette* reported that the council's housing department was seeking permission to convert the house into flats or sheltered accommodation, so that the commanding site off The Ridgeway could be sold with established planning permission. The Preservation Society urged that the handsome Victorian house should be preserved. Local residents joined the protest and feeling ran high. The council's next ploy, as reported by the *Enfield Independent* on 25 July, was to state that the house must be demolished as soon as possible 'to save security costs'. The report continued: 'Enfield Preservation Society say the council has allowed the house to deteriorate, and that in view of this neglect the onus is now on the council to make amends and ensure that this

100. For more than 90 years the former Church School of Industry, Silver Street, housed the offices and printing works of the Enfield Gazette. *When the* Gazette *moved out in 1984 the Preservation Society led a protest against a proposal to demolish the building and replace it with offices and a car park. Offices have since been built behind the original facade. This photograph was taken before 1974, when the ancient brick wall along Churchbury Lane (left) was knocked down and the road widened to give access to the new Civic Centre car park.*

valuable amenity is conserved for the future benefit of us all.' Two years later, the house was pulled down and replaced by 87 flats. The campaign to save the Church School of Industry, a listed building in Enfield Town on the corner of Silver Street and Churchbury Lane, was more successful. The *Enfield Gazette*, which had used the building as its office and printing works for just over 90 years, moved out in March 1984. Two months later, the newspaper reported plans to demolish the building and replace it with offices and a car park. Built in 1876, the distinctive red brick building had housed the Church of England Girls' School of Industry until 1909. With the two neighbouring buildings, it was part of an interesting group. The first, to the south, had been the Duke of Lancaster Coffee Tavern, opened in 1881, while the centre building was Enfield's first cinema. The Preservation Society protested that to demolish the buildings would destroy part of the town's history. Enfield Council compromised by insisting that the façade of all three must be preserved, a condition met with skill and sensitivity when the building was converted into offices.

In stark contrast the council reneged on its promise to preserve the ornate Victorian facade of the old Edmonton Town Hall in Fore Street. The EPS newsletter for winter 1986 pledged the Society's support for the campaign to save the building. The Town Hall, designed by W. Gilbee Scott, who was the architect of Barclays Bank in Enfield Town, held a special place in the affection of local people. Massive, opulent, with some fine architectural details, it stood out as a distinctive, romantic feature in Edmonton's dull urban landscape. In the EPS newsletter for winter 1987 Len Keeble deplored Enfield Council's decision to demolish the Town Hall to make way for a magistrates' court. He

101. Massive, opulent, with many fine architectural features, Edmonton Town Hall held a special place in the affection of local people, many of whom have never forgiven Enfield Council for pulling it down. The EPS condemned the destruction as a philistine act. Here, the Town Hall in 1988, awaiting demolition. The new Edmonton Police Station is taking shape on the right.

complained that no efforts had been made to see if the facade could be preserved, and said the Preservation Society would protest against 'this latest philistine act by the council'. The borough's architectural heritage suffered another grievous blow in 1984 when Broomfield House, a 400-year-old mansion in Broomfield Park, Palmers Green, was devastated by fire. The EPS played a leading part in the campaign to secure its rebuilding but was frustrated at every turn by the determined procrastination of Enfield Council, which favoured the easier option of demolition. This deplorable situation continued to drag on for thirteen years. For most of the Eighties the Preservation Society was also engaged in a protracted battle concerning another important local house, this time in the heart of the Enfield Town Conservation Area.

Brecon House, a large Georgian residence with Victorian additions, was sold by auction in April 1980. This was an unusually important listed building, situated in a commanding position at the north end of Gentleman's Row. The grounds of Brecon House extended from the New River to the footpath skirting school playing fields. They formed, with the gardens of the adjacent The Laurels and nearby Crown & Horseshoes public house, a significant wedge of open space in an outstandingly attractive area. The house was built some time before 1806 on an encroachment from Enfield Chase and had survived with its original stables, outbuildings, walls and gates, giving a unique rural touch to that part of the Enfield Town Conservation Area. Brecon House had been occupied by the Westmacott family since 1890, latterly by two spinster sisters, but had remained empty since the last one died in 1979. The house had later been vandalised and had become so

102. Empty, neglected and vandalised, Brecon House presented a sorry sight when it was bought by a property developer in 1980.

badly dilapidated that the estate agents felt obliged to admit, in the sale brochure, that it was 'in need of complete refurbishment'. But they added, with justified optimism: 'A discerning purchaser with wise expenditure could well make the property one of the finest in the borough'. The house was knocked down for £70,000 to a local firm of property developers and builders, A. C. Nicholas Ltd. They prepared plans for converting Brecon House into flats with a development of nine mews cottages and 18 garages in the back garden, and asked the Preservation Society to comment on the scheme.

The EPS council of management, which at that time was composed of 15 members, most of them opinionated, outspoken individuals, was often a forum for vigorous debate. There was usually little disagreement on matters concerning trees, footpaths or the green belt, but proposals affecting listed buildings were seldom clear cut. Brecon House proved to be an especially sensitive issue and the plans provoked widely differing reactions. It was agreed that the courtyard of mews cottages had been designed with care. (The Royal Fine Arts Commission, to whom the plans were later submitted under the terms of Kathleen Westmacott's will, described it as 'first rate ... a design of skill and charm'.) But however well-designed, any development was bound to destroy the historic significance of the site and spoil the setting of the listed building, and most members of the council of management were strongly against any new building being permitted in the garden of Brecon House. Others, influenced by the builder's claim that some development was essential to finance the restoration of the house (estimated at £150,000) thought the Preservation Society should accept a modified mews scheme. One member of the council of management (who later became a borough councillor) made a proposition to this effect; when it was defeated he asked for his name to be formally recorded as voting for development on the site. Having aired their views, members loyally backed the majority decision to oppose any development and presented their usual united front in public. It was agreed that a letter should be sent to A. C. Nicholas insisting that 'any development of Brecon House should be confined to the creation of high quality flats within the building.' The firm's reply caused some consternation. After giving an assurance that the house would not be altered externally, the letter stated: 'As regards development in the grounds, I am sure you are aware that the local authority made it clear to prospective purchasers of the land that development would be allowed'. The Preservation Society immediately wrote to the Town Clerk asking for clarification, and received a categoric denial that any such assurance had been given.

A planning application for the mews development and conversion to flats was submitted later that year. The borough planning officer (Norman Stonard) noted in his report to the planning committee that arguments for and against were finely balanced, but said he was 'favourably inclined' towards the scheme. Nevertheless, it was turned down by the council. A. C. Nicholas appealed against the decision and the firm was represented by counsel at the subsequent public inquiry at the Civic Centre on 1/2 December 1981. Enfield Council, represented by a solicitor from the Town Clerk's department, was supported by counsel engaged by the Gentleman's Row, River View and Holly Walk (GRH) Residents' Association and by Donald Potter, representing Enfield Preservation Society. The Inspector's opinion was that 'some new development in the rear garden is necessary to provide an economic basis for the retention and conversion of Brecon House'. But he considered the mews scheme would be an unacceptable intrusion and would be detrimental to the character of the conservation area. He therefore dismissed the appeal.

There was a respite of only a few months before the next skirmish. Early in 1982 A. C. Nicholas put forward a plan to convert the house into 4,000 square feet of offices, with

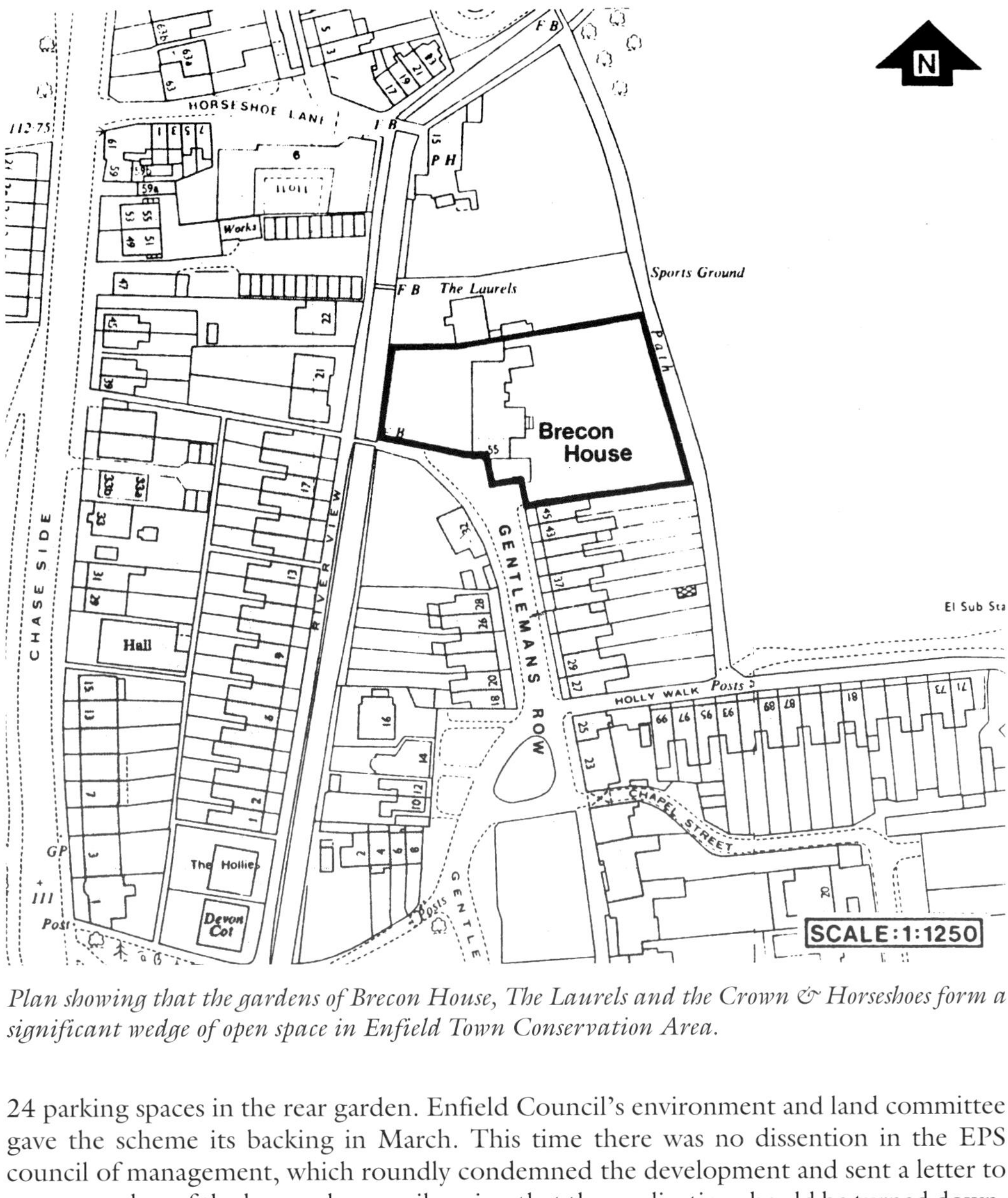

Plan showing that the gardens of Brecon House, The Laurels and the Crown & Horseshoes form a significant wedge of open space in Enfield Town Conservation Area.

24 parking spaces in the rear garden. Enfield Council's environment and land committee gave the scheme its backing in March. This time there was no dissention in the EPS council of management, which roundly condemned the development and sent a letter to every member of the borough council urging that the application should be turned down. The *Enfield Independent* on 12 May 1982 reported: 'Enfield Preservation Society have called on the council to think again; they say the office scheme would be the thin end of the wedge for the conservation area'. The council, unmoved, gave its approval. The EPS urged the Secretary of State (Michael Heseltine) to intervene and appealed to local MPs Ted Graham and Tim Eggar for support. Tim Eggar replied that although he 'had always argued that it was better to have Brecon House as a residential development than as offices', he thought that view was not necessarily shared by many local residents. He added: 'As you may appreciate I have had a number of representations on this particular development and I have decided that it would not be appropriate for me to comment to the Secretary of State'. Ted Graham sent a forceful letter to the DoE saying he was 'deeply

concerned that what will cynically be a commercial exploitation of this site will take place under the guise of retaining and improving a listed building'. Michael Heseltine nevertheless refused to call in the application on the grounds that the case was 'of local significance only'.

Events took an unexpected turn the following year. In September 1983 the *Enfield Independent* reported that the office plan had been withdrawn following the sale of Brecon House to Anthony Webster, proprietor of a local A to Z Stores, who intended to restore the house as a single family dwelling. Was this, the Preservation Society wondered, the end of the Brecon House saga? In the words of Winston Churchill: 'It was not even the beginning of the end. But it was, perhaps, the end of the beginning'. A. C. Nicholas had sold the house, but had retained nearly all the back garden. The firm promptly submitted a plan for four two- and three-storey houses with a new access road onto the land. The EPS council of management agreed that the scheme's architecture was some of the best seen in Enfield for a long time, but voted overwhelmingly against any development. In his letter of objection Len Keeble stressed that the Preservation Society could not support the start of backland development which could set a precedent for further infilling in gardens in the conservation area. He added: 'It seems a pity that we should have to object to a scheme where the architect and applicant have obviously gone to great lengths to produce an interesting and unusual design which might have been a welcome addition to Enfield, but definitely not in the grounds of Brecon House.' Despite a recommendation from the borough planning officer (Norman Stonard) that conditional permission should be granted, the council turned down the application. As expected, Nicholas appealed, but instead of ordering a public inquiry the Department of the Environment decided (at the request of the applicants) that the appeal would be determined by written representations. The official announcement from the DoE, received by the Preservation Society on 9 April 1984, stated that observations must be received by 20 April. The EPS protested forcefully to the Department and to Enfield Council at this ridiculously short notice and asked that 'a proper public inquiry should be held to consider what is locally a very controversial issue.' Bill Issitt, who had been appointed borough planning officer on the retirement of Norman Stonard, supported the Society's request. The DoE thought again, and a public inquiry was fixed for 9 and 10 October 1984.

The Preservation Society once again began the tedious, time-consuming process of preparing a detailed case to confront the professional experts who they anticipated (judging by past encounters) would try to rubbish their evidence at the inquiry. However on this occasion A. C. Nicholas was represented only by Andrew Nicholas (company surveyor) and by the architect for the proposed development. The London Borough of Enfield, on the other hand, had engaged counsel. The GRH Residents' Association, representing 50 households in the conservation area, had prepared an impressive, illustrated, and meticulously detailed document to support their objections. Enfield Preservation Society was again eloquently represented by Donald Potter. The Inspector, though describing the scheme for four houses as 'a sensitive and imaginative design', agreed with the Preservation Society that it would have an adverse effect on the setting of Brecon House and the adjoining properties. In a trenchant report that delighted the objectors, she said: 'In my opinion Brecon House is a building of sufficient architectural and historical importance to require more space about it than would be provided in the appeal proposal. It would be most unfortunate for the long term future of Brecon House and for the conservation area, if at this stage, when after a period of uncertainty the property is being thoroughly restored, it were to be deprived of an appropriate setting. In my view

103. In 1985, after several attempts to build in the spacious back garden had been successfully contested by the Preservation Society and others, Brecon House was being carefully restored by new owners.

although some limited form of development may be found to be acceptable, the present appeal proposal would be too insensitive development, too close to Brecon House, and would seriously prejudice its setting.'

A. C. Nicholas, encouraged by the hint that a smaller scheme might have more success, submitted a plan for two large, linked houses with an access road early in 1985. The Preservation Society complained that the 'undistinguished and unimaginative' design could best be described as 'a hotchpot' reflecting neither the character of Brecon House nor the adjacent Victorian cottages. The borough planning officer also made unfavourable comments. Nicholas withdrew the scheme and a few months later bounced back with a revised plan for two four-bedroomed houses with detached garages arranged formally round a courtyard. The Preservation Society, five other local organisations and several individuals registered objections. To their dismay the planning officer, at the end of a lengthy report, stated: 'I consider that the current scheme would form a worthy addition to the setting of this listed building in this part of the Enfield Town Conservation Area'. He recommended that, subject to several conditions, it should be accepted. The environment and land committee thought otherwise and rejected the application in June 1986. The refusal was endorsed by Enfield Council and the wearisome process began for the third time: A. C. Nicholas appealed, a public inquiry was fixed for 7 June 1987, and members of the Preservation Society spent hours preparing detailed objections which they hoped would withstand cross-examination and convince the Inspector. Donald Potter, the EPS mouthpiece at numerous public inquiries over the years, was now suffering from increasing deafness and Irene Smith reluctantly agreed to speak for the Society.

At this inquiry A. C. Nicholas was represented by counsel. Enfield Council, represented by one of its own solicitors, was supported by Irene Smith and by three veterans who had spoken at both previous inquiries: Anthony Webster (owner of Brecon House) Kevin Hinds (GRH Residents' Association) and Molly Beavan (Enfield Town Study Group). Following Donald Potter's example, Irene Smith had prepared a long and detailed statement describing the Preservation Society's interest in the site, the character of Enfield Town, the conservation area and Gentleman's Row, the history of Brecon House and its setting, and the Society's grounds for objection. To support the claim that local residents and visitors greatly appreciated the special qualities of the area, she produced documentary evidence including several EPS publications: the *Walk around Enfield Town* leaflet, Gentleman's Row postcard and the recently published *Portrait of Gentleman's Row*. Deeply convinced that the Preservation Society was right to insist that nothing should be built at the rear of Brecon House, she dealt coolly and calmly with a taxing cross-examination by counsel for the appellants. The quality of the Society's argument no doubt helped to influence the Inspector, who agreed with his two predecessors and rejected the appeal, adding: 'I have come to the firm conclusion that it is unlikely that in the present circumstances any further residential development would be acceptable on this appeal site'. After a decent interval, A. C. Nicholas, undeterred, made one last attempt. The EPS newsletter for winter 1990 reported that the firm's application to build a four-bedroomed house in the rear garden had been turned down by Enfield Council's planning sub-committee. Nicholas did not appeal. Three years later the saga of Brecon House came to an unexpected but highly satisfactory conclusion with the sale of the rear garden to Anthony and Susan Webster, who had spent nearly ten years (and many thousands of pounds) restoring the house with fastidious attention to correct historical detail. As a token of appreciation the Preservation Society presented them with an EPS historic building plaque for display on the house.

'Hands off St Michael's Green!' was the Preservation Society's reaction in July 1985 when the Enfield District Health Authority announced its intention to build over most of this green oasis in Chase Side. Soon after the Preservation Society was revived in the early Sixties, one of the first actions of the newly formed trees group had been to encourage Enfield Council to lay out the open space in front of St Michael's Hospital. At that time part of the ground was overgrown with rank grass and weeds; the rest, behind a fence, was an unsightly mess of derelict allotments. An anonymous gift of 25 trees, donated by a shopkeeper to mark 25 years of trading in Chase Side, inspired the EPS trees group in 1964 to draw up plans for a traditional village green crossed by tree-lined footpaths. Enfield Council liked the idea and the scruffy piece of waste ground was transformed. The Preservation Society suggested it should be known as St Michael's Green and the name stuck. Situated in a densely populated area, officially classed as being deficient in open space, the green was greatly appreciated by local people. The EPS was outraged when, on 8 July 1985, Enfield Health Authority applied to the council for outline planning permission to build a £680,000 unit for chronically sick children on the green. Within days, 1,000 houses surrounding the green had received a leaflet from the Preservation Society with the warning: 'Enfield District Health Authority wants to build on St Michael's Green, once part of Enfield Chase, which has been used as a public open space for many years. Since the late 1960s the green has been maintained by the London Borough of Enfield at ratepayers' expense and the public has enjoyed free and unquestioned access ....' The leaflet concluded: 'REMEMBER — it was Enfield District Health Authority which only recently sold the War Memorial Hospital site in Chase Side, almost opposite St Michael's Green. The Authority also intends to sell the vast Highlands Hospital site, instead of retaining some of it for future needs.' On 1 August the *Enfield Advertiser* reported that

104. St Michael's Green, Chase Side, subject of a keenly fought battle in 1985 when Enfield District Health Authority announced its intention to build on the green. The Preservation Society's strong campaign against the proposal attracted overwhelming support.

six councillors representing the surrounding wards had condemned the proposals as 'a disgrace'. The newspaper commented: 'The opposition of local councillors reinforces the stand taken by the Enfield Preservation Society, who described the proposals as monstrous.' There was intense public resentment at the health authority's attempt to purloin the green, but the issue was not straightforward.

Although one-third of the land was owned by Enfield Council, it was unclear who owned the rest. The council was known to oppose the building application, but if the health authority could prove its claim to ownership of part of the green, that section would be known as Crown Land and Enfield Council, as planning authority, would be unable to refuse planning permission. Instead, it would merely be able to oppose or support the application; if there was sufficient opposition, the Secretary of State would be asked to make a final decision. The health authority's claim of ownership was dismissed as 'a try-on' by the Preservation Society, which appealed to Tim Eggar MP for support. He issued a firm statement 'following representations from the Enfield Preservation Society and many local residents' which stated: 'I believe that whoever turns out to be the owner of this land should not be permitted to build on it. It is a pleasant, public open space and should be kept as such. I completely oppose building plans for St Michael's Green.' Council officials, historians and clerks administering ancient local charities spent hours consulting their archives, but no record of ownership was found. The health authority tried to exploit public sympathy — a ploy that was to be repeated even more shamelessly ten years later by a health trust trying to build on another green site. On 12 September 1985 Robert Naylor, acting district administrator for Enfield District Health Authority, told the *Enfield Gazette* that the new unit for the young physically handicapped was 'desperately needed'. He challenged opponents of the scheme 'to choose between open land and somewhere for such people to live'. People must decide whether a facility for a group of socially disadvantaged people was more important than maintaining an open piece of land, he said. Bill Issitt, the borough planning officer, had been shrewdly playing a waiting game. In the same issue of the *Gazette* he stated that as soon as the health authority had lodged its planning application in July, he had asked for details of its claim to the land, but had yet to receive a full response. He added: 'Until I am satisfied as to the ownership I would find it difficult to push the application forward'. Enfield Preservation Society presented a petition with 3,260 signatures, mostly from people living near St Michael's Green, to Councillor Frank Nellis, chairman of the borough's environment and land committee. Later that month Enfield Council, having registered its strong objections, referred the health authority's application to the Secretary of State for Health and for the Environment. The council stated that, in view of the strength of nearby residents' opposition, it would expect the application to be dealt with by a public inquiry and not by written representations. The EPS immediately asked Tim Eggar to write to the Secretary of State endorsing this view. The health authority did not pursue its application but neither did it retract its claim to ownership. Instead, it kept it up its sleeve as a threat to be used in future negotiations.

Throughout 1985 the EPS council of management was busy planning events to celebrate the Preservation Society's Golden Jubilee the following year. The centrepiece was to be an exhibition at Forty Hall, using some of the EPS archives to illustrate the story of the Society's day-to-day activities and major campaigns. There was no lack of material. In fifty years the Preservation Society had amassed a unique collection of historic photographs, documents, books, slides and artefacts. A records group had been formed in 1966 to catalogue the then modest archive collection and to maintain a book of press cuttings about the Society. As the existence of the group became known, EPS members and older Enfield residents were generous in donating local handbooks, maps, photographs and other memorabilia to the EPS archives. All such material was (and still is) gratefully received and carefully catalogued and preserved. Members of the group, which was renamed the records and research group soon after Stan Lowen became its leader in March 1977, initiated several valuable projects including a detailed, ongoing survey of changes in the use of individual shops in Church Street since 1899. In 1978 the group began making a photographic record of streets in Enfield, concentrating on roads and their related buildings in areas which were most likely to change. By 1996 more than 80 roads had been covered, plus areas such as Highlands Hospital and the Enfield Chase railway yard, both targets for housing development. All this material, with masses of correspondence, minute books and exhibition material, was stored at home by members of the EPS council of management, some of whom were getting desperate as more and more paperwork invaded their living space and threatened domestic harmony. The EPS publicity committee suggested the Preservation Society should look urgently for rented premises — a room or lock-up garage — where the material could be stored. Even before the proposal was discussed by the council of management, the Society's prayers were answered. Don Gresswell, who had noted the dilemma as he read the committee minutes, offered the Society a gift that both solved the problem and opened up exciting new possibilities.

Don Gresswell, who joined Enfield Preservation Society in 1960, was the anonymous donor who in 1964 had given 25 trees to mark 25 years of trading in Chase Side, where

105. The 1935 poster inviting the citizens of Enfield to protest against the proposal to erect a Town Hall on Chase Green — 'the people's land' — was one of the items from the EPS archives displayed at the Preservation Society's Golden Jubilee Exhibition in Forty Hall. Touring the exhibition with the Mayor (Councillor Win Reardon) are John Marshall MEP, Dr Ian Twinn MP, Councillor Frank Nellis and Valerie Carter (EPS chairman).

he had set up a one-man business as a tobacconist and confectioner. From what was initially a sideline — stationery — he developed a thriving bookselling and stationery empire, supplying hundreds of schools in Enfield and far beyond. The business later moved to Grange Park where, with his two sons, he diversified yet again and built up an international reputation for specialist library equipment. As he prospered, Don Gresswell had made many generous donations to the Preservation Society, often anticipating special needs: money to buy trees, equipment to clear footpaths, loans to help publishing projects. Now came a magnificent and imaginative gift — a freehold site containing a large hut in Parsonage Lane, Enfield. Mr Gresswell had bought the wooden, First World War hut 30 years previously from the Boys' Brigade to use as a warehouse for his bookselling business. It was large enough not only to hold all the EPS records but to serve as a permanent headquarters and meeting place. Don Gresswell suggested it should be named Jubilee Hall, to commemorate the EPS Golden Jubilee. When he accepted the keys on behalf of the Preservation Society on 5 March 1986, Donald Potter (EPS president) recalled Don Gresswell's pioneering work creating footpaths and clearing litter in the 1960s and said he had been a constant inspiration to members. He was a man of ingenuity, resourcefulness and above all, enthusiasm for the countryside.

Chapter 10
Unlocking the Countryside

When Don Gresswell joined the Preservation Society in 1960, most of Enfield's green belt was inaccessible to the public. He had been a keen walker since the age of 16 when he formed a youth club near his home in Wood Green, leading his friends on weekend rambles into the Home Counties. Don Gresswell described himself as 'a life-long footpath addict' and with the full support of Enfield Preservation Society he began making plans for a series of new public paths which would penetrate every part of the nearby countryside. The superb network of footpaths enjoyed by walkers today proves how brilliantly he and his successors in the Society achieved this aim, but it was a long and arduous struggle. Years later, he remarked: 'It was not until we started to do things in Enfield in the early 60s that I realised what was involved, and the effort that was required to achieve any practical effect'.

The first breakthrough came in 1962. Parts of the Forty Hall estate, which Enfield Council had acquired from the Parker Bowles family in 1951, were almost impenetrable and Don Gresswell suggested the Preservation Society should tidy up the overgrown corner of Gough Park at the junction of Forty Hill and Clay Hill. The council welcomed this offer of help. Don Gresswell called for volunteers, pointing out: 'This is the first opportunity for the re-formed Enfield Preservation Society to show that deeds, as well as words, count in the improvement of local amenities'. Among those who responded to the appeal were Christopher Jephcott and Alan Skilton, both still active in the Society today (1996). They, and the other volunteers, were in for a surprise. As the clearance progressed, the working party uncovered traces of a twelve-foot-wide carriageway alongside the old course of the New River, leading from Forty Hill to Whitewebbs Park. With official blessing, the volunteers turned out on 19 freezing weekends throughout a bitingly cold winter to clear the new footpath. Such schemes are now commonplace, but this was one of the first examples in the country of practical co-operation between an amenity society and the local authority. Councillor F. C. Cunneen, chairman of the parks committee, told the *Enfield Gazette* in April 1963 that it was 'a really first class example of a voluntary organisation who have answered an unspoken appeal to beautify Enfield'. The path, which was ready for use the following month, was bitterly opposed by the Gough Park allotment holders, who feared their plots would be damaged by vandals and tresspassers. In October 1964, after lengthy deliberations, Enfield Council agreed to spend £900 on a fence to protect the allotments. The borough refused to hold an official opening ceremony but in June 1965, to inaugurate the new path, Enfield Preservation Society organised a five-mile 'footpath ramble' from the Goat, through Gough Park to Theobalds, then back to Bulls Cross.

106. In autumn 1962, on the first working party organised by Enfield Preservation Society, volunteers began clearing a tangled mass of undergrowth and brambles at the entrance to Gough Park, Forty Hill. Daffodils and other spring bulbs were planted to complete the improvement. This picture, looking out from Gough Park towards Ansells Green and Baker Street, was taken in February 1963. The scene is vastly different today. In 1995 most of the trees near the entrance were cut down by Enfield Council's park ranger service, whose drastic action brought sharp criticism from the EPS and others. The council's plan for ongoing work in the park was modified as a result of these comments.

107. Having tackled the entrance, EPS volunteers turned out on 19 freezing weekends in the winter of 1962/63, undeterred by snow and exceptionally cold weather, to clear a disused footpath through Gough Park from Forty Hill to Whitewebbs. The path, along the old course of the New River, had been revealed when undergrowth was cut back. Working in the foreground are Christopher Jephcott (left) and Donald Potter.

108. *The completed Gough Park footpath, 1964.*

Throughout this time the Society was trying to trace other local paths, some dating back to the early seventeenth century, and have them registered as rights of way. The *Enfield Gazette* reported in August 1963: 'There are more than 100 public paths (24 of them rural paths) within the borough boundaries. Some are well used, others are in danger of being forgotten and lost to the public, having been left unsignposted and fallen into disuse; some public footpaths have become fenced off with barbed wire. It is one of the aims of Enfield Preservation Society to get these opened up to the public again and in this they have the full co-operation of the borough council.' The *Gazette* added that the first new footpath sign and stile, erected at the suggestion of the Preservation Society, indicated a path leading from Coopers Lane Road via Holly Hill Farm to The Ridgeway. The path had been fenced off with barbed wire but was recently 'rediscovered' on the official list of Middlesex footpaths. Enfield Council had agreed to include four new paths suggested by the Society in the following year's estimates. 'Don Gresswell' concluded the report, 'sets off as intrepidly as Marco Polo on Sundays to explore a different footpath and see where it will lead him'.

What the report did not add was that between walks, Don Gresswell spent most of his spare time writing letters, meeting officials and farmers, and consulting maps in his efforts to open up more paths. Society members were keen to help, and an EPS footpaths group was formed in September 1963. Efforts to trace disused paths continued and a large map displayed on the Society's stand at the Town Show that September led to a steady flow of information. It became evident that many paths had been obliterated during the Second World War, when it was permissable to plough up or divert public rights of way so as to obtain the maximum amount of food production from the land. At the end of the war the paths had automatically reverted to their former status, but many were now impossible to follow and the Society began months of painstaking detective work so that the old paths could be reinstated.

In March 1964 the EPS newsletter reported that the footpaths group had signposted all of Enfield's country footpaths, erected two new stiles and dealt with six cases of barbed wire obstruction or misleading notices. Working parties had cleared the view of Wildwoods lake from Flash Lane, and had tidied up St Andrew's churchyard in Enfield Town. Eight new footpaths suggested by the Society had been approved by Enfield Council, and group members had already made one important new path themselves. Describing this venture, the London *Evening News* had reported in February 1964 that Enfield Preservation Society, with the help of youth organisations and using tools provided by the council, was cutting a mile-long footpath along the tree-lined verge of Cattlegate Road. 'The footpath, which commands magnificent views of the green belt, has been forging ahead at the rate of five feet a minute' said the *Evening News*. However, whether or not the clearance work was completed at this breakneck pace, it took two and a half years of concerted effort before this short path (footpath no.1) was opened in January 1966. The negotiations initiated by Enfield Preservation Society involved five local government authorities, the Potters Bar Society, the Ramblers' Association, farmers, local residents, and the Commons, Open Spaces and Footpaths Preservation Society. Although only 400 yards lay within the borough boundary, this path was the key to three miles of walks between Crews Hill and Cuffley.

The Society was determined that the general public should be made aware of this growing access to the nearby countryside, and Don Gresswell agreed to prepare a map of local paths. The first EPS footpath map, published in March 1964, was an immediate success. Five hundred copies (price, one shilling each) were sold in eighteen months. A second edition of 5,000 copies followed.

109. The footbridge erected over the A10 Great Cambridge Road, at the insistence of Enfield Preservation Society, to link the footpath from Turkey Street station with green belt paths in Forty Hill. This picture shows the bridge shortly after its completion in 1970, looking across the A10 into the Dell.

These were years of constant challenge and activity. In July 1964 one of Enfield's rural by-ways was nearly sacrificed to the incessant demands of road traffic. To increase the safety of pedestrians, Enfield Council had proposed straightening the bends in Whitewebbs Lane. Instead, at the Society's suggestion, a footpath was made behind the hedge of this still picturesque, winding lane. In the meantime the volume of traffic on the A10 Great Cambridge Road was growing inexorably. Late in 1964 it was announced that the northern stretch of the A10 through Enfield was to be enlarged into a dual carriageway with a central barrier, thus cutting off the only footpath from eastern Enfield giving access to the nearby green belt countryside. Enfield Council and Middlesex County Council raised no objection, but the Preservation Society demanded that a footbridge should be built over the trunk road to link the footpath from Winnington Road and Turkey Street station with the path which leads from the A10 to Forty Hill near Maidens Bridge. A letter sent by the Society to youth clubs and residents' organisations in eastern Enfield brought massive support for the demand, which was backed by John Mackie, MP for Enfield East. The Society kept up the pressure but it was not until 1969 that the Ministry of Transport relented and promised to build a bridge, which was completed by June 1970.

The Civic Trust had meanwhile asked the Preservation Society to help prepare a report on the recreational development of land in the Lea Valley area. In response, Don Gresswell personally surveyed and classified 253 footpaths between Ware and Edmonton. When the Civic Trust published its visionary report — *A Lea Valley Regional Park: an essay in the use of neglected land for recreation and leisure* — in July 1964 it gratefully acknowledged the help given by various local authorities, national bodies, and Enfield Preservation Society. The report resulted in the formation of what is now the Lee Valley Park, whose name reflects the widespread confusion surrounding the name of the river. Realising how important the Lea Valley development would be for Enfield, the Society organised an open meeting (its biggest to date) in October 1964. A speaker from the Civic Trust explained the proposals and Councillor Ted Graham, chairman of the town planning committee, was loudly applauded when he indicated that Enfield Council would do all in its power to help bring the scheme to fruition.

The Society's detailed plans for an Enfield footpath network were submitted to the borough council in September 1964. Fifteen miles of new paths were suggested, to enable walkers to reach any part of the borough from the Lea to Grange Park or Hadley

110. Miles of open countryside in Enfield's green belt can be enjoyed by walkers today, thanks to the pioneering work of the Preservation Society. This party, on a mid-week walk in November 1993, are on the path between Rendelsham Viaduct and Burnt Farm Ride.

Wood, and to cross the boundary to Potters Bar, Northaw, Cuffley or Cheshunt, without walking on a road. According to the *Enfield Weekly Herald* (30 April 1965) the scheme was the first of its kind to be put forward for London's green belt. The report noted that ten miles of the suggested paths had been accepted by Enfield Council, but warned: 'Earlier proposals of the Society were first approved by the council in June 1963 but are still finding their weary way through the official procedure of footpath creation under the Highways Act of 1959'. Local government changes were to delay the new paths still further. In the EPS newsletter for spring 1967, Don Gresswell reported with exasperation that the EPS footpaths group had been in continuous correspondence and negotiation about paths, still not opened, that had been approved in 1963 and 1964. Fifteen miles of footpath had not yet been implemented. Even more frustrating, the path from Hilly Fields leading under the railway viaduct to Rectory Farm, originally approved by Enfield Urban District Council in 1953, was now to be discussed at yet another site meeting between the GLC Land Agency, the borough planning department, Enfield Preservation Society, and the farmer.

The footpaths group became involved with another innovative project when it waymarked paths on the 500-acre farm at Nazeing owned by John Mackie MP. The technique was then so novel that the *Enfield Gazette* felt it necessary to add an explanation when reporting the pilot scheme on 16 April 1965: 'Waymarking is a system widely used on the Continent to enable visitors to see the best of the scenery by footpath, without fear of losing their way. In this country it is used in some of the National Parks and on long-distance routes, but the Preservation Society is anxious to see if it helps townspeople to obtain greater enjoyment in the countryside'. The following week, the Preservation

Society's waymarking project, coupled with the opening of the Pennine Way on 24 April, was referred to in a letter in *The Times* from the Ramblers' Association 'as a sign that walking has not gone out of fashion'.

The increasing popularity of horse riding was now causing considerable friction with walkers and damage to footpaths. Riders, anxious to avoid the roads, monopolised some rural paths, often intimidating walkers and leaving the paths impassable on foot in wet weather. The Society proposed a route for 10 miles of bridleways early in 1965. Many were constructed, including a complete circuit round the western perimeter of Wilkinson's Woods in Whitewebbs, but the nuisance continued. In 1967, before he relinquished the leadership of the footpaths group, Don Gresswell was able to thank the borough engineer, Frank Ladly, for erecting barriers to prevent horses using the Gough Park footpath and Mile-and-a-Quarter Alley. But the Society's request for a by-law prohibiting horse riding on footpaths throughout the borough, although repeated at intervals for several years, came to nothing.

There were fears that the M25, as it gradually encircled the countryside north of Enfield, would cut off several important footpaths giving access into the green belt. After protracted correspondence, followed by representations from the Preservation Society and Enfield Council at the lengthy public inquiry held at Hertford in November 1969, the Ministry of Transport agreed to construct bridges or underpasses to link the paths and bridleways which would be severed by the motorway.

Enfield Preservation Society was now firmly identified by the public as the guardian of the local footpath network. Instead of contacting Enfield Council, disgruntled walkers complained to the Society when they found that paths were obstructed, impassable because of mud, or badly signed. In the spring of 1971, fired by Peter Woollett, their new, young leader, members of the footpaths group walked all the local paths to check their condition. Working parties were held to clear obstructions, hack back undergrowth, and renew signs. The survey was completed by the autumn, and the group began preparing a revised, three-colour edition of the EPS footpaths map. Published in autumn 1973, it showed more than 40 miles of public paths in Enfield, Cuffley, Goffs Oak and Northaw. Trent Park, which had become a GLC country park earlier in the year, was included for the first time — a particular source of satisfaction to the Society, which had originally attempted to get more generous public access to the park as long ago as 1961. At that time Trent Park was leased to Middlesex County Council by the Sassoon family, but the public was allowed to use the footpaths on only two occasions a year.

The EPS footpaths group continued to organise regular working parties and informal walks for members, but towards the end of 1973 a significant decision was made. It was decided to hold conducted public walks, on the last Saturday of every month, to encourage local people to explore the splendid countryside on their doorstep. These were an immediate success. More than 70 people turned up to join the first walk, from Oakwood to Barnet Church via Trent Park and Hadley Wood, on 26 January 1974. Beginning with modest strolls of three or four miles on local paths, the popularity (and length) of the walks steadily increased. In 1982, the average attendance was 35, although one walk had attracted 65 people. By this time, most of the walking country within 10 miles of Enfield had been covered, and locations further afield were reconnoitered, involving careful planning by the walk leaders, and lengths of up to 16 miles. Walkers on these marathons ranged from 80-year-olds to infants of 18 months carried on a parent's back. Routes were ingeniously worked out so that the weary could fall out before they fell down, but there was a growing demand for a less strenuous programme and in April 1984 the Society

111. Monthly weekend walks conducted by the EPS footpaths group range over a wide area. In August 1995 this party had perfect weather for a nine-mile ramble that included the towpath alongside the River Stort near Sawbridgeworth.

initiated monthly mid-week walks for senior citizens and the less active. These walks, too, proved immensely popular, and still form part of the regular footpaths group programme. Statistics published in the EPS newsletter in 1987 revealed that during the previous year the footpaths group had held 29 public walks, attended by 832 people. Over the previous 10 years, 216 walks and coach outings had been organised, with a total attendance approaching 10,000. The walks (mainly within 20 miles of Enfield) had included several with more than 80 people present, and one with 98. 'All those feet pounding the paths over the years have contributed significantly in keeping our public footpaths open' wrote Stuart Mills, who took over as group leader in September 1978.

One of the most important new footpaths proposed by Don Gresswell in the early 1960s was a route from Hadley Road to The Ridgeway, connecting Trent Park with Enfield's northern countryside. The path, which was an essential link in the Enfield Chace network, had been approved in principle by Enfield Council in 1964, but repeated requests for it to be built met with one official excuse after another. After years of tedious negotiations a route running north from Trent Park (opposite the obelisk) across Parkside Farm to Holly Hill Farm was agreed late in 1975. Then — impasse. The GLC, which owned the land, insisted the path should be fenced before it was opened, and Enfield Council (which had to adopt the finished path) said it could not afford to do the job. Enfield Council did, however, offer to provide the materials if the Preservation Society would supply the labour. Enthusiasts in the footpaths group (then the largest EPS group) needed no further encouragement and with help from other Society volunteers the group began work on the northern section in spring 1976. The task was far from straightfor-

112. EPS volunteers fix plain and barbed wire to complete the fence on a section of the Jubilee Footpath in 1978. More than five miles of wire, secured by 3,500 staples and nails, were used on the path which runs from Hadley Road to The Ridgeway.

ward. The path, which stretched for one and one-third miles over undulating countryside, crossed streams and skirted a copse. Before the fence could be erected, deep-seated tree stumps and roots had to be cleared all along the route. Work progressed steadily, but in the summer of 1977 it became evident that completing the path was going to be a far bigger task than anticipated. The GLC, which had agreed to fence the middle section, withdrew its offer because it had run out of money. This was a major setback but Enfield Preservation Society was so determined to see the path completed that it agreed to instal the entire fence. A grant was received from the Queen's Silver Jubilee Fund to help with the cost of materials, but the amount of voluntary effort involved was prodigious.

Apart from putting in more than 3,000 hours of exhausting physical work, the footpaths group used amazing perseverance and considerable ingenuity to overcome problems ranging from collapsed stream banks to weeks of rock-hard earth in summer and implacably frozen ground in winter. More than 700 posts were driven in, then strung with five miles of plain and barbed wire secured by 3,500 staples and nails. Two streams were diverted, 100 yards of revetting installed, two railway sleeper bridges built and two stiles erected. When at last the work was finished, the Society named the route the Jubilee Footpath in honour of the Queen's silver jubilee. On 3 February 1979, to mark its adoption as a public right of way, the Mayor of Enfield (Councillor John Payne) led 60 triumphant members of the Preservation Society on a walk along the path, accompanied by

113. Walkers in January 1995 crossing one of the bridges on the Jubilee Footpath.

Michael Whitman and his wife, of Parkside Farm. Two years later, in a House of Commons debate on the Wildlife and Countryside Bill, Ted Graham, then MP for Edmonton and Opposition spokesman on the environment, referred to the creation of the Jubilee Footpath. 'I consider that by any standards, it was a major achievement by a voluntary body' he said.

As the Jubilee Footpath was gradually forging ahead, another rural path came under threat. For as long as local people could remember, they had been able to walk freely from Crews Hill to Goffs Oak along Burnt Farm Ride through the Theobalds Park Estate. Unfortunately, however, Cheshunt UDC had neglected to include Burnt Farm Ride in the 1953 definitive map of rights of way and following a change in the agents responsible for managing the estate, people trying to use the path found themselves turned back on the instruction of the landowners. The Preservation Society, anxious to preserve this ancient footpath, appealed for anyone who could prove uninterrupted use for at least 20 years prior to 1972, to complete an official form. There was an impressive response and the forms were used as evidence at a public inquiry the following year to support the Society's case that the entire Enfield/Broxbourne length of the ride was a public right of way. This inquiry concerned only the Enfield section of Burnt Farm Ride, which was soon afterwards given the desired status. In the months that followed, reports of angry scenes between walkers and the estate gamekeeper on the Hertfordshire section became more frequent. Letters to Broxbourne Council brought no result and eventually local organisations decided it was time for a showdown.

Things came to a head in June 1978 when the *Enfield Gazette* reported: 'A quiet countryside stroll on Saturday ended in confrontation between 70 walkers and a gamekeeper, who blocked the path and called the police'. The walkers, led by Stuart Mills of the EPS footpaths group and Sydney Hills JP, secretary of FERAA, included contingents

114. With the law firmly on their side, threatening signs did not deter more than 80 EPS members who enjoyed a victory walk along Burnt Farm Ride shortly after it was officially declared a public right of way in 1981. The Preservation Society fought for five years to keep this path open, supported at every stage by the Ramblers' Association whose national secretary, Alan Mattingly (in dark glasses) is seen here with Stuart Mills, EPS footpaths group leader.

from the Ramblers' Association, Crews Hill Residents' Association and the Potters Bar Society. Among them were two elderly men who had been walking the route all their lives without hindrance until the new agents took charge of the estate. Quietly determined, the walkers marched along Burnt Farm Ride until faced with a newly-erected sign proclaiming 'This is not a right of way'. The gamekeeper, who had no doubt seen the crowd approaching, had completely blocked the path with his van. Red-faced and angry, he now emerged from his cottage, gun in hand — but he quickly concealed the weapon when he saw a press photographer among the crowd. Shouting and gesticulating, the keeper ordered the walkers to turn back. They defiantly replied that they did not intend to budge and would stay there all day if necessary, until he let them through. Threats that he would call the police left the crowd unmoved, at which, his bluff having been well and truly called, the gamekeeper retreated into his cottage to summon the Law. Shortly afterwards, apparently anticipating trouble, police cars raced up the track from both the Enfield and Cheshunt ends of Burnt Farm Ride to converge on the walkers. Having arrived, the officers seemed at a loss to know what to do with so many quiet, orderly people, especially when they recognised a prominent local magistrate, Sydney Hills, as one of the leaders. Eventually, after listening to arguments from both sides, the police sensibly advised the gamekeeper not to cause a disturbance and to let the walkers pass. The vehicle blocking the path was reluctantly removed, and the walk proceeded peacefully.

Pressure for the path to be opened continued, as did individual confrontations with the belligerent gamekeeper. After repeated requests from the Preservation Society and other bodies Broxbourne Council at last took action and in 1980, with the approval of the Secretary of State, a Public Path Creation Order was issued. Objections from the British Horse Society (which wanted the route designated as a bridleway) were not upheld by the minister, and the path was declared legally open along its entire length in the summer of 1981. Public path creation orders are rarely made and this was heralded nationally as a significant achievement.

Another footpath campaign took even longer to reach a successful conclusion. Hours of effort were spent over many years in trying to open up the shortest footpath on the EPS map — the historic Wood Well path. In former days, folk living in cottages in Theobalds Park Road used the path to fetch water from Wood Well, their only source of supply. Originally the path went right through to Flash Lane but in 1963 Don Gresswell found it completely overgrown and disused. So many fruitless attempts were made over the years to reinstate the path and resolve various legal objections and arguments about its use, that many felt this ancient right of way would have to be abandoned. But dedicated walkers are noted for their determination and perseverence and at last, in September 1988, Stuart Mills was able to announce in the EPS newsletter that the Wood Well path was fully open for the first time in at least 15 years. After repeated requests by the Preservation Society and the Ramblers' Association, Enfield Council had cleared the path and had erected a stile and signs at each end. Stuart Mills urged members to use the path, so the EPS footpaths group obediently included the Wood Well path in their Boxing Day walk that year. Describing the day to the EPS council of management in January 1989, Mr Mills said that between 11am when 69 people led by the Society walked the path, and 3.30pm when members of the local Ramblers' Association tried to use the route, two of the three stiles had been removed and replaced by barbed wire. 'We have protested to the council at this deliberate obstruction and have been assured they are pursuing all necessary channels to have the path reopened,' he said. Enfield Council acted swifty and in February it served notice on the landowner to remove the barbed wire. Receiving no response, the council took down the wire the following month and arranged to erect new footpath signs on private property on the opposite side of Flash Lane. In June, more barbed wire was placed across the path. After months of painstaking negotiation, the council secured agreement for a diversion of the path which, it was hoped, would preserve the ancient link and also be acceptable to adjacent landowners. The Preservation Society and the Ramblers' Association gave evidence at the public inquiry to determine the revised route, and both corrected misleading statements and opposed claims from the landowner that the right of way should be extinguished. Work on the proposed diversion was started but was soon abandoned owing to more objections. The council promised to reinstate the path and in

115. The case of the vanishing stile. When Don Gresswell was planning his footpath network he rediscovered the ancient Wood Well path linking Flash Lane with Theobalds Park Road. For at least 15 years, unco-operative landowners persistently blocked the right of way, but late in 1988 the Preservation Society was told by Enfield Council that the path was fully open, with a stile and signs at each end. On Boxing Day morning 69 EPS members climbed over the stile on their Christmas walk.

116. By 3.30pm on Boxing Day afternoon, when the local Ramblers' Association tried to follow the same route, the stile had been removed and replaced by three strands of barbed wire.

the summer of 1994 the EPS footpaths group reported that its members had walked the Wood Well path and had found it fully passable, with new stiles, on its original, legal alignment. Due credit must be given to Enfield Council for its efforts, but had the Preservation Society and others not fought so tenaciously to preserve this ancient right of way, the council would almost certainly have succumbed to a classic example of 'cat and mouse' tactics by an unco-operative landowner and abandoned the path.

Efforts to preserve the character of Carrs Lane were even more time-consuming and finally less rewarding. This ancient lane, formerly classified as a road used as a public path, crosses Bush Hill Park golf course, linking the junction of Old Park Avenue and Old Park Ridings with Bush Hill. In February 1962 Bush Hill Park Golf Club enclosed the lane on both sides with a high fence of concrete posts and wire mesh. The Preservation Society immediately complained to the club and to Enfield Council. When challenged, the club admitted that instead of following the line of the ancient lane, it had 'neatened' it so that the fence straightened and in places narrowed the route. The council instructed the club to remove the fence. The club replied that it had been put up (at a cost of £1,500) to protect a new hedge, and made a successful appeal to the Ministry of Transport for a temporary stay on the council's order. Nearly two years later, in November 1963, the Preservation Society's chairman and vice-chairman (Frederick Hymas and Don Gresswell) wrote to the *Enfield Gazette* and *Enfield Weekly Herald* complaining that a hedge had still not been planted behind the 'ugly and objectionable' fence, which should be taken down. 'This old lane is a gem of rural Middlesex and there is no reason why it should not be preserved in its original state, without the fence' said the letter, pointing out that the lane was situated 'at the heart of the new London Borough of Enfield, with part in each old borough'. The following week the *Gazette* published an angry letter from H. P. Henley, secretary of the golf club, protesting that 2,000 quickthorns had been planted early in 1963, though only a small percentage had taken root. Numerous letters were exchanged between the Preservation Society and Enfield Council about the poor surface of the lane (often impassible to pedestrians in wet weather) as well as the fence. In October 1965 the *Enfield Gazette* reported that the council had repaired the surface so that the route was now usable by walkers again; this was 'in response to repeated Enfield Preservation Society requests since 1963'. By the end of following year the surface was again deteriorating and the council announced it proposed to close Carrs Lane to motor traffic. The golf club was given several 'final dates' to take down the fence. All were ignored. The Preservation Society continued to urge its removal until 1970, then abandoned its efforts in face of the council's reluctance to take enforcement action.

In the years following the opening of the Jubilee Footpath in 1979 Enfield's footpath network was improved and extended, though constant vigilance was needed to ensure existing paths were respected. In May 1979 the Preservation Society was informed that a new tenant farmer who had taken over Holly Hill Farm in March had removed footpath signs, diverted the public footpath and removed a section of hedge. These infringements were taken up with Enfield Council and the GLC. The EPS footpaths group continued its working parties, spending many hours each year clearing encroaching undergrowth and checking paths throughout the network. A more unusual working party took place in autumn 1980, when the group was alerted by complaints that glue-sniffers had defaced most of the large trees beside the footpath in Gough Park. With the approval of Enfield Council the group painted out the offensive graffiti and disposed of the unpleasant litter left behind. Most of Enfield's rural paths needed only routine maintenance to keep them passable and in good order, but the path to Bury Green presented recurring problems on

117. When this new edition of the Preservation Society's footpath map was published in 1989, more than 300 copies were sold in the first week. The map was drawn and revised by Chris Mulvey with a cover designed by Albert Cotton, both EPS members.

the stretch opposite the King & Tinker in Whitewebbs Lane. As a result of poor drainage, the path was usually in an appalling condition in wet weather. With minimal co-operation from the farmer whose land it crossed, the footpaths group and Enfield Council spent many years trying various remedies including digging a drainage ditch, laying a new surface, and erecting a fence to prevent damage by the farm horses, so that walkers could use the route with confidence.

From 1980 Enfield Council was able to employ young people on numerous countryside projects as part of the government's Youth Opportunities Programme. In August 1982 the *Enfield Weekly Herald* reported that the council had approved an £80,000 improvement scheme to lay out new footpaths including a path which had been surveyed by the EPS footpaths group in 1971 connecting Forty Hall, through the walled rose garden, with the Gough Park network. The scheme also included two-and-a-half miles of bridleways and a footpath alternative to Mile-and-a-Quarter Alley so that walkers and horse riders need no longer clash on this popular route. Nevertheless, in May 1985 the Preservation Society was still receiving complaints that horse riders were wandering throughout Whitewebbs, churning up the paths and ruining the surface of the nature trail so that it was no longer accessible for wheelchairs. Enfield Council promised to repair the fences, put an extra barrier at Maidens Bridge, and do all it could to stop riders from using the parks. The Youth Opportunities Programme was phased out in 1983 and replaced by a youth training scheme.

Footpath maintenance is now (1996) one of the activities carried out by Groundforce, an Enfield Council enterprise using volunteers who work under the direction of the council's Park Rangers. Volunteers from Enfield Preservation Society, most of them members of the footpaths group, have been the mainstay of Groundforce since its inception. in May 1990.

118. 'Coach walks' have become a popular feature of the EPS footpaths group programme. Above, 17-year-olds and veterans aged over 70 were in the party that visited East Bergholt Church on a walk to Flatford Mill, Suffolk, in May 1989.

119. A day to remember in the glorious scenery of Dovedale in the Derbyshire peak district, destination of the coach walk in May 1985.

Chapter 11
Operation Clean-Up

As Don Gresswell tramped the lanes prospecting new footpaths, he became increasingly distressed at the sight of piles of rubbish disfiguring the countryside. There was no significant litter problem in rural Enfield before the Second World War but by the early 1960s rubbish dumping and fly-tipping had reached epidemic proportions. After years of austerity, families were improving their homes, replacing furniture and renewing domestic equipment. Many local authorities — though not Enfield — made a charge for removing large household items. The once familiar rag-and-bone man was a dying breed. So how were people to dispose of unwanted goods? For far too many uncaring individuals, the answer seemed simple — load up the car or van and dump the stuff in a quiet, country lay-by.

120. Between 1961 and 1966 Enfield Council used the lakes in Forty Hall woods as a rubbish tip. This photograph, taken in 1962, was one of several sent to the council by the Preservation Society, whose frequent protests were not heeded until the ancient lakes, choked with rubbish, were almost dry.

The dumping was not confined to rural roads or to members of the public. Early in 1961 the Preservation Society was dismayed to receive a report that the ornamental lakes at the foot of the meadow in Forty Hall were being filled with rubbish — by Enfield Council's own workmen. A stiff letter to James Finlay, the borough's chief superintendant of parks, was brushed aside, as was another protest a few months later. The council carried on dumping, and in April 1962 Don Gresswell reported that these ancient lakes, now almost dry, were little better than rubbish tips filled with a sordid mass of water tanks, beds and building rubble. Christopher Jephcott offered to photograph the sorry sight to show councillors how their policy was spoiling a beautiful scene of which they were the appointed custodians, but the council remained unmoved. Protests from the Preservation Society were stepped up in 1965 and more incriminating photographs were taken. But it was not until 1966, after more letters and lobbying, that the message at last got through and the dumping stopped. In November that year, the council minutes noted (in a classic understatement) that 'a member' had requested that consideration be given to improving and landscaping the Turkey Brook and 'the one-time ornamental pools' in Forty Hall park. Council officers were asked to submit suggestions for improving the area.

No sudden action followed, but fifteen years later, in October 1981, Enfield Council made handsome amends for its past vandalism. With the help of labour supplied under the government's Youth Opportunities Programme the main three-acre lake and its subsidiary were dredged, refilled with water and splendidly restored as part of a general improvement scheme in Forty Hall and Whitewebbs. The scheme won a well-justified award from the Civic Trust in 1983 — one of 67 to be chosen from a total entry of 522.

121. Tony Lane and Don Gresswell led the EPS volunteers who cleared five tons of rubbish from Coopers Lane Road on the first clean-up operation in July 1963.

As part of its campaign to encourage more people to enjoy the countryside, Enfield Preservation Society decided in 1963 that it must take the initiative and try to clear some of the rubbish that was disfiguring nearby lanes and footpaths. A survey of Coopers Lane Road revealed sixteen points where rubbish had been dumped. The borough engineer was contacted, and as reported by the *Enfield Gazette* on 12 July: 'Operation clean-up swung into action on Saturday morning in Coopers Lane Road, when a working party from Enfield Preservation Society set out to clear dumped rubbish from two miles of one of the most beautiful country lanes in Middlesex. Dressed in old clothes and armed with dustbins, sacks and shovels loaned by the borough council, the party of six started work at 9.30 am under the leadership of Mr Don Gresswell. Moving slowly down the lane with them as they cleared the rubbish was a three-ton refuse lorry, the driver and vehicle also provided by the council.'

The EPS volunteers were amazed at the variety of rubbish they found — garden refuse, bottles and cans, carpets, plaster ceilings, motor-cycle parts, mattresses and even sections of a shed. Most of the dumping appeared to have been done from private cars or light vans. Members of the working party, who had been asked to keep an eye open for names or addresses among the litter which might identify the dumpers, reported that many of the culprits came from outside the borough. Details were passed to the council for possible prosecution. It later became evident that most of the offenders lived in flats or maisonettes with nowhere to dispose of their rubbish. The volunteers collected about five tons on that first working party, filling two lorry loads before torrential rain forced them to stop. When they returned nine days later to finish the job, they found that in the short time since the first clearance, 24 new dumps had appeared. Even this setback failed to dampen their spirits and with active co-operation from Enfield Council, more EPS working parties continued the onslaught over the next six months. By March, Don Gresswell was able to report with satisfaction that dumping in Coopers Lane Road had been reduced by 90 per cent.

The first blitz on urban litter took place in February 1964. While surveying ancient footpaths, Don Gresswell had tried to walk the path running from Canonbury Cottages in Canonbury Road through to Myddelton Avenue; maps showed that at least 180 years ago this was part of the continuing route of Churchbury Lane from Enfield Town to

122. Brian Proehl of Kenilworth Crescent adds his contribution to the 15 tons of assorted junk removed from the footpath behind Kenilworth Crescent and Inverness Avenue in February 1963.

123 and 124. Parts of Ponders End were disgracefully neglected in the early 1960s. In 1964 the Ponders End Ratepayers' Association asked Enfield Preservation Society to organise a clearance of the most notorious dumping sites. Nearly 17 tons was collected from twelve locations, including Suez Road (above) and Hartsway (below).

Forty Hill. He found the path choked with rubbish and invited ten volunteers from North Enfield Ratepayers' Association to join ten members of the Preservation Society in a Sunday morning working party. Enfield Council again provided tools and a refuse lorry. As the tidying-up proceeded, more volunteers filtered in through back entrances from Kenilworth Crescent and Inverness Avenue, until by mid-morning some 40 people of all

125. Having cleared rural ditches and verges of objects ranging from unwanted furniture to a dead sheep, EPS members thought they were almost unshockable. But they were taken aback when told in January 1965 that this diesel-powered road roller had been dumped in Theobalds Park Road. The massive machine, apparently 'forgotten' by contractors who had repaired the road the previous year, had been rusting for about ten months on the verge near St John's School, where pupils had begun using it as a plaything. Enfield Council was informed and the contractors later removed the roller.

ages were busy shifting old bedsteads, cycles, prams, oil drums, concrete lumps and smaller rubbish, some of it buried well below the surface of the path. Five times during the morning the refuse lorry went back to the Carterhatch Lane depot, where a weighbridge check of each load showed that over 15 tons was collected. After four hours, only about two-thirds of the lane had been cleared. The task was finished by another working party two weeks later and to complete the rehabilitation of the path, the volunteers sowed grass seed in the soil made bare by the removal of the rubbish. News of the Preservation Society's activities spread, and soon afterwards the Ponders End Ratepayers' Association asked the EPS to organise a spring clean in their area, where fly-tipping and dumping had become an increasing menace. With the help of members of the association and several youth clubs, nearly 17 tons of rubbish was cleared from 12 of the most notorious dumping sites, empty plots, waste ground and verges. The EPS newsletter for June 1964 commented: 'This brings our latest anti-litter campaign total to 55 tons in three forays — some litter!'

It became obvious to the Preservation Society that public refuse sites were urgently needed, together with increased and strictly enforced penalties for indiscriminate dumping. In October 1963, following the experience gained in Coopers Lane Road, the EPS had asked Enfield Council to provide 'some convenient places for people to dump their rubbish'. No action was taken. The need became more acute the following year, with the formation of the London Borough of Enfield. The new authority decided to follow the policy of the old Edmonton and Southgate councils, and to make a charge for collecting large domestic articles. The Preservation Society again asked for a refuse depot to be opened, and demanded that the collection charge should be dropped. On 19 November 1964 the *Enfield Gazette* reported: 'In the war against rubbish dumping, Enfield Preservation Society has won a small but significant battle. Under steady pressure, Enfield Council has agreed to collect large domestic articles free, for 12 months'.

Some months later, council refuse depots were opened to the public — but only for a short time on weekdays. The EPS urged that the hours should be longer and should include Saturday morning, and in November 1965 it was announced that the depots

126. Concrete fortifications, part of an anti-aircraft gun site opposite the Jolly Farmers on Slades Hill, were still spoiling the view in 1965, twenty years after the end of the Second World War.

would be open from 7.30am on weekdays and on Saturday mornings. This was a popular move and on 29 April 1966 the *Enfield Weekly Herald* noted that 'since the council decision last November to open their refuse depots on Saturday morning, over 200 deliveries have been recorded, including 35 cars and 70 lots of furniture'. Enfield thus anticipated the far-reaching Civic Amenities Act of 1967, which required local authorities to provide accessible sites where residents could deposit refuse, free of charge. The Act also made it an offence to abandon a motor vehicle or other refuse 'on any land in the open air' and gave local councils new powers and duties regarding the removal of refuse and vehicles. However, hopes that this would solve the problem of rural dumping proved wildly optimistic.

Some of the junk disfiguring the countryside was beyond the scope of voluntary EPS working parties, however willing. Since the end of the war, no attempt had been made to clear up the disused anti-aircraft gun site and army camp opposite the Jolly Farmers on Slades Hill. It was left to the Preservation Society to take action and in 1965 the *Enfield Gazette* reported the Society's anxiety to get the site cleared up because 'a view of Trent Park from 200 homes is being spoilt by the ugly wartime relics in the foreground'. The Preservation Society, which described the site as Enfield's largest eyesore, had discussions with the Ministry of Agriculture. The ministry advised that the owners should apply for a grant under the Requisitioned Land and War Work Act 1945 so that the land could be restored to agricultural use. The problem was unexpectedly solved by a fly-tipper who dumped so many loads of soil on the site that it became completely covered. This illegal act fortuitously relieved 200 households from a grim outlook onto the remains of their wartime defences and at the same time preserved a valuable archaeological record for future generations.

Early in 1964 Don Gresswell had begun trying to get rid of another green belt eye-

127. It was redundant and it spoilt views over the green belt, but it took five years of badgering before the Metropolitan Water Board agreed to demolish the chimney on its Hadley Road pumping station.

sore — the tall, factory-like chimney on the Metropolitan Water Board pumping station in Hadley Road. The chimney was no longer in use and Don Gresswell, in one of numerous letters to the water board, complained that it stuck out like the proverbial sore thumb and marred the view for miles around. The MWB indignantly replied that the chimney had been there for 50 years and nobody had complained before. Don Gresswell persevered and in January 1966 the water board agreed to reduce the height of the chimney if Enfield Preservation Society would bear the cost, estimated at £600. Not surprisingly, the EPS refused this derisive offer. Eventually, worn down by Don Gresswell's barrage of letters, the water board demolished the chimney. Perversely, some local residents who had become used to the chimney as a landmark were sorry to see it go. The pumping station, a typical example of the pleasing architectural style favoured by the MWB, is now a listed building.

In June 1970 the EPS newsletter reported that litter was again causing increasing concern. 'It is not just the dumping of large items in ditches or lay-bys. A sordid sprinkling of small litter — paper, tin cans, plastic bags — seems to mar every open space in the Town. Equally difficult to deal with are the heaps of bricks and builders' rubble casually abandoned in odd corners when a job has been completed and left to become almost permanent eyesores ... There seems to be a growing acceptance of litter as an inescapable background to urban life. We must fight this defeatist attitude.' Instead of relying on spasmodic working parties, the Preservation Society decided to organise a more ambitious event — an anti-litter weekend to clear rubbish from black spots all over Enfield. The borough engineer's department promised to supply plastic sacks and to station skips

128 and 129. Bicycles, prams, oil drums, and water tanks were among the objects cleared from the old course of the New River in Gough Park early in 1965. Top, volunteers pulling out the rubbish before dragging it up the steep banks. Below, EPS vice-president Robert Sykes of Gough Park Cottage with the final haul.

at pre-arranged sites. The Scouts were invited to take part and every branch of the local movement accepted with alacrity. Offers of help also came from the Guides, Boys' Brigade, Forty Hill Study Group, Federation of Ratepayers' and Civic Associations, Edmonton Council of Churches, pupils of Latymer School and many individual members of Enfield Preservation Society. After months of detailed planning it was agreed that on 14 and 15 November these organisations would lead working parties, concentrating first on clearing the Turkey Brook, Brimsdown Avenue (especially near the station), Cooks Hole Road, East Lodge Lane, Coopers Lane Road, the Lavender Hill estate, New River Loop and Slades Hill. Individual EPS members were exhorted to organise small projects of their own or to tidy the area near their home. Infuriatingly, these carefully laid plans had to be abandoned when, in October, council refuse workers went on strike. Throughout the winter, the piles of rubbish grew larger and more numerous. They were not cleared away until March 1971, when the original volunteers were at last able to muster for the anti-litter weekend, which was voted a great success. More than 14 tons of rubbish was collected and the Preservation Society received a warm letter of thanks from Frank Ladly, the borough engineer.

In January 1972 a member telephoned the Preservation Society to report that Tingey's Tops pond at Crews Hill was disappearing under tons of builders' rubble. The pond, adjacent to a public footpath, had for generations been a favourite haunt of youngsters looking for frogs' spawn or fishing for tiddlers. The EPS immediately went to investigate — and sure enough, the pond was nearly half-filled with rubbish, deposited by workmen building an extension to the nearby clubhouse at Crews Hill Golf Club. Enfield Council was alerted. The club, which at first denied all responsibility, subsequently applied for planning permission to fill in the pond completely. The Preservation Society lodged a formal objection, insisting that the pond should be restored as nearly as possible to its former condition, because 'a smaller landscaped pool would be no substitute'. The EPS newsletter urged members to write to the borough planning officer: 'It is no good complaining, in years to come, about what "they" did to the pond, if we do not make strong objections now'. A public outcry followed and Crews Hill Golf Club was instructed to clear the pond. When the rubble had been excavated, the club gratefully accepted the Preservation Society's offer to help restore the surroundings. In January 1973 the EPS footpaths group, in collaboration with John Hannah, leader of the trees group, made several visits to Crews Hill and planted small trees and shrubs round the pond, which has once again become a haven for wildlife.

Later that year the EPS footpaths group made onslaughts to remove accumulated rubbish from Gough Park and from the Strayfield Road bridleway. Several litter clearance sorties were held in 1974, but now that the main dumps had been removed, the appearance of Enfield's rural lanes steadily improved. The official refuse depots were becoming more widely known and used, and Enfield Council routinely cleared small litter from the lay-bys. The improvement continues to this day, thanks to constant vigilance. Odd lapses have occured, as for example in January 1983 when a farmer reported that access to a public footpath and one of his fields off Whitewebbs Lane had been blocked by fly-tipping. On investigation, the Preservation Society found that hundreds of new shoes, some still in their boxes, had been dumped across the path. The following year a three-piece suite was deposited overnight in the car park in Forty Hall park, although the official refuse depots (now renamed civic amenity sites) were open seven days a week. Such incidents are now rare, but keeping the New River Loop and the Turkey Brook free from litter has proved a more intractable problem. The apparently irresistible temptation to

130. Tingeys Tops pond had almost disappeared under a mass of rubble when the Preservation Society was informed in January 1972 that builders working at Crews Hill Golf Club were systematically using it as a rubbish dump.

131. Enfield Council insisted that the pond should be restored and the EPS planted trees and shrubs to complete the rehabilitation. This picture was taken in 1995.

132. Fly-tipping became an increasing problem in Enfield Lock in the 1970s and early 1980s. In 1982 the anglers' car park (shown here) near the Swan and Pike Pool was completely covered by a squalid mess of rubbish.

throw empty cans, bottles and other objects into the water means that these channels are often disfigured by a mass of unsightly rubbish. The Preservation Society has organised numerous working parties to clear these waterways, often in conjunction with local residents, youth organisations and the New River Action Group.

The most ambitious clean-up scheme sponsored by the Preservation Society proved to be the catalyst for the regeneration of Enfield Lock, one of the most remote corners of the borough. Don Gresswell had appreciated the potential of this backwater when making his footpath survey for the Civic Trust in 1963. In April 1966 the EPS council of management agreed he should go ahead with plans for reviving Enfield Lock. The minutes state: 'It was thought that this job would be an arduous one, but finally most rewarding'. Whether any initiative was taken at that time is not clear, because soon afterwards Don Gresswell left Enfield to settle in the Chilterns and nobody else took up the challenge. Enfield Lock had once been a thriving community, dominated by the Royal Small Arms Factory. With the factory's decline the area became more and more run down and dilapidated. The once picturesque area round the Lock House was designated a conservation area in November 1976, but when Don Gresswell visited Enfield Lock early in 1982 he was shocked to see how the district had deteriorated in the 15 years since he moved away. A large, derelict warehouse mouldered on the west bank of the river. The Royal Small Arms Tavern stood boarded-up and empty. The river banks near the lock were hidden beneath waist-high grass. Most damaging of all, the area had become a focus for fly-tipping lorries. Heaps of plasterboard and building rubble had been dumped near the

133. Hilda Dollery (EPS and Eastern Enfield Study Group), Steve Brayshaw (Enfield Lock Residents' Association), Don Gresswell (EPS) and Councillor Peggy Ford clearing litter outside the Royal Small Arms Tavern (now renamed Rifles) at Enfield Lock, autumn 1982.

bus terminus and the lock bridge, piles of rubbish mouldered in every spare corner, abandoned cars, bicycles and prams could be seen protruding from the murky waters of the overgrown Swan & Pike pool.

In March 1982, Hilda Dollery, a member of the EPS council of management who was also secretary of the Eastern Enfield Study Group, became so alarmed at the increase in fly-tipping that she appealed to the Preservation Society for help. The response was immediate and Don Gresswell offered to spearhead a joint clean-up campaign. The study group was also advised to write to Enfield Council, drawing attention to the problems at Enfield Lock. In a written report, the borough's chief executive later tried to explain the sad state of amenities in Enfield Lock Conservation Area with the excuse that the area was 'somewhat isolated from the major part of the urban area'. Don Gresswell countered that this isolation was attractive to many people and gave good reason for

134. Christmas card produced by Enfield Lock Village Clean-up Campaign, 1982. The Civic Trust has described Enfield Lock as 'a gem of waterway detail'.

calling the area a 'village' in future. He promptly initiated the Enfield Lock Village Clean-up Campaign with himself (representing the Preservation Society) as adviser, Steve Brayshaw (Enfield Lock Residents' Association) as chairman and Hilda Dollery as secretary. Writing paper and greetings cards were printed, and a new sense of community was born.

Thirteen working parties were held by the clean-up campaign before the end of that year, clearing accumulated dumping and removing rubbish from the Turkey Brook. British Waterways was asked to cut back the overgrown grass on the river bank. The dismissive reply, after a delay of three months, was that this was a low priority job that could only be fitted in at odd times — so the EPS footpaths group borrowed a scrub-cutting machine and did it themselves in about four hours. The EPS trees group helped to plant daffodil bulbs and more than 100 trees and shrubs, and joined local volunteers in heaving three cars, several bedsteads and other rubbish out of Swan & Pike pool. To focus attention on the area the Preservation Society featured the Enfield Lock Village Campaign in its display at the Autumn Show in the Town Park. Reporting on the first six months' activity in December 1982, Don Gresswell told the EPS council of management: 'The covering of natural vegetation has died back completely and revealed the most ghastly accumulation of litter beneath. We now have the opportunity, until the end of March, to

135. In 1982, to mark the fifteenth anniversary of the Lee Valley Regional Park, the Lee Valley Association invited representatives from boroughs covered by the park to a boat trip on the River Lea. The Enfield contingent, with Sir Lou Sherman at the wheel, set off from Enfield Lock: (left to right) Irene Smith (EPS), Ted Graham MP, Councillor Audrey Lennox, Jessie Sainsbury (FERAA), Councillor Graham Eustance, Don Gresswell (EPS), Sydney Hills (FERAA) and Steve Brayshaw (Enfield Lock Residents' Association).

clear up vast quantities of this before the spring and summer covering returns.' As they tackled the rubbish during the following six months the volunteers waged a constant battle against fly-tipping, which by then had completely covered the anglers' car park. On one Sunday morning alone, five would-be dumpers were turned away and redirected to the council site in Carterhatch Lane.

By the spring of 1983 the success of the campaign was encouraging others to help with the regeneration of Enfield Lock. The Lee Valley Regional Park Authority planted trees and landscaped the towpath from the Greyhound public house to the M25, Enfield Council installed barriers to deter illegal dumpers, and volunteer working parties continued clearing and planting. Later that year, at the suggestion of the campaign, the council agreed that the derelict warehouse site on the west side of the river could be developed for low-cost housing. Following the earlier sale of 23 cottages in Government Row, this transformed Enfield Lock from a run down industrial zone into a residential area. Even greater changes were in store, but thanks to the clean-up campaign the foundations of a village community had been firmly established. On the nomination of the Keep Britain Tidy Group, Don Gresswell received a Queen Mother's Birthday Award in 1980 'for a high level of achievement in the field of environmental improvement and litter abatement, and particularly for his work with the Enfield Lock campaign'. His years of effort on Enfield Preservation Society projects and in the Chilterns were acknowledged in the 1983 Birthday Honours when he was made MBE 'for many years of dynamic conservation work'.

Chapter 12
Rescuing the New River

Celebrations to mark Enfield Preservation Society's 50th anniversary began in January 1986 with a walk along the Gough Park footpath and into the green belt. In February the youngest EPS member — four-year-old Claire Butler, granddaughter of Irene and Stanley Smith — helped the Mayor (Councillor John Reed) plant a Dawyck beech tree in the grounds of Capel Manor Centre, Bullsmoor Lane. Other events followed, culminating in an outstandingly successful exhibition, *Pride in Place*, in Forty Hall Museum. The thousands of visitors who flocked to the gallery throughout August saw an

136. A headquarters at last! Don Gresswell cuts the ribbon before handing the keys of Jubilee Hall to Enfield Preservation Society on 5 March 1986. Left to right: Albert Cotton, Wally Woodfield, Bob Errington, Mary Woodfield, Valerie Carter (EPS chairman), Stanley Smith, Don Gresswell, Donald Potter (EPS president).

137. In 1986 Jubilee Hall was in a sorry state. In addition to internal alterations, EPS volunteers renovated the exterior, repaired guttering, installed a boundary fence and laid a concrete path. The roof was later tiled by professionals — one of the few jobs for which the Preservation Society had to enlist outside help.

array of pictures, assembled with great skill and professionalism by Alan Skilton, which gave them a new appreciation of the achievements of the Preservation Society. The other high point in the golden jubilee celebrations was a dinner at the House of Commons hosted by Tim Eggar MP. Sadly, Don Gresswell was not able to attend any of the special events. He was taken ill early in the year and died in June on the day of the EPS annual general meeting, greatly mourned by the Society he had done so much to help and inspire.

Meanwhile, the refurbishment of Jubilee Hall was under way. Though Don Gresswell's gift had been accepted with alacrity and gratitude, members of the EPS council of management were dismayed when they entered the building for the first time. The simple wooden hut, a survival from the First World War, was dark, dilapidated and devoid of any decoration. Daylight could be seen through several gaps in the thin walls, the floor was burnt, the roof timbers were exposed. Irene Smith told the *Enfield Gazette* in December 1985: 'The hut needs rewiring, replumbing, re-equipping — in fact there's not a single thing we can use'. Some members of the EPS council of management had misgivings and warned that the annual membership subscription would have to be increased to help pay for the rates, standing charges and other running costs. But as usual, the Preservation Society rose to the challenge. Planning permission was sought and received to allow the premises to be used for meetings. Len Keeble personally carried out a detailed survey and prepared plans for converting the hut into a main hall, smaller hall, office, kitchen and toilets. An appeal in the EPS newsletter brought offers from members eager to help with carpentry, rewiring, plumbing and painting. The refurbishment cost £7,500 and took two

138. The slow transformation of Jubilee Hall from cavernous hut to comfortable headquarters began even before the keys were handed over. Here, after several months of hard work, a ceiling has been fitted, the electrical system renewed, and a frame erected (right) for the wall to the office and bookshop.

years, but after putting in more than 4,000 hours of work the volunteers had transformed the barren wooden hut into a bright and comfortable headquarters. Members were so generous in offering their special skills and donating time that almost no outside help was needed. Fully insulated, carpeted, equipped with gas central heating, built-in projection and audio systems, a secure office, bookshop, ample storage space, toilets and a fitted kitchen, the building was opened on 5 March 1988 by Eileen Gresswell, exactly two years after her husband had handed it over to the Preservation Society. After the ceremony engraved pewter tankards were presented to the five volunteers who had borne the brunt of the two-year refurbishment: Len Keeble, Albert Cotton, Bob Errington, Stanley Smith and Wally Woodfield.

Membership of the Preservation Society was now more than 1,700 and within weeks of the opening of Jubilee Hall, activities began to expand. The main hall seated 70 people in comfort and a programme of fortnightly morning and afternoon meetings was instigated for EPS members. These meetings uncovered a rich vein of local talent. A seemingly inexhaustible supply of interesting speakers were persuaded to take part in the programme, together with veterans like David Pam with his talks on local history and Eric Smith, whose photographic quiz on Enfield had been a popular (and always different) annual event since 1972. These sociable gatherings became so popular that 'house full' notices were posted on several occasions. The EPS council of management, which since the death of Godfrey Groves had been meeting wherever it could find a large enough room, free of charge, thankfully settled into the permanent headquarters. More informal social activities were organised, thus increasing members' involvement with the Society. To help cover expenses, local organisations were invited to hire the hall for meetings or quiet activities

139. EPS volunteers tackled nearly every job themselves in the conversion of Jubilee Hall. Here, Stanley Smith prepares the ground for a disabled ramp at the side entrance, watched by (left to right) Wally Woodfield, Roger Dormer and Albert Cotton.

(jumble sales, discos and musical entertainments were barred). Within two years the annual income from lettings covered the running costs of Jubilee Hall and it became necessary to introduce a regular 'no lettings' policy on some evenings so that time could be reserved for EPS activities.

The Preservation Society was relieved to find that the new programme at Jubilee Hall did not affect attendance at the EPS main meetings, which had moved to the conference room at the Civic Centre. The long-established pattern of three meetings every year, in spring, summer (the AGM) and autumn, continued to attract large audiences to hear a stimulating variety of speakers on topics ranging from *The secrets of the River Lea* to *Does architecture need art?* A joint meeting with the Edmonton Hundred Historical Society had become another eagerly awaited annual fixture. Then, as now, local residents expected Enfield Preservation Society to take the lead in campaigning on environmental issues and a capacity audience was assured whenever it called a meeting on a matter of public concern. These large meetings, which could have been difficult to control, were always well organised and effective, thanks partly to an efficient public address system. Since he was a 16-year-old schoolboy, EPS member David Fisher has operated a public address system (often with a roving microphone) at every big meeting. One embarrassingly successful meeting, which could easily have got out of hand, occurred in March 1987 when the Preservation Society hosted a meeting, supported by organisations from

140. Soon after it was opened in March 1988, EPS headquarters became a popular meeting place and a focus for the Preservation Society's activities. Here, the scene in May 1992 when members collected their copies of A Victorian Suburb, *second volume in David Pam's History of Enfield.*

all over north London, to launch the New River Action Group. Scores were unable to get into the packed conference room at the Civic Centre. Throughout a long Saturday afternoon, from 2pm until 6pm supporters stood round the walls, unmoved by warnings from Civic Centre staff that they must leave because the hall's capacity had been exceeded. 'Residents fight to save river' was the front page headline in the *Enfield Advertiser* on 19 March with a report which began: 'Over 250 people packed Enfield Civic Centre at the weekend to ensure the preservation of the New River and its reservoirs. Thames Water is planning to implement drastic changes to the waterway over the next five years, which in places could cut the water flow to a trickle.'

The first hint of a threat to the New River had come in June 1985 when Thames Water revealed its plan to build a £7.2 million tunnel ring main for London. Water from the New River, still an integral part of London's water supply, was to be diverted into the new underground system at a point near Cheshunt. The announcement added that the rest of the historic watercourse would not be needed as a water supply after about 1990 and would therefore be redundant as far Thames Water was concerned. This statement had set alarm bells ringing from Broxbourne to Hackney. There were fears that within a few years, stretches of the river could become dry, be filled in, or be sold off for development. Residents in Enfield were particularly apprehensive about the future of the New River Loop which, as well as being a valuable wildlife habitat, made a vital contribution to the character of Enfield Town and the Town Park.

The New River was constructed between 1609 and 1613, under the direction of Sir Hugh Myddelton, to carry fresh water from springs at Chadwell and Amwell in Hertfordshire into the City of London. Cut out by hand, the original course of the aqueduct took

141. A favourite view of the New River Loop as it flows through Chase Green Gardens, with the Methodist Church spire in the background.

many detours around the countryside, following the 100-foot contour in order to maintain its level until it discharged into the Round Pond at New River Head just below Sadlers Wells. When it was inaugurated on Michaelmas Day 1613 the New River measured 38.8 miles. The course was later shortened to about 24 miles by ending the river at reservoirs in Green Lanes, Stoke Newington, and straightening the course of the channel. Some of the detours, such as the loop through Myddelton House, Whitewebbs and Gough Park, were cut off and abandoned. Though clearly discernible, this section is now dry apart from a short stretch in Gough Park. Other detours, including the Enfield Loop which runs from Southbury Road, through Enfield Town Conservation Area and the Town Park, to Bush Hill, though no longer part of the water supply, became valuable but vulnerable environmental features. The condition of the Enfield Loop, which had always been entirely dependent on water pumped in from the New River, was causing concern before Enfield Preservation Society was formed. In August 1933 it became known that the Metropolitan Water Board (which had taken over the New River Company in 1904) intended to abandon the loop. The board was so eager to get rid of it that when Enfield Council demanded that the loop should be retained as an amenity the MWB offered to hand it over, free of charge, on condition the council agreed to maintain the banks and bridges. In 1935 the council decided to accept a free conveyance of the loop and began negotiating with the board about a supply of water. At least one member of the newly formed EPS council of management appreciated what Enfield Council was taking on. In a letter to the Preservation Society in September 1936, Ambrose Wiseman warned that 'when (if ever) the council take over the loop ... unless great interest is taken, it will become a noisome ditch'. He went on to point out that expert advice would be needed 'to keep it beautiful'. His colleagues were more sanguine and at the EPS council of management meeting in September the following year H. H. Collier reported that preliminaries for taking over of the loop were nearly complete. He added, with considerable optimism, that when this had been done, 'the water would not be stagnant, but would flow'.

A formal agreement between the MWB and Enfield Urban District Council was signed on 1 March 1938. The board would supply, at an accepted charge, a daily input of filtered water which would pass over a flume near Southbury Road to replenish the Enfield Loop and Carrs Basin in the Town Park. Unfortunately the system did not work well when levels in the New River fell and the supply to the loop was reduced, a frequent occurrence in dry weather. Without a good flow the level in the loop dropped, the water became murky and deposits of silt built up. In addition, the banks grew dilapidated through inadequate maintenance and this led to a large number of leaks. Complaints about the run-down appearance of the loop, unpleasant smells in summer and the amount of rubbish in the water, became frequent.

In 1974 Enfield Preservation Society decided it must take action before the loop became a nuisance rather than an asset. The autumn newsletter appealed for volunteers to help with a pictorial and written survey 'to confront the authorities involved and show what improvements are needed'. There was an enthusiastic response and in November a group of 22 volunteers, led by Brian MacDonald, began a yard-by-yard survey of the loop from the ornamental gardens in Southbury Road to the Town Park. The condition of the banks, footpaths, fences and bridges, the amount of rubbish and the state of plant and animal life in the water were all recorded in detail. The final report, illustrated with nearly 40 photographs, was a damning indictment of years of inadequate maintenance. The introduction stated: 'It is important to point out that those conducting the survey were ordinary citizens of Enfield, having a responsible concern for the environment in which

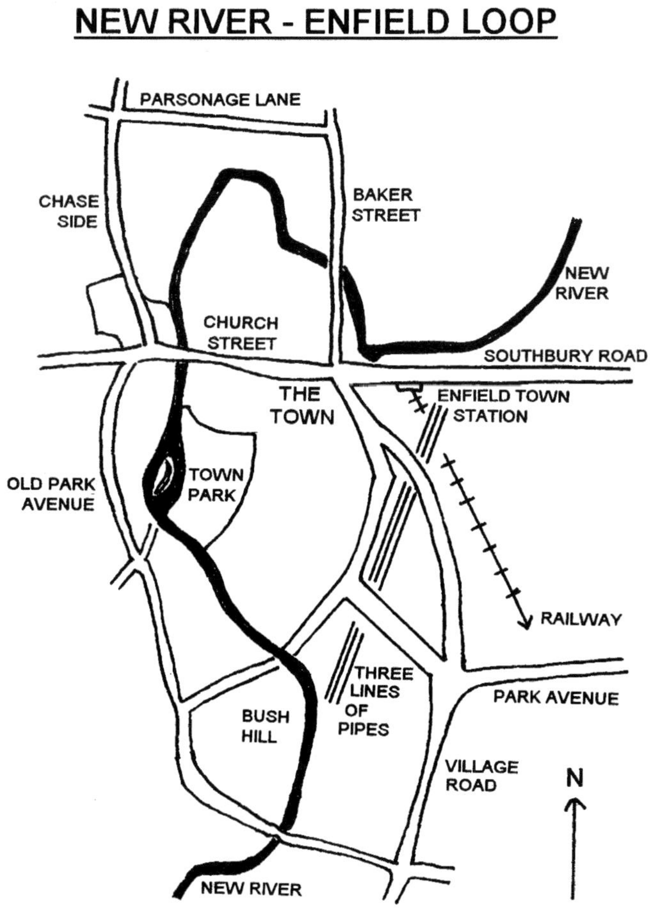

they live. They were not experts with any particular axe to grind'. Experts or not, the volunteers had no hesitation in stating that while not beyond redemption, Enfield's New River Loop was deteriorating and certainly could be much improved. The Preservation Society's report warned that unless positive action was taken and pressure kept up, the inhabitants of Enfield would witness the decay and eventual disappearance, in a very short time, of this unique and beautiful amenity in the heart of their borough. This loss would be especially tragic at a time when Enfield was losing so much of its individuality and historic heritage, stated the report. It pointed to the unsightly culverted section of the loop used as a car park behind St Andrew's Road, as a stark warning of what could come about through lack of regard for this ancient waterway. Trying to be practical and recognising the perennial difficulties of any action which involved local public expenditure, the Preservation Society's recommendations were divided into short-term aims which would halt deterioration and ensure maintenance and long-term proposals for preserving and improving the loop.

Rubbish along the banks and in the river was identified as 'probably the most unsightly feature of all' and regular clearance was recommended. Retaining timbers, especially to sections in the Town Park, needed urgent attention where banks were collapsing. The extensive use of weedkiller on the banks should be ended. The iron bridges and

142. A postcard of River View in the 1950s, showing the banks of the New River Loop in need of attention.

143. Generations of Enfield families have enjoyed strolling beside the New River Loop in the Town Park. This view was taken in about 1929 when there was plenty of water in Carr's Basin.

railings should be repainted and the council should apply for them to be listed. Footpaths along the loop should be levelled and maintained and various eyesores and clutter should be removed. The survey found that the loop was suffering from bad erosion and pollution despite an undertaking from the water authorities to provide 100,000 gallons a day and to keep it topped up. The most important long-term recommendation was therefore to ensure that sufficient water was entering the loop and being retained: if water loss was the problem, the cause ought to be investigated and appropriate remedies taken. The report recommended that once the flow had been restored, water plants should be provided and the loop restocked with fish as soon as conditions were suitable, but it warned that a major dredging operation to remove accumulated dead leaves might be needed first. There were also suggestions for planting flowering shrubs and bulbs along the banks, installing seats and providing signposts and maps.

The survey was well received by Enfield Council and the Preservation Society was warmly thanked for its constructive comments, but the outcome was predictable. It was the same old story of not enough water, and no money for maintenance. After a meeting with council officers, Preservation Society representatives reported to the EPS council of management in April 1976. The minutes record: 'All the points raised in our survey were dealt with at great length and there was complete agreement and sympathy with the issues raised. Unfortunately there is very little money available at the moment, although the parks department is setting aside a small yearly sum to repair the banks. In view of the drought conditions prevailing, there is no possibility that the Thames Water Authority would allow an increased amount of water into the loop and alternative methods of supply are being considered, including the diversion of the Sadlers Mill Stream.' A full report and recommendations from council officers was to be presented to the LBE environment and planning committee.

144. A tricky job, but EPS volunteers enjoyed the challenge of painting railings and bridges along the New River Loop in 1977. In the boat, Stuart Mills; near the bank, wearing fisherman's waders, Stan Lowen.

Meanwhile the Preservation Society offered to help paint the cast iron bridges and railings along the loop. The offer was gratefully received and by autumn 1977 working parties organised by Stan Lowen had completed the job without council assistance, although Enfield Council did provide the paint. Note was taken of several of the recommendations in the EPS survey. In due course, the bridges were listed. Less weedkiller was used and sporadic clearance of the watercourse was carried out — but in January 1979 the Preservation Society had to ask the council to improve its procedures because the muck and rubbish cleared from the loop was usually left on the bank, from where it often fell, or was pushed, back into the water. In the spring of 1981 the EPS newsletter reported that Enfield Council had allocated limited finance for revetment improvements in the Town Park, where the river banks needed urgent improvement. It also welcomed the news that Thames Water (owners of the New River since the demise of the Metropolitan Water Board in 1974) planned to instal a new pump to improve the flow into the loop; this would replace the flume in Southbury Road at the junction of the loop with the New River. Despite these measures, the state of the Enfield Loop continued to cause concern, especially during summer months when the usual meagre supply of water was reduced still further. In June 1983 the EPS council of management learned that more than one hundred fish had died in Carrs Basin, probably because the extremely hot weather, with temperatures in the nineties, had depleted the oxygen in the water.

In June 1985, when Thames Water revealed its plans to divert most of the water from the New River to boost London's new ring main system, the implications for the Enfield Loop were all too obvious and Enfield Council, as well as local residents, became seriously alarmed. An internal council memo, dated 16 August 1985, warned: 'Currently, approximately 200,000 gallons per day are passing into the Town section, but even so, the Borough Engineer and Surveyor estimates that 1,000,000 gallons per day would be necessary to produce any obvious movement in the water flow'. The memo also noted: 'One disturbing aspect is that despite the current input, very little water comes out at the other end.' This was thought to be due to the amount of bank leakage caused by the lack of maintenance in the past, and to 'rat holes and such similar deficiencies'.

There was widespread opposition to Thames Water's plan to shrug off responsibility for the New River. It would, said its critics, deprive three London boroughs — Enfield, Haringey and Hackney — of a valuable green corridor which brought a rich assortment of plant and animal life into the suburbs and inner city. The historic aspect of the New River with its charming Victorian bridges and interesting relics of industrial archaeology would be put at risk, and hopes of creating a linear riverside footpath (first envisaged by Don Gresswell in 1963) would vanish for ever. The front page of the EPS newsletter for winter 1985 proclaimed: 'New River — we must take the lead' and went on to reveal that the Preservation Society was alerting as many local and national bodies as possible to the threat of this environmental disaster so that Thames Water would be made aware of the strong public feeling. The Preservation Society had already contacted local MPs, who all agreed the New River must be saved. Lord Graham of Edmonton included a rousing item in his column in the *Enfield Gazette* with the exhortation 'Go to it, EPS — I'm right behind you!' Tim Eggar contacted Roy (later Sir Roy) Watts, chairman of Thames Water, who informed him there would be 'obvious difficulties' in preserving the southern part of the New River because there was no natural flow and maintenance costs were very high. Individual organisations in the three London boroughs (and also in Broxbourne) protested, but after some months it became clear to Enfield Preservation Society that a concerted campaign would be needed to combat a body as powerful as Thames Water, which

145. *Engraving from the* Illustrated London News, *17 May 1884, showing scenes along the route of the New River. 1. Chadwell Springs, Ware. 2. New River Gauge, Hertford. 3. Footbridge, Amwell. 4. Turnford pumping-station, Cheshunt. 5. Behind Theobalds House. 6. Sluice House, Bush Hill Park. 7. Hornsey pumping-station. 8. Stone at Chadwell Springs. 9. The Castle pumping-station, Green Lanes. 10. Engine room in the pumping-station. 11. New River Head, Sadlers Wells.*

was forging ahead with its plans, apparently totally unconcerned about the environmental aspects.

The Preservation Society, embarking on its most ambitious initiative to date, decided to hold a delegate meeting for organisations based near the New River. Invitations were sent to historical societies, residents' associations, archaeological societies, angling clubs, amenity societies, wildlife trusts and ramblers' associations, from Ware to Islington. Kenneth Baker (Secretary of State for the Environment) cut the first turf for London's ring main on 7 March 1986. A few weeks later, on 30 April, representatives from 34 organisations all over north London met at Enfield Civic Centre in a committee room provided free of charge by the council and agreed to form a New River Action Group (NRAG). Its aims were to safeguard the New River and its reservoirs, preserve them as wildlife habitats and secure more access for the public. Valerie Carter, who had presided at the meeting in her capacity as EPS chairman, was later elected chairman of the action group with Denis Smith (Greater London Industrial Archaeological Society) as vice-chairman, Audrey Lennox (Southgate Civic Trust) secretary and Frances Mussett (EPS) treasurer.

As part of the campaign to increase public awareness of the threat hanging over the New River, NRAG organised a series of 'action days' involving local communities along its length. The first, held at Enfield on 14 March 1987, began with a conducted walk along the Enfield Loop before the meeting which packed the Civic Centre in the afternoon. Similar programmes — a walk along a local stretch of the New River, followed by a meeting — were later held in Hornsey and Stoke Newington, with a particularly memorable event at Islington where the meeting, in Sadler's Wells Theatre, was addressed by Dr David Bellamy. Thames Water, at the invitation of the action group, provided a spokesman at each meeting and these hapless individuals found themselves confronting large and hostile audiences at every location. EPS members were strongly represented at all the meetings and the Preservation Society made several generous cash donations to NRAG, which quickly established itself as a powerful campaigning force. Support for the campaign increased until a total of 40 organisations and more than 100 individual 'friends' had joined the New River Action Group. Local authorities were supportive, providing premises for meetings free of charge. Nearly every Member of Parliament in north London gave active help to the campaign.

This concerted action was to some extent effective. In February 1987 the *Enfield Gazette* reported that Thames Water had changed its plans. Instead of being diverted near Cheshunt, the New River would remain untouched until it reached a point just north of Maidens Bridge, Forty Hill, where a new tunnel would take most of the flow into reservoirs at Coppermills in Waltham Forest 'leaving a greatly reduced but as yet undecided volume in the rest of the river'. This let Broxbourne off the hook, but meant that the threat to the rest of the New River and the Enfield Loop was as great as before. The next surprise came in June, when Thames Water, having tried unsuccessfully to persuade the three local authorities (Enfield, Hackney and Haringey) to take over responsibility for the New River, announced it would retain ownership. Increasing public pressure had evidently ruled out the earlier policy of abandoning the river. However, a dependable supply of water was essential if the river was to remain a viable watercourse and Thames Water refused to state its intentions.

The New River Action Group stepped up its campaign and made renewed attempts to secure a face-to-face meeting with Roy Watts, chairman of Thames Water. Michael Portillo MP agreed to chair a meeting at the House of Commons and thanks to his intervention Roy Watts and his technical advisers met Valerie Carter, Audrey Lennox and Denis Smith

146. Church Street, Enfield Town was used as background in this ingenious Thames Water advertisement, which appeared in national newspapers to publicise its recharge scheme, unique in Britain. The text explains that up to 33 thousand million gallons of surplus water can be stored in the naturally porous sand and chalk that lies up to 60 metres below Enfield and Haringey — enough to provide over 50,000 North Londoners with 30 gallons of water a day each. When needed, 'the stored water will be pumped out into the New River (making a new use for a beautiful 17th century aqueduct) which will channel it onwards for treatment'.

on 2 March 1988. Lord Graham of Edmonton and Chris Smith MP (Islington South) were also present at the meeting, which proved to be a turning point in the campaign. Like conjurors producing rabbits from a hat, the Thames Water officials drew from their briefcases a set of new proposals for sending a flow of 60 megalitres per day down the New River and building a series of weirs to help retain the vegetation and wildlife habitats. Encouraged by this news, the action group pressed for more. By July 1988 Thames Water had agreed to increase the daily flow to 80 megalitres.

As London's underground ring main took shape, the plans were revised yet again. Thames Water engineers had realised that the natural chalk layer below Enfield and Haringey could be used to store up to 150,000 million litres of water — more than even its largest reservoir near Heathrow could contain. To make the most of this natural resource the water authority therefore decided to spend £7 million on a series of 15 boreholes with small, unmanned pumps, eleven of them in the Enfield area. When supplies were plentiful, water would be pumped down into the chalk acquifer and stored until there was a shortage, when it would be brought up into the New River which would take it to Coppermills for purification. Water levels in the New River would be controlled by the recently installed weirs. Describing this innovative plan, the EPS newsletter for spring 1992 thankfully announced: 'The New River is safe at last'. The recharge scheme came into operation three years later. *Thames Water News* reported in August 1995 that Robert

Atkins (Minister for the Environment and Countryside) had switched on one of the new borehole pumps at a ceremony in Wood Green. The paper commented: 'The £7 million project guarantees the long-term future of the historic New River, which plays a vital role in the scheme'. The scheme later received a Civic Trust commendation.

By 1994 the New River Action Group, which had become a registered charity, was supported by 50 affiliated organisations and several hundred individual 'friends'. Although its main objective had been achieved, the action group was still working to secure more public access to the waterway and to preserve the wildlife habitats. In both these aims it enjoyed the full co-operation of Thames Water plc, which since its reorganisation had adopted an enlightened and positive policy on environmental matters. (It had even taken the trouble to incorporate specially designed bat boxes in the unmanned pumping stations erected for the recharge scheme). In July 1994 the second stage of the New River Path (from Amwell to Broxbourne) was opened along part of a route first surveyed in 1986 by ramblers' groups affiliated to NRAG. It is hoped the path will be extended south of Enfield, thus realising the New River's potential as a green chain. The New River Action Group remains active in the longstanding campaign to save the reservoirs and filter beds at Stoke Newington and Hornsey from development, and in other planning controversies affecting the river. Audrey Lennox eventually succeeded Valerie Carter as chairman, but today (1996) a member of the EPS council of management, Frances Mussett, is chairman of the action group and Enfield Preservation Society continues to give strong support to the vigorous and widely respected organisation it helped to bring into being.

Although the New River had been saved, the future of the Enfield Loop continued to give anxiety. The damage done by the accumulation of silt, algae and rotting vegetation which had built up on the river bed was glaringly obvious in the long. hot summer of 1995. Long stretches of the loop became covered with green slime. In other parts of the loop the water was so shallow that grass could be seen growing through the surface of the water. The Preservation Society decided it must take action yet again to save one of Enfield Town's finest features. At the 1995 AGM Colin Pointer (EPS chairman) announced that as its main diamond jubilee project the Preservation Society intended to launch a rescue plan for the New River Loop, an ambitious initiative that would have to be phased over several years.

Chapter 13
Planting & Perseverance

Ambrose Wiseman, whose shrewd warning about the Enfield Loop proved so accurate, also lived up to his name in his far-sighted efforts to persuade the Preservation Society to initiate a programme of tree planting. The minutes of only the fourth meeting of the EPS council of management, held on 29 September 1936, record that Mr Wiseman (who was the proprietor of the *Enfield Gazette*) put forward the suggestion for an arboreal day, the Preservation Society working with the consent and co-operation of the Urban District Council and education authorities to plant trees in Enfield's parks and other open spaces. The suggestion was adopted in principle and it was left to the executive committee to arrange details. Sir Henry Bowles, who was present at the meeting, probably told his brother, because records show that some months later Ambrose Wiseman received a letter from E. A. (Gussie) Bowles of Myddelton House saying that he

147. E. A. ('Gussie') Bowles, standing beside a bridge over the New River as it flowed through his garden at Myddelton House, Bulls Cross. In 1960 this part of the New River was filled in, but its route in the garden is still clearly discernible, as are other sections of the old course through Whitewebbs Park and Gough Park.

might have a few unusual trees in his nursery ground and inviting him to go round and see what there was to spare. Mr Bowles suggested that in the meantime the Preservation Society should look round for likely sites. It was decided to bring this to the attention of Enfield Council, but nothing came of the proposal.

Mr Wiseman, unable to attend the EPS council of management in May 1937, sent a letter asking the meeting to consider 'the orgy of tree felling which is going on under the auspices of the District Council, who seem to have given their woodman a free hand to do as he likes'. He requested that his letter should be sent to the council, 'who should be pressed that for every tree cut down, another should be planted and that the person responsible for the cutting down be made to plant it and look after it'. The council's response, if any, is not recorded. The Preservation Society, according to the *Enfield Gazette,* had decided by May 1939 that it must do everything it could 'to prevent the unnecessary destruction of trees resulting from the rapid building development in the district'.

Enfield Preservation Society renewed its protests when it resumed activities after the war. In July 1961 a member reported that large oak trees were being bulldozed 'on the building site between Gordon Hill and Lavender Hill'. As a result, it was agreed to feature trees in the EPS exhibit at the Enfield Show in the Town Park and to ask all members 'to report any menace to local trees'. The Preservation Society began taking positive action in August that year, when a trees sub-committee was formed. One of its four members was a newcomer to the EPS, Christopher Jephcott, who soon became a driving force on the council of management. The following year saw the start of the long struggle — still continuing — to secure a higher standard of tree pruning in local parks and streets. In February 1962, supported by Christopher Jephcott's photographs of mutilated specimens, protests were made to Enfield Council about badly lopped trees. James Finlay, the parks superintendent, blamed lack of funds, an excuse which was to be echoed by his successors for the next thirty years or so.

As he drove round the district visiting his patients, Dr Jephcott became increasingly concerned at the bleak appearance of eastern Enfield, where there was scarcely a tree to be seen on the barren housing estates and industrial areas. In the rush to rehouse families after the war, the preoccupation had been to build as many homes as possible and there had been little time to consider the quality of the surroundings. The result was a depressingly dull and drab environment, and the EPS council of management urged that the situation should be remedied. At this time there were no local authority schemes for tree sponsorship and National Tree Week had not been invented. The Preservation Society decided to take the initiative and to tackle the industrialists first. In January 1963 the Society invited the Enfield & District Manufacturers' Association to a cheese and wine party in the Tudor Room. In a persuasive speech, Donald Potter (EPS chairman) stressed the need for more trees in eastern Enfield and said he hoped plantings would be included in every new factory scheme. The response was encouraging. Ronald Peachey, managing director of International Flavors and Fragrances of Southbury Road, immediately promised 50 trees which were later planted in or near Albany Park. The planting was carried out by Enfield Council parks department, which also gave full co-operation to the Preservation Society's next imaginative project. Following a detailed survey of possible planting sites carried out by Christopher Jephcott, the EPS formed an ambitious plan. It would raise enough money to buy 1,000 trees to beautify the borough's neglected areas and would then organise a special Tree Planting Week. The EPS trees group, which was formed in November 1963 with Christopher Jephcott as leader and the renowned horticulturist Frances Perry as a member, offered to organise the appeal.

148. The bleak expanse of Albany Park in 1960, with Brimsdown Power Station dominating the skyline. Since 1964, when 25 trees were planted in the park, EPS has promoted several schemes to improve this open space in eastern Enfield. The Power Station was closed in the mid-1970s.

Enfield Tree Planting Week was fixed for 15-21 November 1964. It at once caught the public imagination. In August 1964 the Preservation Society sent appeal leaflets to over 400 societies, organisations and businesses. The leaflets pointed out that although the EPS stand at the previous year's Town Show had boasted that Enfield was 'the borough of a million trees', the majority were growing in Whitewebbs, Hilly Fields and Forty Hall. Many roads and open spaces, particularly in eastern Enfield, were windswept and bare. 'A sapling of reasonable size costs an average price of one guinea' said the leaflet. 'Will your organisation be prepared to subscribe for five, ten, fifty or even more trees for a gift that will last a lifetime?' The leaflet explained that Enfield Council's parks committee had agreed to order, plant, stake and maintain all the trees given for planting in areas under their control, and there was an assurance that the trees would be chosen with care so that they would not outgrow their sites and become a nuisance. Within days of the leaflets going out, offers to buy 60 trees had been received. As the fund mounted, the local press printed long lists of subscribers every week. News of the appeal even reached Ontario, Canada from where Bob Kenny, a former Enfield resident, sent a donation for six maples. Nearly 10,000 local schoolchildren subscribed one penny each to buy seedlings supplied by the Forestry Commission for planting in their school grounds. Enfield Preservation Society donated 95 saplings to mark the 95th birthday of its president, Ebenezer Rees (described by the *Enfield Weekly Herald* as 'the grand old man of Enfield'). At his request, 40 of the trees were reserved for gardens being laid out for the nurses' homes at Chase Farm Hospital; the rest went to eastern Enfield. The appeal target was reached by December and when the fund closed, enough money had been raised to buy 1,103 trees.

The Mayor, Alderman Ernest Mackenzie, opened Enfield's Tree Planting Week in November 1964 by planting a Norway maple alongside Hertford Road, just inside the grounds of Ambrose Fleming School. A young cedar was planted nearby by Sophie Hymas, wife of the EPS chairman. This species had been chosen as the emblem of the appeal to commemorate the magnificent tree (claimed by some to be the first cedar in this country) planted in

149. Enfield Tree Planting Week in November 1964 began with a ceremonial planting on the frontage of Ambrose Fleming School. Left to right: Christopher Jephcott, Sophie Hymas, Frederick Hymas (EPS chairman), the Mayor (Alderman Ernest Mackenzie), and James Finlay (superintendent of parks). Don Gresswell noted on the back of the photograph: 'The tree was subsequently cleared away to make room.'

1670 by Dr Uvedale in the grounds of the old Enfield Palace, where Pearsons department store now stands. The appeal leaflet carried a photograph of the large cedar in Forty Hall; to drive the message home, the same picture was used for the EPS Christmas card in 1964.

Several industrialists responded to the appeal and Johnson Matthey of Stockingswater Lane held their own tree planting day. On a Saturday early in December, members of the firm's sports club and football team, helped by factory managers and members of Enfield Preservation Society, spent all day planting 156 trees round the borders of the firm's sports ground in Goldsdown Road, Brimsdown. The cost, about £400, was borne by Johnson Matthey. Thorn Electrical Industries announced they would plant trees around their factory on the Great Cambridge Road and on their sports ground in Bulls Cross. With some satisfaction, Christopher Jephcott told the *Enfield Gazette*: 'It looks as if Tree Planting Week may last for several months, and with the support received from manufacturers, the original target of 1,000 trees may be doubled.' Fifty trees were planted along the Hertford Road between Green Street and Bullsmoor Lane by Middlesex County Council, shortly before it was merged into the GLC.

The outstanding success of the week overwhelmed Enfield parks department, which was still struggling to plant hundreds of saplings many months later. The Civic Trust described the Preservation Society's appeal as 'a model to pass on to other amenity societies'. However, the EPS newsletter for May 1965 warned that against these gains must be set the loss, which the Preservation Society had been unable to prevent, of some fine trees on building sites. The warning was reiterated by the *Enfield Gazette* in August, with the

150 and 151. An EPS working party (above) about to start digging up a derelict 45-yard swathe of rough grass at Southbury Station in October 1966. Left to right: Mr Beckett, D. Wood, Joyce Ball, Edgar Artiss, Christopher Jephcott, Harold Ball, Maurice Connolly, Ursula Jephcott, Mrs Beckett, A. Caven, R. Durrant. The flowering trees and shrubs they planted in spring 1967 still delight passengers and staff at the station. Below, laburnum and lilac in bloom in May 1995.

comment that 'Tree Preservation Orders seem useless when builders get to work ... Enfield Preservation Society cannot look after every valuable tree in Enfield on its own. It has done a grand job in awakening residents' awareness of their leafy heritage, now it is up to residents everywhere to be their own watchdogs whenever trees are threatened'.

One of the earliest direct planting schemes carried out by the Preservation Society still provides an oasis of green to welcome passengers arriving at Southbury Station, Ponders End. As part of the plan to beautify the eastern parts of the borough, the EPS offered to plant trees and shrubs on a wide, 45-yard strip of rough grass and weeds alongside the 'down' platform. The first approach to British Rail, in 1965, brought the unbelievble reply that BR intended to make a 'special charge' to Enfield Preservation Society of three guineas a year for the use of the land. The Society protested with some indignation. Although no further mention of payment was made, it took more than eighteen months of careful negotiation before BR gave its full consent to the planting scheme. At last, in October 1966, ten members of the EPS trees group began clearing the ground, a task which was to take many weeks. Planting took place the following spring. The transformation of this derelict land was appreciated by passengers and by the rail staff, and the message was no doubt passed up the line to BR headquarters. Three years later, no difficulties were put in the way when the Preservation Society offered to plant eight trees and several shrubs at Enfield Town station. This scheme was completed by the spring of 1970.

For well over 30 years members of the EPS trees group, often helped by other Preservation Society volunteers, turned out on working parties every autumn and winter to plant thousands of trees, shrubs and hedgerows. Great care was taken to choose the appropriate species for each site, whether to hide an eyesore, brighten a drab area or relieve a barren expanse of grass or tarmac. Specimen trees bought with Preservation Society funds were augmented by seedlings donated by members. Soon after its formation, the EPS trees group began receiving offers of small trees of all types. Many had seeded themselves in the gardens of members, who usually demanded that the seedlings should be collected as soon as possible; the group then faced the problem of keeping the plants alive until a suitable planting site was found. The difficulty was resolved when Robert Dugdale Sykes, one of the Preservation Society's vice-presidents, offered the use of part of his garden at Gough Park Cottage, Forty Hill, as a tree nursery. Until he moved house in 1988 hundreds of seedlings were 'grown on' in the EPS tree nursery there, until they were large enough to plant out.

At times it seemed as though malign forces were conspiring to put a jinx on the efforts of the EPS trees group. Drought, storms and vandalism were not the only hazards members had to contend with. In January 1967 the group spent many hours laboriously cutting 120 willows, each twelve feet long, from a disused osier bed in Forty Hall. They were later planted at Enfield Lock, with help from the Enfield Lock Residents' Association — only to be eaten the same day by horses which had been left by their gypsy owners to forage for food in Warwick Field. Barely a handful of the willows survived. In a typically busy planting season two years later, the group put in more than 50 trees and hedges. One of the hedges, planted in York Terrace with the approval of Enfield Council, was cut down a few days later by the council's parks department owing to a bureaucratic blunder. Undaunted, the group adopted the motto 'You can't win them all' and kept on planting.

These early losses, however, came to be seen as mere irritations compared to the ravages of Dutch elm disease, which reached Enfield in 1971. An anxious watch had been kept for the tell-tale patches of yellowing foliage that were the first signs of the disease, and the EPS autumn newsletter warned that 20 elms appeared to be dying on Bush Hill,

152. The culprits! In January 1967 members of the EPS trees group spent hours cutting 120 willows from an osier bed in Forty Hall, but when the 12-foot trees were planted in Warwick Field, Enfield Lock, they were eaten the same day by horses owned by gypsies.

in Old Park Avenue, and in Forty Hall. The disease spread with frightening rapidity and on 3 September the *Enfield Gazette* reported that during the previous five weeks, one-third of local elms had become affected.

Meanwhile, the Preservation Society was fighting a losing battle to save scores of magnificent trees which were being cut down in some of the borough's most gracious areas, as blocks of flats and terraces of 'town' houses replaced substantial Victorian and Edwardian villas set in mature gardens. Road widening schemes and the new Civic Centre development also took their toll. The EPS newsletter complained in autumn 1969: 'Enfield's trees are under constant attack from private developers and official planners' . There was particular concern about trees which had been cut down in Village Road, Bycullah Road, Private Road, Quakers Walk, Windmill Hill, Wellington Road and The Ridgeway. Trees were also lost in Brimsdown Avenue, where they were badly needed. John Hannah, who in 1968 had succeeded Christopher Jephcott as leader of the EPS trees group, told the *Gazette* in October 1970 that he was 'appalled' at the rate trees were being lost. He complained that several had been felled in Cecil Road when the one-way system was introduced, 30 were moved from the junction of Southbury Road and the Great Cambridge Road, and a fine old yew and other mature trees had been cut down on the Civic Centre site. In the autumn of 1971 EPS representatives met Enfield councillors and council officers to express concern at the continuing loss of trees on private and council developments and the dearth of official planting. The Preservation Society urged the council to embark on a 10-year planting programme to offset the losses that were occurring and to plant more trees in eastern Enfield and on council housing estates.

The destruction continued. That winter, as the Civic Centre took shape, the Preservation Society vainly tried to save several splendid trees on the site, including a holm oak. Christopher Jephcott, the EPS representative on Enfield Council's Conservation Advisory Group, reported with fury that only four days after the group had been assured that the borough engineer's department was investigating schemes for saving the trees, they were felled by the contractor. 'We are perturbed that this unchecked vandalism could take place on the council's doorstep' he said. Donald Potter, the EPS chairman, was even more scathing about another council development. He told the *Enfield Gazette* in February 1972 that in planning to cut down more than 40 trees by the roadside at St James's Vicarage, Hertford Road, to build two blocks of old people's flats, Enfield Council was behaving 'in the way we would expect an avaricious private developer to act'. The council was destroying 'a very important amenity in an area where there is an acute shortage of trees' he complained. The Preservation Society tried to persuade the council to realign the flats so that more trees would remain, but in this it was not successful. In June 1973 the *Gazette* reported: 'The Society's fight to save the trees has ended in defeat.' A total of 42 would be felled. Christopher Jephcott was quoted as saying: 'The real villain is the ministry cost-yardstick, which forces local authorities to develop sites up to a certain density so that the costs are kept within the yardstick. They don't make allowances for things like trees which ought to be preserved.'

However, the message was beginning to get through, both locally and nationally. In 1972 Enfield Council initiated a tree sponsorship scheme; the Preservation Society immediately donated £100, requesting that most of the money should be spent in eastern Enfield. The first sponsored tree, one of a group of maples paid for by the EPS, was planted by the Mayor on The Ride, Ponders End, on 20 January 1973. The ceremony was chosen to mark the borough's participation in Tree Planting Year, which had been set up by the government in an attempt to make good some of the losses caused by Dutch elm disease. Nevertheless, it was often one step backwards for every two steps forward. In March the EPS newsletter thanked members who had contributed to the Preservation Society's tree fund and happily announced numerous projects for the year, including plantings to be carried out by the EPS trees group at Grange Park Primary School, Merryhills School, Forty Hill Vicarage, and in London Road, with sponsorships (many of them memorial plantings) on Chase Green and in several local parks. Only a few months later, the autumn newsletter bemoaned the imminent destruction of some fine oaks on building sites near The Ridgeway and warned: 'unless adequate replanting takes place, the names High Oaks and Oak Avenue may soon have nothing but a historical significance, instead of marking some of the most noble trees in the borough'. In the same issue, Christopher Jephcott regretted that because of staff shortages it sometimes took Enfield Council more than a year to take action on requests by the EPS for preservation orders on important trees, or to investigate apparent contraventions of tree preservation orders.

Dutch elm disease continued its relentless sweep through Enfield. In October 1974 the *Enfield Gazette* reported that the disease had made such serious inroads into the borough's elms that the total disappearance of the tree from local parks and countryside now seemed inevitable. Attempts to halt the spread had been unsuccessful and the majority of local elms were now affected. A survey by the borough parks department revealed that 1,667 trees on council land had fallen victims to the disease in 1974. The estimated cost of removing the trees was nearly £40,000. The report added that according to Douglas Stacey, the borough's chief parks and recreation officer, efforts to immunise 300 of the finest elms in the borough with a course of injections 'had produced mixed results'. The national slogan for Tree Planting Year — *Plant a tree in '73* — was followed by exhortations to *Plant some more in '74* and *See them thrive in '75*. Cynics added *By '76 they'll all be sticks!* and in Enfield, as elsewhere in the country, this proved sadly true. At the end of June 1976 temperatures in the south-east of England soared; 90 degrees Farenheit was recorded in Central London, the highest since the London Weather Centre opened in 1940. As the heatwave continued, young trees wilted. For weeks, there was no break in the hot weather. In Enfield, pubs ran out of lager and on 20 August the *Enfield Weekly Herald*, reporting government restrictions on watering and vehicle cleaning, noted that the 'desperate' water shortage had forced Enfield Council to take drastic action. Staff had been instructed to use the absolute minimum water necessary to keep sports grounds open. According to the *Enfield Gazette* (26 August) it was the worst drought to hit Eng-

153. National Tree Week 1975 saw one of the Preservation Society's frequent efforts to involve young people in tree planting. Here, watched by councillors, council officers and EPS representatives, pupils from Albany School help Bryan Davies (MP for Enfield North) plant £50 worth of trees in Albany Park.

land and Wales for 250 years. Most of the newly planted trees died and to add insult to injury the EPS autumn newsletter reported two additional and avoidable losses of hedgerows during the summer: a hedge north of Whitewebbs Road had been deliberately grubbed out, and uncontrolled stubble burning had set fire to another in Cattlegate Road.

By the end of 1977, in addition to the drought casualties, Enfield had lost more than 10,000 elms. A number of mature wych elms on Chase Green were the last local victims of Dutch elm disease and to help fund their replacement, the Preservation Society decided to involve local residents. This procedure was later used with success in other parts of the borough. Letters were sent to people living in houses overlooking Chase Green, inviting contributions towards replacement trees. A total of £74 was subscribed which, when made up to £100 from EPS funds, was enough to sponsor 14 limes and a number of small pines. In March 1978 the Mayor, Councillor Amy Emsden, helped to plant three of the lime saplings along the frontage to Chase Green Avenue. The Preservation Society provided or sponsored more than 100 trees in the 1977/78 planting season, and by spring the tree fund was nearly exhausted. This presented a problem because the EPS trees group was determined to support the 'Stop the Rot' campaign which had been launched by Ponders End Residents' Association in a plucky attempt to brighten their part of the borough, which was long overdue for a face-lift. The Preservation Society decided to raise money by renting a stall in Enfield Market. EPS members responded

154. Snow did not deter an EPS working party who planted groups of trees round the playing field at Chace Boys' School (now Chace Community School) in 1976, and it did not stop the trees from flourishing. This picture shows the junction of Baker Street and Tenniswood Road before Carlton House surgery was built, with (from left) Rex Harvey (headmaster), Councillor Peter Perryman, Gordon Macfarlane and Les Dixon .

generously to an appeal for saleable items and provided an amazing assortment ranging from a four-piece silver teaset to home-made cakes and jam. Over £278 was raised and for several years the market stall became an annual fund-raising event to boost the Preservation Society's tree fund.

Efforts to improve neglected parts of eastern Enfield continued. The EPS newsletter for spring 1980 reported that thanks to the proceeds from the market stall, 40 trees would be planted to hide eyesores and enliven council estates in Ponders End, 'including the ironically named Orchard Road, which is completely devoid of trees'. Later that year the Preservation Society dug deep into its funds and raised £600 to provide 80 trees as part of the local response to the Queen Mother's birthday appeal. Unfortunately the commemoration turned sour. The EPS newsletter for December 1980 described National Tree Week that November as 'something of a sick joke in Enfield'. While the Mayor appealed to residents to sponsor trees to commemorate the Queen Mother's 80th birthday and the EPS gave generously to finance new plantings, the GLC had allowed several magnificent oaks to be felled in Enfield's green belt and had marked others with ominous white crosses. The local papers were united in their condemnation. 'The GLC celebrated National Tree Week by felling three 100-year-old oaks', said the *Enfield Weekly Herald* on

155. In an initiative launched by the Preservation Society in 1978, residents living near Chase Green subscribed enough money for 14 lime trees and several conifers to replace some of the trees lost on the green through Dutch elm disease. Near the massive stump of a Dutch elm casualty the Mayor (Alderman Amy Emdsden) plants a sapling, watched by (from left) Rogan, Jonathan and Brian Macdonald and Councillor Peter Perryman.

20 November. 'It seems they are felling living trees to avoid the expense of a proper maintenance programme'. The *Enfield Gazette* carried an interview with Irene Smith, who indignantly proclaimed: ' The GLC contend these trees were dangerous, but the few dead limbs could easily have been expertly removed, allowing the trees to make an important contribution to the landscape for the next 100 years'. She added: 'More than 200 oaks have been felled [on GLC farms] over the past 10 years with little or no replanting, in spite of a written promise to replace felled trees by planting twice the number on the holding — not that two saplings in any way compensate for the loss of a mature oak.'

Even more destructive, and more difficult to prevent, was the disappearance of hedgerows. The *Enfield Independent* reported in June 1981 that the Preservation Society wanted the new Wildlife and Countryside Bill (then going through Parliament) to include provision for grants to maintain, replace and repair hedgerows. This proposal was supported by Ted Graham, MP for Edmonton and Opposition spokesman for the environment. He told the House of Commons that the situation around Enfield was 'extremely disturbing'. On the Enfield Chase estate owned by the GLC there were 3,000 acres of farmland, he said. In 1937 the average size of a field was 10.9 acres, but by 1980 this had been increased to 17.9

156. A 'stag-horned' oak in Hadley Road, about 1980. Throughout the 1970s Enfield Preservation Society complained that the GLC was felling healthy but neglected trees to save the expense of regular maintenance.

acres through grubbing out hedgerows. 'The loss of Enfield's hedgerows amounts to a startling 13.4 miles — a colossal 25 per cent', he said. The position was just as bad for hedgerow trees. In 1946 there were 2,560 semi-mature or mature trees on the estate, but by 1980 the number had declined to 1,956. 'There is one farm of 97 acres where 118 trees have been removed and only 110 remain' he claimed. The Preservation Society tried to make good some of these losses. In the 1980/81 planting season more than 200 forest trees of various species, many of them donated by EPS members, were planted on Botany Bay Farm to screen slurry pits and provide areas of natural cover for wildlife. Four years later 75 forest trees were planted on Rectory Farm to screen the view of the plant yard and farm buildings from the nearby Chase Farm Hospital and The Ridgeway.

Mature trees were constantly coming under threat in urban parts of the borough. Roughly one-third of Enfield's 20,000 street trees had been planted in the early part of this century and by the mid-1970s some of the limes, planes and maples had grown to majestic proportions. In November 1977 the *Enfield Gazette* reported that the previous year's drought had produced claims totalling £40,000 against Enfield Council for damage caused by tree roots. This was £15,000 over the council's insurance limit and it therefore proposed to replace so-called 'suspect' trees. Douglas Stacey, borough parks officer, told the newspaper that many trees had now reached an age and size disproportionate to their surroundings and said the council was considering a five-year programme for the removal and replacement of 250 trees a year at an annual cost of £13,500. The Preservation Society urged that no tree should be cut down unnecessarily and demanded details of the replacement programme.

In November 1978 the EPS trees group received a list of 300 trees, mainly London planes in Edmonton and Southgate, which were to be cut down and replaced with 260 ornamental species. It was agreed that Wally Woodfield (then trees group leader) and Christopher Jephcott would monitor and photograph every stage of the scheme before the EPS made further comments. No unexpected snags occurred. The EPS newsletter for spring 1980, reporting that the current replacement programme had included Sketty Road, Enfield, commented that residents in the road had complained when the trees were removed, but added: 'the replacements are sturdy specimens, so we hope last year's virtual 100% success rate will be equalled'. This smooth start to the replacement programme was unfortunately not maintained. The Preservation Society received frequent complaints that trees had been felled without reason and that replacements had died because they had not been watered. For a number of years, members of the EPS trees group devoted an enormous amount of time and money to Enfield's street trees, trying to get more planted, to improve the standard of after-care, and to secure better pruning of established trees. By 1985 the replacement programmed had affected 40 streets. The trees group surveyed them all and reiterated the Preservation Society's policy that no mature trees should be felled where there was enough space to accommodate them. Enfield Council was urged to replace dead trees and to resume planting in roads with no trees, and offered a list of suitable varieties.

The Preservation Society had meanwhile been going ahead with its efforts to encourage residents to sponsor trees for their own roads. In November 1981 Enfield Council had launched a new sponsorship programme: for a fee of £7.50 the parks department would provide, plant and stake a tree. The EPS lost no time in sponsoring twelve trees at the northern end of Ladysmith Road, greatly improving its appearance. Two years later, neighbours asked for planting to be extended along this long, straight road. The Preservation Society, already committed to a heavy programme, wrote to 120 residents in November 1983 inviting them to share the cost, which had now risen to £10 for each tree. Donations totalling £72 were received from 13 households. This was made up to £150 from EPS funds and 15 sorbus were planted, but not everyone was pleased. A number of properties in Ladysmith Road had trees in their front garden and on 2 February 1984, two weeks after the street trees went in, the *Enfield Gazette* published a complaint from a pensioner. She claimed that when the letter from the Preservation Society arrived 'we were ankle deep

157. Trees sponsored by the Preservation Society and residents in 1983 add colour, life and interest to Ladysmith Road in May 1995.

in fallen leaves and the drains were blocked'. She and her neighbours, she wrote, 'spent hours of back-breaking time and energy trying to collect and sack the leaves and rubbish'. In a subsequent issue a resident in Balmoral Road joined the controversy, complaining that damage to pavements and the cost of sweeping up and disposing of leaves meant that street trees were 'of great expense to ratepayers'. Members of the Preservation Society found it difficult to understand this churlish attitude but in autumn 1987 the EPS trees group admitted that there had been a rather disappointing response to its latest street tree appeal. In Pembroke Avenue 138 letters had been delivered, bringing only 12 replies, three opposed to any planting and nine enclosing donations totalling £24. In Bell Avenue, 27 letters had brought six replies — two against planting and four with donations amounting to £14. If the response from these roads was typical, it seemed that a stubborn minority of Enfield residents preferred to live in a bare street devoid of trees; a larger number enjoyed trees and were prepared to help pay for them, but the vast majority were either indifferent to their surroundings, or expected others to foot the bill for planting schemes.

However, this apathy was swept away in 1987 when the full impact of the great October gale became apparent. More than 3,000 trees were lost in Enfield on the night of 16 October. Over 2,000 were uprooted in the borough's parks and woodlands, changing the landscape for generations. The famous lime avenue in Forty Hall was ruined. Paths in Whitewebbs were blocked by the 200-year-old giants that crashed to the ground. There were devastating losses in the Town Park. Ancient oaks came down on Chase Green and in Hilly Fields. More than 1,000 street trees were uprooted and many of those that survived were so badly damaged that they were later removed. Private sports grounds and gardens also suffered. Jubilee Hall, the new EPS headquarters in Parsonage Lane, was among scores of buildings damaged by falling trees. One of the two 50-foot Monterey Cypresses growing on the frontage crashed into the narrow space between Jubilee Hall and the neighbouring church hall. Fortunately the tree caused only minor damage, but it took volunteers two days to saw it up and clear the site. The other cypress remained upright but had become so dangerous that it was removed professionally.

The EPS newsletter for winter 1987 announced that the Preservation Society had launched a Tree Disaster Fund and would add £1 for each £1 subscribed up to the first £1,000. Membership had just reached 2,000 and the announcement concluded: 'It would be splendid to celebrate our 2,000 membership total with a fund which topped £2,000'. The magnificent response was a heartwarming endorsement of the Preservation Society's dogged efforts to preserve and improve the borough's tree cover. More than £800 was subscribed in the first eight days. With £1,000 donated by the EPS, the fund continued to grow until it reached a total of nearly £5,000. Spending the money proved more difficult. Enfield Council officers made it clear that it would be months before they could consider sponsorship proposals from the Preservation Society. For many weeks following the October gale, staff in the parks department worked flat out, coping with the massive clear-up. Then came a race to plant 700 street trees funded by the Department of the Environment, which had imposed a condition that planting must be carried out by 31 March 1988. Explaining the situation in the EPS newsletter for spring 1988, Wally Woodfield pointed out that with the planting season nearly over, heavy demand all over the south of England meant that suitable tree stock had become scarce and expensive. Enfield Council was anxious not to rush into piecemeal replanting and had asked the Preservation Society to help assess sites in parks and open spaces where mature trees had been lost so that new trees could be positioned where they would enhance the landscape.

During the first months of 1988 senior parks officers in Enfield were also heavily

158. Scenes of desolation greeted Enfield residents when they awoke on 17 October 1987, the morning after the great gale. Irene Smith (extreme left) was dwarfed by one of the giants that crashed down on Chase Green.

159. After the great gale, it took two days to saw up and remove the 50-foot Monteray Cypress which fell between Jubilee Hall and the neighbouring church hall.

involved with preparations for tendering. The government had decreed that numerous local government services must be put out to competitive tender by July 1988 and parks staff were busy working out the criteria for maintaining street trees, shrubberies and verges. The EPS Tree Disaster Fund was placed on deposit, in a high interest account, until a programme for the 1988/89 planting season could be agreed with council officers.

In September 1988 the Department of the Environment made Enfield Council an offer too good to miss: to help the tree replacement programme, the DoE would make an additional grant, possibly up to 50%, to augment public subscriptions. The amount subscribed by the public to the borough's tree replacement fund, opened after the October gale, was comparatively small. Enfield Council made an approach to the Preservation Society — was the EPS willing to have its Tree Disaster Fund added to the borough's total, to maximise the government grant? The Society agreed to make £4,800 available, subject to two conditions: that the planting sites should be mutually agreed, and that the council would replace any trees that died. This latter obligation was felt essential, because the Preservation Society had become increasingly concerned that lack of after-care for council plantings was resulting in heavy losses. One assumes that the money was gratefully received. A letter of thanks was received from the council's arboricultural officer but no official acknowledgement of this generous gift was received from the Mayor or even from the borough parks and recreation officer. To this day not a single plaque indicates any of the plantings paid for by the EPS Tree Disaster Fund.

The first tranche of the EPS fund, £3,500, provided 424 trees which were planted on 71 sites in spring 1989. Fifty schools, including several in Edmonton, were included. Always optimistic, the Preservation Society hoped this would foster an interest in trees among the pupils. Alas, the plantings were doomed. After an unusually wet winter and spring, 1989 saw the hottest, driest summer for 13 years. The local papers published letters from the Preservation Society urging people to water newly-planted saplings near their homes, but at least 50% of the trees died. In August the EPS informed Enfield Council that it would sponsor no more trees until all the losses had been made good. The council honoured its agreement and Frances Mussett, newly appointed leader of the trees group, announced in the EPS newsletter for winter 1989 that the replacement planting

160. Trees uprooted in Essex Road on the night of 16/17 October 1987 dislodged paving stones and damaged walls, roofs and parked cars.

was nearly complete. It was hoped, she said, that the trees would become well established in time to withstand any repetition of the previous summer's severe drought. But it was not to be. Another scorching summer followed, and in the newsletter for autumn 1990 Frances Mussett reported: 'Most of the newly planted trees appear not to have survived the last two dry summers. We have therefore decided not to sponsor new trees until Enfield Council reviews its planting programme to include provision for watering the trees'. It was suggested that upright lengths of pipe should be inserted near the tree roots, ready for watering by a tanker, as was done in Oxford and other places.

By autumn 1991 the cost of a sponsored street tree had risen to £25. No policy on watering had been adopted by Enfield Council, and the Preservation Society decided that in future it would sponsor street trees only if it received a written undertaking from a resident willing to 'adopt' them. This would involve regular watering during dry spells, checking the stakes and reporting any damage. On this basis the EPS sponsored five trees in Ordnance Road, the residents paying for another seven. The following year, although the price had gone up to £30, the Preservation Society, helped by contributions from local residents, sponsored several plantings including eleven trees in Parsonage Lane.

Dissatisfaction at the poor standard of tree pruning, often carried out at the wrong time of year, increased when the council put the work out to tender. The EPS newsletter complained that after being subjected to the 'Enfield lop', street trees frequently resembled lollipops . In August 1991 EPS representatives again expressed concern to council officers but the response was most unsatisfactory. 'It was clear', said the newsletter, that 'there were no long-term management plans for tree pruning, which was opportunistic when sums of money became available ... it appeared that the degree of severity of pruning was largely in the hands of the man up in the tree with the chain-saw ... the consequences, considering the contract had to be completed on time and the decision as to whether to cut a branch close to the trunk or just take out the tips would be made by the man in the tree, were obvious'. An urgent meeting was sought with councillors. In November 1991 the Preservation Society was informed that the council had allocated an extra £20,000 for tree maintenance and pruning for the current year. This gesture did little to solve the problem and in 1993 and 1994 the EPS continued to follow up numerous complaints from residents who were upset at the drastic and unseasonal pruning of nearby trees. No replacement planting was carried out in 1993/4, the familiar excuse being 'shortage of money'. At last, in December 1994, the Preservation Society learnt with relief that Enfield Council had voted a substantial increase in the highway trees budget and had adopted a management plan. Another hopeful sign was the council's decision to participate in the London Tree Forum, a capital-wide organisation launched by the Countryside Commission to press local authorities to draft tree strategies and improve the care of London's tree stock.

As part of the Preservation Society's continuous efforts to stimulate an interest in trees among children, questionnaires were sent to local schools in 1990 asking if they would welcome new trees or hedgerows in their grounds and would be willing to water any new plantings. The response was so enthusiastic that the programme had to be staggered. In the first stage, trees costing £1,500 were planted at 18 schools, with new hedgerows (well over 600 whips of hawthorn, blackthorn and wild cherry) for three schools the following year. The hedge planting, carried out on three consecutive days by members of the EPS trees group and the Enfield Conservation Volunteers, was dogged by one problem after another. The first project, carried out at Albany School in relentless rain, was vandalised within hours, involving tedious arrangements to replace the uprooted whips. At Forty Hill

161. Among the 700 varieties of trees and shrubs in the famous Beale Arboretum at West Lodge Park are several choice specimens donated by Enfield Preservation Society. In 1987 a group of members watched Donald Potter (EPS president) hand a commemorative plaque to Trevor Beale to identify the golden cedar planted to mark the Preservation Society's Golden Jubilee. In the left foreground is Wally Woodfield (EPS trees group leader); on the right, Irene Smith and (between her and Mr Beale) Douglas Stacey, the borough's chief parks and recreation officer.

Church of England School, where some 260 whips were planted round the sports field, the ground on the south boundary was so dry and stony that a trees group member returned the following morning to carry over 200 buckets of water to give the hedge a good start. The final day was spent at Galliard Primary School where the exhausted volunteers had to give up after planting more than 200 whips because the ground contained so much building rubble that it was unsuitable. In the EPS newsletter for summer 1993, Frances Mussett wrote: 'The hedges will be a lasting monument to all that hard work and will provide a valuable environmental resource for future schoolchildren to enjoy in the form of a more diverse wildlife'. One hopes her optimism will be justified. This was one of the last planting schemes carried out by the trees group, which in 1994 amalgamated with the EPS anti-litter group to expand its scope as the natural environment group.

Enfield Preservation Society provided or sponsored nearly 3,500 new trees between 1964 and 1996, all of them planted in the confident hope that they would give pleasure to future generations. But when Irene and Stanley Smith toured Enfield in 1995, hoping to photograph some of the early plantings to illustrate this book, they were disappointed to find that many of the trees had failed or had been cut down. Unfortunately the destruction was especially noticeable in eastern Enfield, sometimes because the ownership of the site had changed, occasionally because roads or buildings had been extended or for no apparent reason. Despite these and other losses, the hedges, trees and shrubs planted by the EPS have brought beauty, colour and interest to hundreds of places all over the borough. The Preservation Society continues to initiate planting schemes of various types and remains vigilant in trying to protect and increase the trees that grace Enfield's streets, parks and other open spaces.

Chapter 14
The Changing Scene

The demand for housing sites became intense during the 1980s. The building industry, which had made no attempt to regenerate existing housing areas, had organised a vociferous campaign, concentrated mainly in south-east England, urging the release of green belt land. The house builders' persistence was rewarded in the autumn of 1983 when the Department of the Environment issued a draft circular which proposed 'rationalising' green belt boundaries. All over the country, the amenity movement took up the challenge and rallied to the defence of green belts. The EPS newsletter for November 1983 reported that a deputation from Enfield Preservation Society had spoken to Tim Eggar MP 'but we were not encouraged by the outcome'. Christopher Jephcott commented: 'The circular threatens to strike at the whole basis of the green belt in a way that has not been done since this universally admired policy was introduced'. Members were urged to send protests to their MPs.

The GLC, which was under threat of abolition, milked the situation for as much political capital as possible. The *Enfield Gazette* reported on 8 December 1983 that Illtyd Harrington (deputy leader of the GLC), accompanied by councillors and representatives from amenity and conservation groups, had toured London's green belt in an open-top bus. The report explained that the GLC had direct management control over 10,442 acres of green belt land including farms, smallholdings, parks and golf courses. 'All this will be divided and passed on to the London boroughs who, the GLC say, might be tempted to sell to private developers when the GLC is disbanded in 1986.' There was also the threat of industrial development along the M25. The report added that Wally Woodfield, the EPS chairman, had joined the bus for the Enfield section of the tour. He had made it clear that Enfield Preservation Society was not a political group but was concerned at any developments that might affect the preservation of green belt land. Later that month Wally Woodfield told the EPS council of management that the 'circus tour' had taken place in pouring rain. Locally, the bus had stopped only at Holly Hill Farm and Trent Park. While waiting for the bus to arrive at Holly Hill Farm he had spoken at length to the *Gazette* reporter, mentioning the Society's intention to fight for the retention of the green belt and its disquiet at the government circular. 'The reporter's notes got soaked but the report in the paper was not too garbled' said Mr Woodfield.

Six months later, an official statement about the transfer of green belt land owned by the GLC was still awaited. On 28 June 1984 the *Enfield Gazette* reported that the Preservation Society had written to Enfield's chief executive and Town Clerk, Wilfrid Day, asking what plans had been made for managing the green belt when it was handed over by the GLC. The letter stressed that this vast estate, 'some of the finest landscape within the

Metropolitan green belt' and comprising more than half the farmland within the borough, must be used not only to benefit the tenants who farmed it, but also to benefit the people of Enfield who enjoyed its beauty and valued its potential for informal recreation. 'Such an opportunity is unlikely to come again', said the letter. The same issue of the *Gazette* carried a report of the 1984 borough monitoring seminar at which council officers had admitted they were 'not quite sure' what would happen to the green belt land when it was released from GLC control.

Later that year the government, taking note of widespread criticism, revised the disputed circulars and appeared to confirm its commitment to existing green belt policies and boundaries. The revised wording was so convoluted that even Tim Eggar (as reported in the *Enfield Independent* on 10 October) admitted that the circular was 'somewhat unclear'. He conceded that while lack of clarity left room for flexibility, it often gave rise to unjustifiable concern and he promised to speak to the Secretary of State when he had received the views of the EPS and FERAA. These were readily forthcoming. Not surprisingly, Patrick Jenkin, Secretary of State for the Environment, assured Tim Eggar that the green belt land would be better run once it was in the hands of the London boroughs. He agreed, as might be expected, that capital's green belt was 'a priceless possession and must be protected for London and the region as a whole'. The Preservation Society nevertheless remained unconvinced. Its scepticism appeared well founded when on 25 October 1984 the *Enfield Gazette* reported: 'Crews Hill Residents' Association and the Enfield Preservation Society are up in arms about an Enfield Council letter they fear may open the way for a residential development on green belt land'. The row concerned the pumping station in Whitewebbs Lane, a massive building which had not been used since the 1950s. Enfield & District Veteran Vehicle Trust had been granted planning permission by the council to convert the pumping station into a museum but the owners, Thames Water, had refused to sell direct and intended to auction it the following week. The report stated that the Veteran Vehicle Trust now expected to be squeezed out. Their fears followed a letter from the borough planning officer (Bill Issitt) to Thames Water, advising that 'subject to a number of reservations' a suitable scheme for conversion to residential purposes would receive his favourable recommendation. The Preservation Society strongly opposed this 'peculiar' decision. As anticipated, the Veteran Vehicle Trust

162. The former Metropolitan Water Board pumping station in Whitewebbs Lane, unused since the 1950s, standing empty and deteriorating in 1983. Enfield Preservation Society, having tried unsuccessfully to have the handsome building listed, was horrified by a suggestion from the borough planning officer that housing might be approved on the site. The Enfield & District Veteran Vehicle Trust have now converted the pumping station into the Whitewebbs Museum of Transport.

was outbid at the auction, but Enfield Council's green belt policy was not put to the test on this occasion because within a few weeks the buyer had pulled out of the deal. The trust was able to acquire the pumping station for £126,050 and begin the rewarding task of converting it into a transport museum.

Although recognising the problems caused by the shortage of building land, the Preservation Society refused to deviate from its policy of opposing all developments in the green belt. It also continued to protest at attempts to build housing estates on urban green spaces or in spacious gardens (so-called 'backland' development). This intransigence brought criticism from a usually sympathetic quarter. The *Enfield Gazette* reported on 19 July 1984 that the Mayor of Enfield (Councillor John Jackson) speaking at an EPS cheese and wine evening in Forty Hall, admitted he had been 'very alarmed indeed' by the government circulars. He was pleased that the minister had, to some extent, now retracted and had agreed that the green belt was largely sacrosanct. Nevertheless, provision had to be made for housing needs and developers were hungry for land. 'We cannot have our cake and eat it' the Mayor warned the EPS. 'Some backland development is perhaps inevitable. I applaud your efforts to protect the green belt, but you must remember there is a price to be paid. Occasionally we have to provide land within the urban landscape for development, which may not always meet with your approval.' His prophecy was soon fulfilled. Backland development became harder to resist as householders succumbed to tempting offers to sell off part of their property. In parts of Gordon Hill, Clay Hill, and other established areas, clusters of closely packed flats began to cover what had been gracious, mature gardens.

163. The closure of Ripaults factory on the corner of Southbury Road and Crown Road triggered a lengthy dispute about the fate of the buildings and the extensive site, which included a sports field and miniature golf course for employees. Ripaults Cableworks, which made electrical wiring systems for cars, was a major employer in Enfield from 1936 until the 1980s. The distinctive office block (shown here), with its red and white colour scheme, was listed by the Department of the Environment on the day demolition was due to start. Later, in 1989, an application to demolish the building was turned down; at the public inquiry the EPS pointed out that the sleek office block, with its landscaped forecourt, was characteristic of the Art Deco factory buildings which sprang up on the A10 and nearby roads in the 1930s. Development was eventually allowed on most of the site. New hope for the empty office block, which for several years was included on English Heritage's register of buildings at risk, came in February 1996 with a planning application from a vehicle company eager to renovate and extend the buildings.

Pressure on private playing fields increased; their owners, eager for revenue in the prevailing recession, were often thankful to sell. Within the next three years the Ruberoid sports ground in Carterhatch Lane had gone for housing, industrial development had been approved on the Ripaults sports ground in Crown Road, Sainsbury's had obtained permission for a supermarket on the Langham Playing Field, Winchmore Hill, and the Arundel Tennis Club in Radcliffe Road had vanished under bricks and mortar. In 1985 Enfield Council had expressed strong resistance to the selling of private recreational land and sports grounds for building, but several of these developments, which had all been opposed by the Preservation Society, were won on appeal. Because the stakes were so high, developers who had been refused planning permission were quick to appeal, knowing that there was an excellent chance a DoE Inspector would overturn the council's decision. The borough planning officer's report for 1985 revealed that of 109 planning appeals lodged since September 1983, 40% had been allowed and the council had won 60%. This proportion was to remain fairly constant until 1990, when the council's success rate dropped to 56%. As Stuart Mills asked in the EPS newsletter for autumn 1988 — with odds like that, why should a developer take local policies seriously?

Enfield Council was faced with a dilemma. Although the population of the borough was falling, the number of households was increasing, partly because of the high proportion of people living on their own. (In 1984, about 23% of local households comprised just one person, and two-thirds of those were pensioners.) With local house prices rising faster than the national average, pressure on open land became acute. Allotments were the next target. The EPS newsletter warned gardeners to 'use them or lose them' but in 1988 the council decided that over the coming three years, thirty acres of allotments would be developed for housing. The borough planning officer's report stated: 'It is clear that there is a considerable supply of housing land within the built-up area of the borough'. To the consternation of the Preservation Society, streets as well as open spaces became blighted by 'town cramming'. Most of the new developments consisted of blocks of flats or a number of small housing units cramped into schemes which were frequently criticised by the EPS for overcrowding and mundane design. Christopher Jephcott, the Preservation Society's eloquent spokesman on town planning matters, voiced concern in two successive EPS newsletters in 1989. In the spring issue he condemned the spate of recent planning approvals which had allowed slightly larger than average houses, sometimes only a few years old, to be demolished to make way for densely packed mini housing estates. 'The implication of this trend for the future appearance of the borough is ominous', he warned. Enfield Council was stung by this criticism, and councillors and council officers made their displeasure known in a series of sharp exchanges with members of the Preservation Society.

The EPS council of management, which had become seriously alarmed at the damage being done to some residential areas, held a special policy meeting. It was agreed that representations from the Preservation Society and from local residents were having little or no effect on the council's planning decisions and that Enfield's character was being radically changed by the erection of three- or four-storey blocks of flats where houses had once stood. In the latest example in Queen Anne's Gardens, Bush Hill Park, the council had even ignored advice from English Heritage that 22 units would be overdevelopment on such a small site. Another protest was sent to Enfield Council, and with the unanimous backing of the EPS council of management, Dr Jephcott expanded on the theme in the summer newsletter. The Preservation Society was, he wrote, 'extremely worried' that in the more attractive areas of the borough 'even moderately sized and recently built houses' were being pulled down and replaced by large blocks of flats. 'These are usually higher than the buildings they replace and those which surround them and, because of the permitted densities, there is usually too little amenity space left on the site to allow any satisfactory landscaping to soften the impact' he complained. Recent examples had occurred on four separate sites in Crescent Road and Waverley Road, with others in Southbury Road and Queens Road.

Dr Jephcott conceded that a major factor was the need, imposed by new strategic planning guidelines, for the borough to find space for 7,000 additional dwellings by the year 2001. 'Enfield Preservation Society', he wrote, 'was taken to task because the mention of this subject in the last newsletter was regarded as an attack on Enfield Council. It was no such thing. We accept that this is a problem with no easy solutions and that councillors of all political persuasions share our concern. However, we think it is important that, in the pursuit of this housing target, the need to protect the green belt does not become an excuse for permitting the redeveloped areas to become featureless and dull. A varied and interesting mix of dwellings, greenery, formal and informal pockets of open space, with undeveloped pockets to harbour wild life, should be our aim for the residential areas in this outer London suburb. All new planning applications should be considered in this light. The designation of further conservation areas, as recently with Hadley Wood, can help in this process, but the concept needs to extend wider than that, so that the whole of Enfield gains a reputation as a pleasant place in which to live.' This well-reasoned argument no doubt prompted local councillors to take a critical look at the effects of their housing policy. The borough planning officer's report for 1990 admitted that 'the number of house conversions into flats is beginning to have an adverse impact on the character and appearance of some areas'. The following year, when the borough's draft Unitary Development Plan was published, with policies intended to take Enfield

164. The EPS campaign against street clutter and eyesores began in 1936, when Middlesex County Council was persuaded to remove empty sand bins from Hertford Road. These galvanised iron bins, rotting on Chase Green in 1964, were scrapped after complaints from the Preservation Society.

165. The Preservation Society has been trying for 60 years to persuade Enfield Council to improve the design of its notice-boards. Heavy concrete structures, criticised by the Society in the 1960s, are still in use in several areas, but some have been replaced by equally unsatisfactory structures. The EPS newsletter for winter 1989 showed this dismal scene at the corner of Dryden Road and Queen Anne's Place in Bush Hill Park Conservation Area, where a dilapidated metal frame with peeling paint and tattered posters shielded a vandalised seat.

into the 21st century, the Preservation Society noted with approval that, although the demand for smaller dwellings continued, policies in the UDP would not permit cramped or excessively intensive developments, and also sought to limit the proportion of conversions so that the character of an area was not adversely affected.

The determination that the whole of Enfield should be seen as a pleasant place in which to live, as reiterated by Christopher Jephcott, has motivated the Preservation Society since its formation. The Society has always been keenly aware that apparently insignificant changes or intrusions could insidiously destroy the charm of a residential road, the appearance of a shopping centre, or the attractions of a park. The Preservation Society's major campaigns on emotive issues have always earned headlines in the local press. Its persistent attempts to encourage good design in new developments and to prevent buildings being spoilt by unsympathetic alterations are well respected. But the general public remains largely unaware of its dogged and often successful efforts to improve the everyday street scene. This time-consuming campaign has continued week in, week out, demanding constant dedication from members of the EPS council of management in writing letters or lobbying various authorities on apparently trivial matters. Efforts to improve the street scene had begun in the 1930s, but the first real drive to get rid of street clutter was launched in 1963, when the Middlesex County Council was persuaded to remove empty sand bins from the Hertford Road and Enfield Council agreed to take down redundant noticeboards. Unused and dilapidated noticeboards were the subject of another onslaught by the Preservation Society in 1989. Photographs of advertisement eyesores were first sent to Enfield Council in 1968 and numerous complaints about garish illuminated signs, especially in the green belt and in conservation areas, were made in subsequent years. The level of response from the council tended to vary according to the manpower available in the planning department. The design and siting of bus shelters, lamp standards, bollards, litter bins and other street furniture also came under frequent scrutiny from the Preservation Society, sometimes with unexpected results. In 1966 it complained that a pillar box had been placed directly in front of the listed Public Offices (now the Register Office) in Gentleman's Row, spoiling the view of the handsome Ionic door frame.

166 and 167. A quaint survival in Enfield's main shopping street, the Old Vestry House, 22 The Town is now used as an office by a firm of solicitors. It was built for the parish beadle, with cells each side, and was taken over as a sub-divisional police station in 1840. In 1942 the Preservation Society successfully opposed an attempt to remove the decorative iron railings and melt them down for use as 'munitions of war'. In 1965 the EPS again came to the rescue when a bus shelter was sited directly in front of this unusual little building (above). To the Society's delight, Enfield Council soon afterwards prohibited advertising on flank walls in sensitive areas, and the large poster was removed.

168. In 1966, with complete disregard for the effect on the surroundings, the Post Office placed a pillar box directly in front of the handsome Ionic door of the Public Offices (now the Register Office) in Gentleman's Row. When the Preservation Society suggested the box should be moved to a less obtrusive position, it disappeared from the scene.

The Society's suggestion that the box should be moved resulted in its complete disappearance from the scene, to the irritation of some residents.

Together with its active support for street trees, the Preservation Society always strongly encouraged the retention of the grass verges. In December 1976 the *Enfield Gazette* reported a complaint by the EPS that verges were being damaged, possibly irreparably, by parked cars, without the council making any attempt to prohibit this abuse. The borough engineer, Donald Treweek, replied that there was no possibility of the council taking action 'during the present limit on local government spending'. Less than five years later the Preservation Society's forebodings were realised and Enfield Council decided to save on maintenance costs by covering narrow or damaged grass verges throughout the borough with concrete or tarmac. The EPS asked the council to reconsider. In an attempt to gain wider public support, Christopher Jephcott sent a letter to the *Gazette* pointing out that 'even a narrow strip of grass makes a vast difference to the attractiveness of a street'. Roads where verges had been covered in tarmac or concrete generally had a dusty, drab appearance, he said. Having no doubt forgotten the Preservation Society's earlier complaint, the borough engineer blandly replied that 'in some areas a lot of grass doesn't exist on verges because of parked cars'. But he promised that if residents in a particular area were willing to maintain their verges, the council would not concrete over them. It was only after numerous patches of grass had disappeared under cheerless hard surfacing that people fully appreciated the living verges they had taken for granted.

Since Don Gresswell's spectacular clearances in the early Sixties, the Preservation Society has waged constant war on litter and its dispiriting effects on the local environment.

The amount of litter in the streets has often been a been a sordid indication of the state of the borough's finances. Over the years, the Preservation Society has been forced to fight this same battle many times, with varying success. There was a quick response in the summer of 1972, following a tour of Enfield by the council's deputy cleansing superintendant and EPS representatives. They pointed out the uncollected litter which was disfiguring the 'no man's land' on greens around council houses and new developments, and asked for an agreement on who was responsible for keeping them tidy. Within six months the cleansing department had formed a mobile caretaking unit to care for

169. The white surface under the Grammar School windows in Church Walk in 1977. The wall was a magnet for graffiti in the 1970s, spoiling an otherwise delightful corner of Enfield Town.

170. The pleasing result in 1979, after the Preservation Society had paid for the rendering to be removed.

these areas. Ten years later, in May 1982, the general level of litter had become so noticeable that Christopher Jephcott complained in the *Enfield Independent* that although the Preservation Society accepted the need for economies in council spending, it felt that the current expenditure of 5p a head was insufficient to keep the streets clean and tidy. An election was imminent, and he hoped the new council would be more conscious of the need to make Enfield a place we could be proud of. The following month, the *Enfield Weekly Herald* reported: 'In a week when the London Borough of Enfield has mysteriously received a Keep Britain Tidy recommendation, the borough engineer (Donald Treweek) admits that the standard of street sweeping in the borough has fallen to an unacceptable level because of economies.' The council agreed to resume Sunday sweeping and clearance in shopping areas, but the general situation failed to improve. In 1989 the Preservation Society organised a special meeting to discuss the litter problem. Reporting the event, the EPS newsletter commented that looking at the squalid mess in some local streets, car parks and open spaces, it was hard to believe that Enfield Council was spending £1m a year on rubbish clearance and disposal, and that 70 people were employed on cleaning streets and emptying bins at an annual cost of £100,000.

During the 1970s and '80s EPS representatives served on the council's Keep Enfield Tidy Group and made valiant efforts to stimulate this well-meaning but ineffectual body. Councillor Richard Stacey, its last chairman, told an EPS meeting in 1989 that the group had concentrated its annual budget of £3,000 on education, starting with schoolchildren. He felt its efforts had not been successful because of the attitude of the public With considerable justification, the Preservation Society did not agree. The previous year, under the heading 'What a load of rubbish!', the EPS newsletter for summer 1988 had reported: 'April 23 this year was designated Clean-up Day throughout the country. The ideal opportunity, one would have thought, to organise a massive onslaught to clear the rubbish littering Enfield's streets, car parks and open spaces. But to the amazement of our representatives, the March meeting of the council's Keep Enfield Tidy Group (which meets only three or four times each year) was cancelled "through lack of business" '. There were few regrets when the Keep Enfield Tidy Group was disbanded late in 1989, and true to its traditions, Enfield Preservation Society decided it would take action itself. The winter newsletter asked whether members were interested in forming a group to tackle the litter problem. There was an encouraging response and in January 1990 the EPS anti-litter group met for the first time. Led by Prue Lambert and Beryl Dorrington, the group carried out monthly 'litter-picks', concentrating at first on squalid corners of Enfield Town where rubbish had been allowed to accumulate. There was almost too much litter to cope with. In one-and-a-half hours on a Sunday morning in April, nine members picked up more than 70 kilos of rubbish and retrieved nine supermarket trolleys. More ambitious schemes followed.

'Operation Eyesore' was the national theme for the Civic Trust Environment Week in 1990 and the EPS anti-litter group responded with two projects. The first, with other volunteers from the Preservation Society, was an attempt to clean up the former Chapel of Rest in Chapel Street. This quaint building behind St Andrew's Church in Enfield Town was built in the early nineteenth century to house the parish fire engine. It had later been used at various times as a Chapel of Rest and a church 'Meet a Need' office, but it had recently become defaced by graffiti, most of it sprayed from aerosol cans. Undeterred by youths who taunted them as they painted, with shouts of 'It will soon be just as bad again!', the EPS working party laboriously applied three coats of paint, followed by an anti-graffiti layer. The building looked superb but, alas, the improvement was short-lived.

171. Operation Eyesore was the national theme for Environment Week 1990. The EPS anti-litter group bravely decided to clean the former Chapel of Rest in Chapel Street and treat it with anti-graffiti paint, but the task was far more difficult than they anticipated. Getting down to work: Beryl Dorrington (right) and Prue Lambert, with John Pecorini and Stan Dixon up the ladders.

The volunteers had been badly advised, and their well-meaning enthusiasm was no match for the ancient bricks, oozing with moisture and without a damp course. Within weeks, bubbles appeared on the side walls and patches of paint began to slough off. The paint suppliers were called in and to the dismay of the volunteers the experts recommended that to achieve a better result the problem walls should be stripped down to the brickwork, which must then be treated with a fungicide followed by a sealer, primer and top coat. Fortunately the front of the building was not badly affected and it was agreed that as the sides were relatively unseen by the public, further treatment would be deferred.

The second project chosen for Environment Week in 1990 went more smoothly and was an encouraging example of what can be achieved with a little inspiration, co-operation and good will. The EPS anti-litter group suggested to Enfield Council that the neglected corner of the Library Green by the public telephone at the corner of Cecil Road and Church Street, should be improved. Within a commendably short time a scheme had been agreed, the planning department had allocated money from its fund for environmental improvements, the engineer's department had laid paving, and the parks department had planted trees. Enfield Preservation Society agreed to sponsor a litter bin and British Telecom donated a seat to the Society to complete the transformation. The result was a remarkable improvement to this entrance to the Town. Shoppers appreciated the

172. In 1990, inspired by the Preservation Society, Enfield Council and British Telecom co-operated in an Environment Week project which made a dramatic improvement to a corner of the Library Green. The prime movers, shown here, were: (left to right) standing, Nicola Rossi (British Telecom), Steve Jaggard (borough engineer's department) and Nigel Tomers (borough planning department). Sitting on the seat (later stolen) which was donated by British Telecom, Prue Lambert and Beryl Dorrington.

seat — but so, unfortunately, did others. It was stolen the following year. British Telecom declined to provide a replacement, so the Preservation Society stumped up for another seat and made sure that this time, it was securely bolted into the ground.

Continuing their brave efforts to improve St Andrew's Churchyard, members of the EPS anti-litter group spent much of 1991 removing graffiti from the walls of the parish church, painting railings, mending broken graves and filling gaps in the yew hedge with new planting. With the help of sponsorship from local firms, litter bins were provided and two new seats were installed. This face-lift scheme won a prize in a national gardening magazine — 5,000 spring bulbs, which were later planted in the churchyard. But it was an uphill struggle and the volunteers received scant thanks and no physical help from the church congregation. In April 1992 the group reported that 300 daffodils had been vandalised and initials had been scratched on a new seat. Volunteers had laboriously collected and stacked slabs from a vandalised grave, only to find the pieces of stone strewn all over the churchyard on their next visit. Beryl Dorrington, the group leader, told the EPS council of management that her helpers were becoming increasingly frustrated because their efforts were negated on so many occasions. Nevertheless, the group refused to throw in the towel and a few months later, in August 1992, volunteers made a renewed onslaught on the former Chapel of Rest. Several layers of peeling paint were painstakingly removed from the walls and a coat of anti-graffiti paint was brushed on. Over the last four years, although the surface is far from perfect, this unusual little building, a landmark in the heart of Enfield Town, has remained almost free of graffiti thanks to the perseverance of the EPS anti-litter group. Sadly, litter and vandalism remain continuing problems in the churchyard.

The introduction of the Environment Protection Act in 1992 made local authorities legally responsible for removing litter from their own land. It also gave them power to direct landowners to clear rubbish from their property within a given time. The EPS autumn newsletter therefore advised members to report badly littered areas to Enfield Council, instead of cleaning them up themselves. Hoping that they were thus relieved of their main — and never pleasant — self-imposed task, members of the EPS anti-litter group thankfully began looking for other ways to improve the local scene. At this time, as so often before, financial constraints were forcing Enfield Council to make drastic reductions in spending. One of the first services to be cut in the 1993/4 budget was the spring and summer planting of flower-beds. In an attempt to keep street beds and containers filled with flowers and shrubs, the Enfield in Bloom organisation stepped into the breach and announced it would co-ordinate an 'Adopt a Flower-bed' campaign throughout the borough. At first, this initiative did not meet with universal approval. Some local firms and organisations resented being asked to sponsor planting schemes and the *Enfield Advertiser* reported the launch of the campaign in August 1993 under the heading 'What a blooming nerve'. Enfield Preservation Society, through its anti-litter group, was one of

173. Frances Perry addresses EPS members from the doorway of Myddelton House, Bulls Cross, before leading a conducted tour of the garden in April 1985, watched by her husband, Roy Hay (seated). Mrs Perry, a protegee of E. A. Bowles, had an unrivalled knowledge of the famous garden he created. Myddelton House is now the headquarters of the Lee Valley Park Authority, which is restoring the garden (listed Grade II on the national register of historic parks and gardens) with guidance from an advisory group whose members include an EPS representative.

the first organisations to offer help, thus continuing an involvement with local planting schemes which began in 1963 when EPS volunteers planted 1,000 crocus bulbs on the Library Green in Church Street.

Enfield in Bloom, which had always been staunchly supported by the Preservation Society, was the brain-child of Roy Hay, the horticultural journalist who set up the Britain in Bloom movement. When he married Frances Perry (one of the Preservation Society's vice-presidents) in 1977 and moved to Bulls Cross, he was shocked to find that his work

174. One of the first initiatives in Enfield in Bloom's 'Adopt a Flower-bed' scheme was undertaken by the EPS anti-litter group, who in autumn 1993 planted small shrubs in the wall in front of the Church of Our Lady of Mount Carmel and St George in London Road. The church, initially criticised by some parishioners as resembling 'a miniature cathedral' replaced a smaller church which suffered extensive bomb damage during an air raid in November 1940.

175. The original Church of Our Lady and St George soon after it was opened in 1901, with the clergy house.

for Britain in Bloom had not reached Enfield. Roy Hay firmly believed that as well as lifting people's spirits, flowers and plants in public places encouraged a sense of civic pride and reduced both litter and vandalism. He relentlessly lobbied, badgered and cajoled the local authority until Enfield in Bloom was set up in October 1982. Since then, Enfield in Bloom has planted thousands of daffodil and crocus bulbs throughout the borough and has encouraged shops, public houses and individuals to enter an annual floral competition. In 1988 the Preservation Society sponsored an additional class in the competition, for 'Best completely new front garden'. Later changed to 'Best new front garden or transformation of a derelict site', the class attracts an encouraging variety of entries each year.

Under the Adopt a Flower-bed scheme, the EPS anti-litter group first cleared and planted the wall in front of the Catholic Church in London Road. Next, in November 1993 it planted the walls around the London Road car park with more than 200 specimens of ivy, lavender and euonymous. Just before Christmas, all the lavenders planted in the wall opposite the Townhouse were stolen, so the group, which had undertaken to maintain the site, filled the gaps with ivy.

To reflect its changed function, the anti-litter group amalgamated with the EPS trees group in 1994 to form the natural environment group. Despite the good intentions of the Environment Protection Act, litter clearance remains one of the preoccupations of the new group. Although a marked improvement in the standard of street cleaning took place in 1994 after the service was handed over to private contractors, these public-spirited EPS volunteers have resumed regular 'litter-picks' to collect rubbish from problem areas such as car parks and alleys in and around Enfield Town.

176. Clad in red sweatshirts bearing the EPS logo and the slogan 'Enfield Preservation Society Cares', members of the natural environment group filled ten plastic sacks with litter in a two-hour blitz on Holly Walk during National Spring Clean Week in April 1996. Left to right: Pam Bull, Ginny Billett, Beryl Dorrington, Frances Mussett and Gill Pointer.

Chapter 15
Spreading the Word

Membership of Enfield Preservation Society passed the 2,000 mark in 1988 and continued to increase, as did the Society's range of activities. Its reputation, already considerable, grew still higher and reached a wider public with the national publication of *Amenity in action,* the Civic Trust handbook of community initiatives. This listed over 200 projects carried out since 1970 by some of the 1,000 local amenity societies registered with the Civic Trust. The handbook, published in 1988, described ten of the many campaigns and projects initiated by Enfield Preservation Society, the highest number attributed to any single organisation, with a whole page devoted to the campaign to save the New River.

In that same year the EPS lost an activist who had participated in many of these campaigns and had played a dominant part in its affairs since the early 1960s. In March 1988 an illuminated address expressing the Preservation Society's 'gratitude and affection' was presented to Donald Potter on his resignation as EPS president. A widower for some years, he had remarried at the age of 80 and moved to Wheathampstead with his wife Daphne. Barely a month after the presentation, members of the Preservation Society were saddened by news of his sudden death. Donald Potter had played a prominent part in Enfield affairs since 1956 when he and his first wife Kathleen moved from Winchmore Hill to Gentleman's Row. At that time Mr Potter was secretary and actuary to the Canada Life Assurance Company, positions he retained until his official retirement date. The company then asked him to supervise the transfer of their administrative offices to a new building, Canada Life House, in Potters Bar. When the offices opened in June 1973, he retired and was able to devote more time to his other interests. Donald Potter was president of the Enfield North Liberal Association and a life elder of Christ Church, Chase Side, but he was best known for his long involvement with Enfield Preservation Society. The *Enfield Gazette* described Donald Potter as 'a mild-mannered man, quietly spoken, with an old-world charm' and commented: 'It is hard, at first, to see him as a tough-armed campaigner for the environment'. The EPS newsletter for summer 1988 recalled that the role Donald Potter most enjoyed, and at which he excelled, was acting as the Preservation Society's advocate at local planning inquiries. His evidence, meticulously prepared, delivered in his usual courtly style with wit and authority, always had a strong influence on the proceedings. His shrewd advice, lively mind and courteous, kindly presence were greatly missed by the EPS council of management. As a memorial to its late president, the Preservation Society offered to plant a small wood on farmland adjacent to the Naybur Garden Centre on The Ridgeway. Miscellaneous goods stacked in the garden centre were visible over a wide area of the green belt and the EPS had long wished to have the eyesore screened. A wood seemed a neat solution and the plan found favour with Enfield Council's land agent. The proposal was made in June 1988 but it was not until March 1994, after years of tedious negotiation, that Potter's Wood was planted.

Shortly before his death Donald Potter had been deeply involved with the compilation of *A Portrait of Gentleman's Row*, a lavishly illustrated book featuring the elegant and historic buildings in the showpiece street where he lived. The book, published by Enfield Preservation Society, was designed round photographs taken in 1979 and 1980 by Reginald Williams, an EPS vice-president. Reg Williams first became interested in photography in

177. Reginald Williams, whose superb photographs of Enfield have enriched EPS publications and archives.

178. In August 1984 Enfield Preservation Society had a seat placed on the Library Green in memory of Reg Williams, one of the Society's vice-presidents. A group from the EPS council of management tested the seat the following month: (left to right) sitting, Irene Smith, Priscilla Lowen, Christopher Jephcott, Hilary Stone, Velma Byford. Standing: Stan Lowen, Gordon Macfarlane, Donald Potter, Alan Skilton, Derek Needham, Wally Woodfield, Stuart Mills.

his teens, but it was only after his wife died in 1963 and he joined the Enfield Camera Club, that it became a major hobby. Through his membership of the Preservation Society Reg Williams became keenly aware how rapidly Enfield was changing and he set himself the task of making a pictorial record of historic features and endangered buildings. He also spent a great deal of time copying and enlarging pictures and prints of buildings already lost to the local scene. The photographs in *A Portrait of Gentleman's Row* were selected from the large and valuable collection he gave to the Preservation Society before his death in 1982. The book, superbly produced, was of an exceptionally high standard for a local amenity society and was one of a stream of publications produced by Enfield Preservation Society since 1965.

EPS books and booklets, footpath maps and walk guides, Christmas cards and local view postcards have advertised the borough's attractions throughout the United Kingdom and carried Enfield's name all over the world. The series of hardback books represent an ambitious and costly enterprise unattempted by any other amenity group in the country. The high standards reached have enhanced the prestige of the Preservation Society, but it was perhaps just as well that initially the EPS council of management did not realise how easily things could go wrong. Encouraged by the success of three photographic reprints of Cuthbert Whitaker's *History of Enfield*, each of which sold out within a few months of publication, the Preservation Society decided in 1977 to publish *Enfield's Architectural Heritage*, a unique pictorial record of the borough's best listed buildings. Designed by Alan Skilton, with help from Peter Perryman and Valerie Carter, this was an original and comparatively expensive production. To make it widely accessible it was published in softback as well as the dearer hardback edition. The book was an immediate success, ordered by local libraries and snapped up by historians as well as the general public. But even as glowing reviews appeared in the press, the Preservation Society began receiving complaints from disgruntled purchasers whose hardback copies were falling to pieces, with pages coming loose each time the book was opened. The trouble was due to a fault with the so-called 'perfect' binding (a misnomer if ever there was one — this was the first and last time the EPS specified this type of binding for its publications). It was only thanks to the dogged perseverence of Irene Smith, who relentlessly pursued the bookbinders and printers over the ensuing months, that the Preservation Society was fully compensated. In December 1978 she told the EPS council of management that she had at last had a meeting with those responsible, who had conceded that the hardbacks were 'useless'. They had agreed to provide satisfactory copies, to refund the costs on 200 unsold books and to replace any faulty books returned to them. However, although five weeks had elapsed since the meeting, the promised confirmation had still not been received. It took several sharp letters before the matter was resolved and the printers kept their bargain. In 1995, when *Enfield's Architectural Heritage* had long been out of print, the EPS historic buildings group, in response to frequent requests, began preparations for a new publication on listed buildings in Enfield.

It was an exciting day for the Preservation Society when local historian David Pam asked if the EPS was interested in publishing his first full length book, *The Story of Enfield Chase*. As the local history and museums officer for the London Borough of Enfield, David Pam had become widely known to members of clubs and organisations throughout the borough, to whom he had given countless talks. He was the author of numerous papers published by the Edmonton Hundred Historical Society and had retired as a council officer in 1982 with the intention of writing local history. *The Story of Enfield Chase*, which was well received, was a foretaste of the feast to come. In 25 years of research,

179. The Enfield Cedar and 'Palace', from a print dated 1821. The magnificent tree was cut down in the 1920s to make way for shops on and around the site now occupied by Pearsons department store. In 1982, when the Palace Gardens shopping precinct opened, this print, reproduced on a striking red background, formed the EPS Christmas card.

David Pam had studied thousands of documents relating to the parish of Enfield. Many of the papers and parchments had probably not been read since the day they were used two, three, four, five or more centuries ago. As he pored over the inventories, court records, letters and legal documents, he became determined to write the story of the parish from its first recorded beginning up to the outbreak of the Second World War. Enfield Preservation Society agreed to publish the trilogy and its initial trepidation about the heavy financial outlay soon vanished as sales of the first volume soared. *A Parish near London* (Enfield before 1837) was published in 1990, followed by *A Victorian Suburb* (1837-1914) in 1992 and *A Desirable Neighbourhood* (1914-1939) in 1994. David Pam's blend of scholarship and sly humour, and his ability to relate changing historical events to the lives of ordinary men and women living in the parish, made the trilogy immensely popular with local readers. National journals were unanimous in their praise for this scholarly but readable history, for the high standard of production and the numerous illustrations, many of which came from EPS archives. Even before the series was complete, *The London Topographical Society Newsletter* commented: '... it is a real cause for celebration when a borough finds itself a local historian, positively pickled in the records, who can write at one and the same time a coherent and gripping account of one of London's northern suburbs. David Pam is that man, and the second volume of his magisterial history of Enfield is the achievement of a lifetime.' The newsletter could have added, with equal justification, that it is also a cause for celebration when a borough contains an amenity society which can provide not just the funds, but also enough volunteers with the dedication and professional expertise needed to publish and market a major work of this quality.

Another outstandingly successful publishing venture has been the series of EPS local view postcards. The first, showing White Lodge, Silver Street, was issued in December 1984. A total of 26 different views had been published by early 1996, with total sales reaching more than 129,000. In addition to well-known gems such as Forty Hall, Gentleman's Row and Trent Park, the cards have featured scenes in Enfield Lock, Ponders End, Bush Hill Park and other less obvious parts of the borough. The superb colour photographs were all taken by Stanley Smith, an EPS vice-president, who has generously allowed the Preservation Society to use his pictures without a copyright fee. New views are regularly added to this popular series. Although some EPS publications have been sold direct to members, the majority have been retailed through local shops. Thanks to the dedication of Doris Connolly, a member of the Society, this sales operation has been carried through without the expensive intervention of a wholesaler. Since 1970 she has voluntarily acted as the Preservation Society's link with local shops, visiting them several times a year to deliver many thousands of cards, books and other EPS publications.

Since 1964 a growing band of volunteers have delivered the EPS newsletter to addresses all over Enfield. Initially published three times a year to give notice of the Preservation Society's main meetings, the newsletter has been issued quarterly since 1970. In recent years, as news reports in the local press have rapidly (and regrettably) declined, the role of the EPS newsletter has expanded. In addition to carrying announcements of Jubilee Hall meetings, coach outings and group activities, it has become an important channel to keep members informed about local planning decisions and Enfield Council's environmental policies. The newsletter distributors save the Preservation Society a huge annual

180. Delivering the quarterly EPS newsletter to more than 2,200 members involves a dedicated band of packers and distributors. Very few copies are posted, saving the Preservation Society an enormous annual expense. Here, volunteers pack newsletters in 1971 under the watchful eyes of Trudy Maunder (seated at back) and Harold Howson. In front of them (right) are Maurice and Doris Connolly, with Joyce and Harold Ball side by side at the front table.

181. A children's painting competition was held in conjunction with Fagin's bookshop in 1990 to promote the new Junior EPS organisation. Enfield's Mayor John Jackson presented prizes to the winners, who had painted pictures entitled 'My environment'. Outside the bookshop with their prizes: (left to right) Matthew Stevens, Prue Lambert, Rebecca Catanach, Denny Harvey, Mayor John Jackson, Felix Acquah (who designed a poster for Young EPS), Gill Soutar (chairman of Young EPS) and Laura Billings.

postage bill and are typical of the scores of willing members who quietly, dependably and unobtrusively help and support the EPS in many different ways.

In 1992 the Preservation Society broke new ground with a publication for schoolchildren, *The Enfield Book.* This lively mixture of puzzles, quizzes, articles and pictures was designed to stimulate an interest in Enfield's history and the local countryside. It was produced in conjunction with Young EPS, an organisation launched by Enfield Preservation Society in 1990. Believing in the 'catch 'em young' principle, the EPS council of management had for many years discussed the possibility of forming an organisation for young people. No leaders were forthcoming until, early in 1990, Prue Lambert volunteered to start a Young EPS group. She set about the task with enormous enthusiasm. The launch took place in the conference room at the Civic Centre where the Mayor (Councillor John Jackson) showed the youngsters the borough's civic regalia. Prue Lambert assembled a small committee which produced a Young EPS newsletter and began an inventive programme of activities that included talks, conducted walks and visits to local places of interest. As a group project it was decided that if Enfield Council could provide a suitably neglected site, Young EPS would transform it into a 'pocket park'. A derelict area between Hamburger Halt and the Bulldog public house in Bullsmoor Lane was suggested. Little more than a long, thin strip of threadbare grass with a public footpath

182. Enfield Preservation Society, the Department of Transport and Enfield Council organised a competition in 1993 for pupils from schools all over the borough to design tiled murals to brighten the walls of the underpasses under the A10. The entries included a Noah's Ark theme, circus frieze, underwater scene, and a panorama of sports and wildlife in local parks. The winning designs, some of which are reproduced here, now enliven the underpasses.

running through it, the site was covered with litter and looked most unpromising. The decision was left to the young people, who after visiting the site with their parents in December 1990 decided to go ahead. Enfield Preservation Society gave £150 to help the project and after a lot of hard work by the youngsters and their parents the litter was cleared, the grass relaid, and flowerbeds created and planted. Enfield Council repaired the boundary fencing, installed lighting and provided seats to complete the creation of this pocket park, now known as Little Gate, which in 1991 won an award in the Enfield in Bloom garden competition.

Despite the enthusiasm of its leaders, Young EPS failed to attract a large membership. This was partly because, in a misguided attempt to include as many young people as possible, an unmanageable age range — 'anyone aged six to 18' — had been set. The group had undoubted potential. Those who joined enjoyed the activities and the Little Gate project showed what could be achieved, but as in any youth group, the demands on leadership time and ingenuity were considerable. When Prue Lambert resigned from the EPS council of management towards the end of 1992 nobody felt able to take up the challenge. There was no response to an appeal in the EPS newsletter for a new leader, and the following year Young EPS was reluctantly disbanded. However, the Preservation Society did not abandon its attempts to involve young people. In 1993 schools all over the borough were invited to submit designs for a tiled mural to brighten the dingy pedestrian subways under the A10. The competition, organised by Enfield Preservation Society, the London Borough of Enfield and the Department of Transport, was a great success. Winning designs from Oakthorpe Junior School and Latymer School were among those used to decorate some of the cheerless subways to great effect, although within a short time two of the murals had been badly vandalised. In August 1994 and again in 1995 the Preservation Society set up a stall in the Palace Gardens shopping precinct and conducted a summer holiday quiz for children, with prizes provided by the EPS and local shops. The enthusiastic response to these initiatives made the Preservation Society determined to continue its efforts to interest young people in their local environment.

183. Enfield District Scouts are among many organisations which have asked the EPS to conduct special walks round the historic heart of Enfield Town. In August 1995, Cub Scouts studying for their local history badge were shown the sights by EPS representatives Len Keeble, Stan Lowen (on right) and Maire Newton.

Chapter 16
The Whitewebbs Affair

Towards the end of the 1980s it became evident that politicians both in and outside Parliament were once again becoming insistent that the government should relax its green belt policy. Enfield Preservation Society was made embarrassingly aware of the danger at its annual dinner in December 1987. The guest of honour was Lord Harris of High Cross, chairman of the Institute of Economic Affairs, who was known to have the ear of the Prime Minister and government policy makers. Lord Harris (who had local connections) began his speech by saying that he had long been an admirer of the Enfield Preservation Society, but the council of management's delight at having secured such a high-powered speaker turned to mortification as he launched into a biting attack on the government's green belt policy. As an economist, he felt that in this changing world preservation could sometimes be taken too far. If there had been such rigid guidelines 200 years ago as there were today, there would have been no industrial revolution, he asserted. The realities of economics must be taken into consideration when discussing the green belt. 'Some parts of the green belt are greener than others' said Lord Harris. 'There is a great deal of green, but some of the green belt is brown and grey. We must not create an unnecessary obstacle to the mobility and prosperity of a thriving community.' The EPS chairman, Wally Woodfield, was too taken aback (and perhaps too polite) to make a firm disclaimer at this heresy, which was reported at some length in the *Enfield Gazette* on 17 December.

Fears that the public might gain the impression that the Preservation Society agreed with Lord Harris and was wavering in its defence of the green belt led to angry recriminations at the January meeting of the EPS council of management, when it was reported that letters of protest had been received from members expressing dismay at the choice of speaker. Calm was restored when David Pam pointed out that it was the mark of a civilized organisation that members listened to views other than their own. It was left to Denis Hoy, the EPS representative on the London Green Belt Council, to set the record straight in a firm letter published in the *Gazette* on 21 January 1988. Pointing out that he and most of those attending the Preservation Society dinner had been 'astonished and appalled' at Lord Harris's remarks, Denis Hoy continued: 'With the vast disparity between the prices of farmland and development land, it is easy to see that, if building were allowed on the so-called "brown and grey" green belt, the greener areas would very quickly be allowed to deteriorate and become "brown and grey" so that the owners could profit from the offers of the developers.' The protection of designated green belt was all the more important in the light of the recent decision by Nicholas Ridley to release 350 acres of 'interim' green belt (proposed but not yet designated) near Harlow for housing developments connected with Stansted Airport. In Enfield, continued Mr Hoy, councillors had warned that to enable them to protect the green belt, the EPS must be flexible regarding developments elsewhere. 'This reiterates the view of the Enfield Preservation Society and the London Green Belt Council that the green belt must be preserved in its entirety'.

The local green belt became even more vulnerable as the M25 rapidly carved a concrete swathe through Enfield's countryside. The section of motorway between the A10 and the M11 opened in January 1984; by the following year the M25 reached south of the Dartford tunnel. Industrialists and retailers, keen to take advantage of the improved communications, joined house builders in demanding that more development should be allowed within the road's perimeter. The Preservation Society received little comfort from a government circular on the green belt issued in 1984. Despite saying that 'the strongest restraint' on development around the M25 should continue, the circular went on to give strategic guidance on provision for the growth of industrial and distribution activities which required 'well located sites' — by implication, close to the M25.

Against this background, there was considerable foreboding when, in February 1985, B & Q applied to build a massive DIY retail store on the Kingswood Nursery site at the junction of Bullsmoor Lane and the Great Cambridge Road, a stone's throw from junction 25 on the M25. The Preservation Society protested that the prominent nursery site, situated in the green belt, adjacent to Capel Manor Centre and the Forty Hill Conservation Area, was totally unsuitable for B & Q's proposed 55,000 square foot retail store and 12,000 square foot garden centre with 339 parking spaces. Enfield Council refused planning permission, B & Q appealed and a public inquiry, which lasted five days, was held at the Civic Centre in February 1986. B & Q thought it prudent to be well represented. Accordingly a QC appeared with four expert witnesses: a chartered surveyor, town planning consultant, landscape architect and a civil engineer. The arguments and evidence used on the need for such a DIY superstore had obviously been put forward at other inquiries which had produced successful results for the developer. However, they were comprehensively refuted by a solicitor and officers from Enfield Council. Supporting evidence was given by members of Enfield Preservation Society, Forty Hill & Bulls Cross

184. South Lodge, Whitewebbs Park, an ornate Victorian cottage with decorative barge-boards, unusual chimney pots, and interesting window detailing. The lodge had fallen into such disrepair in 1971 that it was threatened with demolition, but after receiving a deputation from the Preservation Society, Enfield Council extended and carefully restored the building, which is now in use as a dwelling.

Study Group, the London Green Belt Council, FERAA, Capel Manor and others. To the astonishment of B & Q, who were confidently anticipating another success, and to the delight of the Preservation Society, the Secretary of State dismissed the appeal in May 1986.

Before the GLC agricultural holdings were passed to the London boroughs, Patrick Jenkin, then Secretary of State, had emphasised that he regarded this green belt land as inalienable (i.e. not transferable to another owner). In a statement made on 7 November 1984, he had recalled that the consultation paper on the transfer of GLC interests made it clear that no change in policy was proposed. He had urged authorities with holdings acquired under the 1938 Act to manage this land carefully so that the countryside was enhanced. This stricture clearly applied to Enfield's green belt estate, but early in 1987 the Preservation Society was dismayed to learn that under the government's recent 'right to buy' legislation, several tenants of residential properties formerly owned by the GLC had applied to buy their houses and the surrounding green belt land.

The 'right to buy' legislation had been introduced to enable council tenants to own their own homes. Some of the green belt properties that had been transferred to Enfield Council from the GLC were modest properties with gardens in keeping, but two holdings were in a totally different category and could not be equated with ordinary council houses. The sale of Parkside House with nearly seven acres in Hadley Road opposite Trent Park, and Parkside Coach House in Ferny Hill, Hadley Wood, was strongly opposed by Enfield Council, which described the properties as 'set in substantial grounds of considerable landscape importance'. Enfield Council was vigorously supported by the Preservation Society, which enlisted the help of the London Green Belt Council. This body was assured by William Waldegrave (Secretary of State for the Environment) that the right to buy legislation would affect 'only a tiny part' of the capital's green belt and that 'the assurance that the land would normally be regarded as inalienable remains substantially valid'. The Preservation Society was not impressed by this classic example of political doublespeak. A long and costly dispute followed. Enfield Council took the matter to the High Court, which upheld the council against the Secretary of State and decided that the Housing Acts 1980 and 1987 had not impliedly repealed the provisions of the Green Belt (London & Home Counties) Act 1938. The tenants of Parkside House and Parkside Coach House both appealed against the refusal to allow them to purchase the properties. This resulted in two local planning inquiries during 1988, at which Irene Smith stated the Preservation Society's conviction that the green belt estate should be managed as a whole, and that ownership should not be passed to a variety of people with different motivations and standards. The Inspector recommended that although the tenant of Parkside Coach House (by far the smaller of the two holdings) should be permitted to buy the property, the purchase of Parkside House should not be allowed. The Preservation Society's relief at this decision was short-lived. In July 1989 Nicholas Ridley, then Secretary of State, notified Enfield Council of his intention to overrule his Inspector's recommendation and to allow the sale of Parkside House. The EPS sent a strong protest to Mr Ridley and was later disappointed to learn that the council, which had asked for a new public inquiry, had in the meantime reached an agreement with the tenant and bought the property. The house and its freehold were later sold to a private individual, but Enfield Council retained the freehold of the grounds.

Evidence given by the Preservation Society at the Parkside House public inquiry had undoubtedly strengthened the council's case. Irene Smith was able to quote a recommendation made a few days earlier in a joint report by the Countryside Commission and the

185. Rear view of Whitewebbs House, built in 1791 by Dr Abraham Wilkinson. After being used as an old people's home for many years, the house was closed by Enfield Council in 1989 It stood empty, suffering from vandalism and general deterioration, until 1995 when it was sold for conversion into a country house restaurant.

Nature Conservancy Council. The report had stated: 'The finest landscapes in the Greater London area are generally acknowledged to be those areas such as the North Downs and Enfield Chase, which have strong visual characteristics'. It recommended that Enfield Chase should be identified as heritage land, which it defined as 'extensive areas of open land that are of strategic importance in London because of their combined value for landscape, historical interest and nature conservation, and which should be protected and managed accordingly'. The London Planning Advisory Council (a quango set up after the demise of the GLC) had also recommended that Enfield Chase should be designated 'an area of special character'.

The Preservation Society became wary, but not unduly alarmed, when in June 1989 Enfield Council announced that Whitewebbs House was to be sold 'to benefit social services'. Whitewebbs House, which was built by Dr Abraham Wilkinson in 1791, took its name from a much older property which once stood on the opposite side of Whitewebbs Lane. Some years after its construction, the present house was fitted with ornate fireplaces and restructured in the style of a French chateau. This handsome edifice, a familiar landmark in its green belt setting, had never been listed, despite numerous requests by the EPS. Dr Wilkinson, who owned land to the east of the house, purchased Whitewebbs Wood after the Enclosure Act of 1803, forming a sizeable estate. In 1931, under the Public Health Act, the Whitewebbs estate was bought jointly by Middlesex County Council and the Enfield Urban District Council for the benefit of the residents of Middlesex, for public open space and recreational use. The purchase price was £23,000. Enfield took over the woods and the parkland, part of which was opened as a public golf course in 1933, and the MCC used the house for an old people's home. With the reorganisation of local government in 1965 ownership of the estate passed to the newly formed London Borough of Enfield, which continued to run the house as a home for old men until it was closed in May 1989. The official announcement issued by Enfield Council the following month, said it was intended to dispose of Whitewebbs House 'on the basis of a long

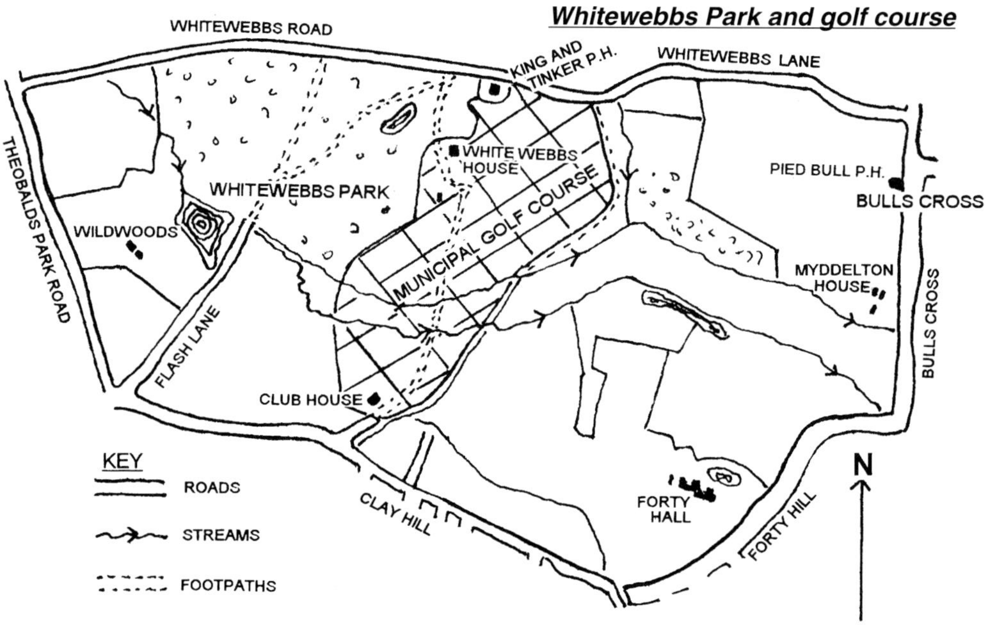

leasehold'. Access to the property would be from Whitewebbs Road only, and the municipal golf course would be excluded from the sale. Members of the EPS council of management who toured the deserted house soon after it was put up for sale were impressed by its fine internal features. The Preservation Society hoped a suitable use could be found for the imposing building, but as the months passed, no purchasers were forthcoming. Rumours began to circulate and early in January 1990 the Preservation Society wrote to Enfield Council expressing its concern that the golf course must not be included in any sale. Brian McAndrew, Enfield's chief executive, replied: 'I will be happy to involve the Society before matters are formally considered and I accept that widescale and careful consultation will be necessary if any significant changes are proposed for this area'.

There was widespread consternation and disbelief when, on 28 June 1990, headlines in the *Enfield Gazette* proclaimed: 'Whitewebbs House and golf course set to be sold off in multi-million-pound package'. At first, many local people assumed the newspaper had got hold of the wrong end of the stick. Whitewebbs was the only municipal course in the borough and the course itself, surrounded by publicly owned green belt parkland, was crossed by footpaths which for more than 60 years had been favourite walkways for local families. But confronted with this leaked report, Enfield Council confirmed that earlier that week its property committee had studied a consultants' report which stated that 'the sale of Whitewebbs House and its grounds together with the Whitewebbs Golf Course, offers an opportunity to the London Borough of Enfield to raise capital on an exciting asset'. The report suggested that a replacement golf course could be built elsewhere with part of the proceeds from the sale. Rectory Farm, on The Ridgeway, was identified as the proposed site for the new course. The committee asked the consultants to submit a further report and authorised the borough valuer to start negotiations with the tenant of Rectory Farm for the surrender of his tenancy. At its July meeting the EPS council of management resolved that the Preservation Society 'would use all its powers to stop the London Borough of Enfield selling Whitewebbs golf course' and immediately set about organising what was to become one of its most effective campaigns. Two thousand hastily printed handbills were distributed at the Trent Park Show in early August. Under the heading SAVE WHITEWEBBS GOLF COURSE, the bright green leaflets stressed that the golf course was an integral part of Whitewebbs Park and warned that the popular footpaths across the course were not statutory rights of way, but permissive paths which could be closed at any time. The leaflet added: 'The Enfield Preservation Society is totally opposed to any attempt to sell or lease the golf course which is a cherished part of our local heritage'.

One thousand green car stickers, provided free by a local firm, were soon carrying the message: 'Tell Enfield Council NO SALE OF WHITEWEBBS' to all parts of the borough. The EPS campaign made front page news in the *Enfield Herald & Post* on 16 August under the headline 'Group slams Council sale'. The report said the public outcry had provoked Enfield Council into stating it was 'keen to clarify any misunderstandings about the options being considered and to get public feedback before any decision is made'. However, this supposed willingness to consult residents was dismissed as 'a load of nonsense' by Irene Smith, who said: 'They have been keeping us all in the dark'. She told the *Herald & Post* that despite assurances given in January by Enfield's chief executive, the council had made no attempt at consultation. The Preservation Society later learned that on 13 September 1989, months before that assurance was given, Enfield Council's property and land committee had appointed Humberts (Leisure) Estate Agency to carry out a feasibility study on the sale of Whitewebbs House and adjoining council land holdings.

Having alerted the public, the Preservation Society invited local organisations to a meeting in Jubilee Hall at the end of August. Although this was the peak holiday season, all the main residents' and amenity associations were represented, with delegates from FERAA, the Ramblers' Association, Enfield Sports Advisory Council, Enfield Archaeological Society, Edmonton Hundred Historical Society, Whitewebbs Golf Club, Enfield Natural History Society, the London Wildlife Trust and others — a total of 20 organisations. A steering committee was formed to co-ordinate the campaign to save Whitewebbs and it was agreed to seek an urgent interview with Councillor Graham Eustance (leader of Enfield Council) and key committee chairmen. In a report on 30 August the *Enfield Gazette* quoted Valerie Carter, who chaired the meeting on behalf of the Preservation Society, as saying: 'As part of their property review, Enfield councillors have felt duty bound to consider all the borough's assets. They now have a duty to consult the electorate and to listen to the residents of the borough. It is quite clear from this meeting that the people of Enfield do not want any part of Whitewebbs Park to be sold or leased to a private concern'. This was putting it mildly. Feeling at the meeting had run so high that some delegates proposed staging a demonstration outside the Civic Centre on 4 September, when the council's planning and transportation committee was due to meet. The Preservation Society, which had never organised or participated in public manifestations, was not in favour, but the proposal was carried by an overwhelming majority. The resulting protest was orderly and non-political, but councillors had to run the gauntlet of scores of banner-waving families who were clearly upset at the prospect of losing some of their favourite local walks.

As news of the threat to Whitewebbs spread, public anger increased. The local papers were inundated by letters expressing outrage and resentment that Enfield Council should consider selling a public golf course which was heavily used by young people and pensioners, a sale which would cut off access to public paths. The Preservation Society featured Whitewebbs in its display at the Town Show and ordered 2,000 more car stickers. Coun-

186. Play continued as usual on Whitewebbs golf course in July 1990, when Enfield Council shocked the borough by trying to sell the course, with Whitewebbs House, to private bidders. A determined campaign initiated by the Preservation Society attracted such massive support that the council was obliged to withdraw the golf course from sale.

cillor David Conway (chairman of Enfield Council's property committee) received a hostile reception when he told a packed meeting at Whitewebbs Golf Club in September that by investing £9million from the disputed sale, the council could knock £6 a year off individual poll tax bills 'for the forseeable future'. At the same meeting Irene Smith was loudly applauded when she reminded the audience that public access to the golf course was a condition of the 999-year lease granted to Enfield Council in 1931. 'None of Enfield's parks and amenities will be safe if the council is allowed to dispose of Whitewebbs Park in this way', she stressed. In a long letter published in the *Enfield Advertiser* on 13 September, Councillor Graham Eustance vainly tried to woo public opinion with extravagant promises of the delights being planned for the Rectory Farm site: 'two 18-hole golf courses, with extensive footpaths, bridleways, a nature reserve and the planting of 40 acres of woodland'. The public remained unmoved, while the Preservation Society voiced its strong opposition to the creation of golf courses on farmland which was so important to the landscape.

With still no sign of the promised public consultation, the Preservation Society cancelled the speaker booked for the EPS members' meeting at the Civic Centre in October and invited the Mayor and key council chairmen to address a public meeting on the Whitewebbs issue. Having listened to Councillor Eustance and others, the packed meeting, with many standing, passed a resolution demanding that Enfield Council should safeguard the existing status of the golf course, should exclude it from any sale or lease of Whitewebbs House, and should safeguard all permissive paths adjoining the grounds before any sale. But when he was asked by the council's property committee to report on the meeting, Councillor Eustance made no mention of this. He merely stated that he had explained the council's plans (which he had) and that the audience had appeared satisfied that green belt criteria would be upheld (which they certainly had not). The EPS winter newsletter noted that the Preservation Society had lodged an official protest at this misrepresentation, which made no reference to the resolution nor to the total opposition, expressed by every speaker, to the council's proposals. 'Enfield Preservation Society and the Whitewebbs Campaign Committee will fight this ill-conceived plan every step of the way', the newsletter promised. In December a petition with 10,500 signatures opposing the sale was handed to the council.

In January 1991 the *Enfield Independent* organised a phone-in vote on the sale of the golf course. Only 25 callers were in favour of the sale, with 1,158 against. The Whitewebbs controversy deluged Enfield councillors with a larger protest mail than they had received on any previous issue. But regardless of public opinion, and despite opposition from a significant number of its own members, the council instructed Humberts (Leisure) Estate Agents to 'test the market' for Whitewebbs House and golf course. In April the *Enfield Advertiser* reported that although there had been no official decision to press ahead, Humberts had issued a sales brochure. John Mason, the borough valuer, assured the *Advertiser* that a decision to sell would only arise if a sufficiently attractive offer was made. He suggested a minimum of £9million, bringing a response from Irene Smith that no amount of money would compensate for the sale of land that the public had been using freely for 60 years.

Disquiet about the sale had meanwhile been growing within the Conservative majority on the council. Influential members, led by Councillor John Jackson, refused to toe the party line and in April the property committee finally decided not to sell the golf

187. Intricate plasterwork surrounds the elegant windows of this imposing reception room in Whitewebbs House, photographed in May 1989 shortly after the building became vacant.

course. Banner headlines in the local papers reflected the widespread jubilation. 'Whitewebbs sale ditched!' shouted the *Enfield Gazette* on 25 April, reporting that the decision 'met with cheers and a general sense of disbelief from about 100 stunned members of the public'. The *Enfield Advertiser* proclaimed: 'Delight at decision on Whitewebbs', and stated: 'Enfield Council's decision not to sell Whitewebbs golf course is being hailed as a success for Enfield Preservation Society and the thousands of people who supported its campaign'. Councillor David Conway, who had recommended that the sale should not go ahead because of the strength of opposition and the difficulty of providing an alternative course within a restricted timescale, told the *Advertiser*: 'This is a win for the Enfield Preservation Society and the individuals who wrote to us expressing their concerns about this issue'. The marketing exercise had not been without cost. Reports later revealed that Humberts Leisure was paid £17,000 for an advertising campaign. Labour Councillor David Mason was quoted in the *Enfield Gazette* as demanding that the council 'should apologise to chargepayers for wasting £32,000 in consultants' fees and £36,000 in extra security during the delay in selling the house'. The 24-hour security had unfortunately not deterred squatters from invading the premises. On a visit to Whitewebbs House in April, members of the campaign committee had been shocked at the deterioration in the two years since their last inspection.

By common consent, the Whitewebbs Campaign Committee was not disbanded; it continued in being, with a wider remit, as Enfield's Countryside Action Group. In September 1995 Enfield Council announced it had gone into partnership with a private firm, Sunley plc, who would manage and improve facilities at the public golf course and who had arranged a deal with Whitbread to convert Whitewebbs House into a country restaurant.

Barely three months later, public fury flared again at the revelation that the council was still intent on developing Rectory Farm for golf and was working on new plans to build three 'pay and play' 18-hole golf courses and a driving range on this 348-acre farm off The Ridgeway. The scheme, which would have devastated a wide tract of farmland and involved the destruction of five miles of hedgerows, was bitterly opposed by the Preservation Society and others. Land owners in the green belt were rushing to profit from the apparently insatiable demand for golf courses around London, and within weeks the *Enfield Gazette* reported (15 August 1991) that the owner of the 346-acre Vicarage Farm, Hadley Wood, intended to turn 212 acres into a golf and tennis centre. The newspaper calculated that between one-fifth and one-sixth of Enfield's green belt land could be turned into golf courses under plans currently being considered by the council. However, nothing came of the Vicarage Farm proposal and on 25 September the *Enfield Independent* announced that the council had withdrawn its plans for Rectory Farm. Councillor Terence Neville, chairman of Enfield's environment committee, admitted there had been 'a high degree of public opposition'.

Whitewebbs continued to be an environmental battleground. Throughout the winter of 1990 and for much of 1991 the Preservation Society urged Enfield Council to stop a series of car boot sales and markets in Whitewebbs Lane. Well over one thousand visitors had flocked to 300 stalls on Guy Lodge Farm on most Sundays and Bank Holidays, choking the narrow lane with traffic and disrupting the rural peace for miles around. Unable to take effective, speedy action to stop the markets, the council successfully lobbied the planning minister (Sir George Young) who subsequently asked local authorities and others to suggest changes in the law. The Preservation Society supported the Council for the Protection of Rural England in its request that the legislation should include a new

188. One of the paths in Whitewebbs Park, where the tranquil woodland walks have been enjoyed by Enfield families since the estate became part of London's green belt in 1931.

clause to control car boot sales in the green belt. Hampered because the Guy Lodge farmer was not a council tenant, Enfield Council was obliged to invoke cumbersome legal procedures to put an end to the Sunday markets and boot sales. With this case still unresolved, there was widespread alarm when Councillor Neville announced that Enfield Council might sell its green belt farms to the tenants. This new threat to the green belt was reported in the EPS newsletter for winter 1991, which revealed that the council was considering selling, on long leases, the tenancies of all the agricultural holdings inherited from the GLC. 'This would put some 3,500 acres of open countryside at risk' warned the Preservation Society. 'The effect would be to break up the ownership of an estate which was acquired to be managed as a whole, for green belt purposes. Many permissive paths which are not statutory rights of way could be in jeopardy ... wildlife protection would be problematic ... Because existing controls do not give adequate protection, hedgerows could be destroyed, new buildings erected and unauthorised activities spring up'.

To reinforce its concern the Preservation Society organised a public meeting in the conference room at the Civic Centre on 29 November, under the title 'What price Enfield's green belt?' The response was a resounding endorsement of the Society's green belt policy. The hall was filled to capacity long before the meeting was due to start. Security staff, reinforced for the occasion, turned many people away. Councillor John Jackson, one of the principal speakers, admitted that existing planning regulations were not strong enough to protect Enfield's green belt if it passed out of council control. 'Long leases might seem an attractive option,' he said 'but what is a leasehold tenancy today could become a freehold tomorrow, at the whim of the government.' He wisely suggested that putting Enfield's green belt agricultural land into a trust might be a safeguard.

In spring 1992 the EPS newsletter was able to announce, with relief, that plans to sell the farms on Enfield Council's agricultural estate had been abandoned, following a strong campaign by the Preservation Society and the Countryside Action Group. The EPS enthusiastically seized on the idea of setting up an independent trust to manage the council's green belt holdings, and began working hard behind the scenes to further this aim. Within Enfield Council there was a willingness to explore the possibilities and in autumn 1993 the property sub-committee asked council officers to prepare a full report. Thanks to the tenacity of the EPS chairman, Colin Pointer, a meeting was held at Jubilee Hall in November 1993 to discuss the proposal. Representing both political parties, Councillors Richard Course, John Jackson, Jeff Rodin, Stephen Wortley and John Yates were present at the meeting, which was attended by 15 organisations. The delegates unanimously supported the concept of setting up a trust 'to own and manage in perpetuity the entire Green Belt Estate at present in the ownership of the London Borough of Enfield, for the benefit of the residents of Enfield, visitors to the area, and to protect the landscape'. A steering group was formed to press the council to agree the principle of establishing a trust, and to work with officers at the Civic Centre towards setting it up. But if, as Harold Wilson once suggested, a week is a long time in politics, six months can bring in a new era. In May 1994 the Labour Party swept into power in the council elections, ousting the Conservative majority for the first time in 26 years. Jeff Rodin was elected council leader and Richard Course became chairman of the environment committee.

At the May meeting of the EPS council of management it was agreed that a letter should be sent to all Labour councillors, setting out the Preservation Society's view on a green belt trust and enclosing a copy of recent comments by Michael Portillo MP, who had recommended that farmers should be given the right to buy their agricultural holdings. The officers' report on setting up a trust was submitted in June, but shortly afterwards Enfield Council decided not to proceed with the idea. It did, however, take a step in the right direction by setting up a consultative forum, on which the EPS was invited to participate, to consider future management policy of the council's green belt estate.

The pressures on green belt land were particularly acute at Crews Hill. Following the unsuccessful attempt by nurserymen to sell their land for housing in the 1970s, a gradual change came over the area. Garden centres and aquatic centres, selling direct to the public, began to replace the nursery gardens and commercial greenhouses. By the late 1980s, the biggest concentration of garden centres in Greater London was established at Crews Hill and Theobalds Park Road, which together had become known as 'the gardeners' mile'. Taking advantage of the crowds of shoppers who descended on the garden centres every weekend, some firms began flouting green belt planning regulations by selling items which had little or no connection with horticulture. In the scramble to attract customers, garish advertisements and excessively bright lighting soon defaced the once rural road. Despite frequent complaints from the Preservation Society and other bodies, no adequate enforcement action was taken. A half-hearted attempt to tackle the problem was made in June 1984 when Enfield Council drew up a set of policies for Crews Hill, covering dwellings, horticultural units, horses and intensive livestock keeping, and garden centres. This remained mainly a paper exercise and in 1988 Martin Jewell, Enfield's new borough planning officer, lamented in his annual report that 'a particular problem is apparent at Crews Hill in the number of unauthorised developments which have been taking place without planning permission'. Fresh efforts were made to get to grips with the problems, but with scant success. The garden centres continued to draw large crowds, especially at weekends, and some householders in Crews Hill's small residential community complained that heavy traffic, noise and unattractive commercial activities, including a scrapyard, were blighting their surroundings. At the same time, Crews Hill continued to attract a steady stream of planning applications. Every year throughout the 1980s, at least one-third of the requests for development in the green belt were concentrated on Crews Hill, reaching a peak in 1983 when this area received 52% of all the green belt applications. It was known to the Preservation Society that some councillors, although unwilling to say so in public, were anxious to see the green belt policy relaxed so that houses could be built at Crews Hill, which they regarded as second-rate green belt. Tim Eggar MP supported this view in an interview he gave to *Business Talk*, a magazine for north London businesses, in January 1990. 'Where there is an opportunity to develop low cost housing in what I call "marginal" green belt, we must grab it', he said. The Preservation Society challenged him to define what he meant, but he refused to be drawn.

Soon after it took control of Enfield Council in 1994 the Labour majority decided to review the future of the Crews Hill area. Consultation leaflets and maps were distributed, listing the problems and suggesting solutions. The first public reaction came in the EPS newsletter for winter 1994, describing the review as 'dubious'. The main criticism concerned the future of a large tract of land at the junction of Theobalds Park Road and Whitewebbs Road, which was labelled clumsily in the document as 'an area with a variety of uses which are generally unattractive to the location'. The consultation guidance for this land continued: 'Persistent breaches of planning control means that a long-term solution is required. One option could be to use the area for low density housing. Such developments would substantially improve the landscape and highways in the area.' An accompanying questionnaire asked for 'yes' or 'no' answers to questions which seemed to

189. An old postcard showing Flash Lane, Wilkinson's Woods.

be loaded in favour of residential development. In the EPS newsletter, Christopher Jephcott stressed the need for consultation exercises to be carefully designed so that the form of question did not pre-empt the answer. The Preservation Society, he said, considered that the Crews Hill leaflet could be falling into that trap. 'We all agree that the area as it exists, with its ever more innovative garden centres, does not enhance the green belt', he continued, 'but it does perform a useful function, as the numerous visitors attest.' He pointed out the mistaken reasoning in the council's argument that, because a portion of green belt had been abused or neglected, it should have its protected status removed. This same argument had always been seen as providing an incentive to those who might be hoping to profit from enhanced land values, for they had only to run down a piece of green belt in the hope that it would be released for development.

Overwhelming support for the Preservation Society's view that the whole of Crews Hill must remain within the green belt was expressed at a public meeting organised by the Crews Hill Residents' Association the following January. The option of releasing some land for housing, which was put forward by Councillor Richard Course, met with strong opposition, as did proposals for building leisure facilities on some of the glasshouse sites. On 9 February 1995 the *Enfield Gazette* reported that Councillor Course had told the meeting: 'This area deteriorates as every year goes by, with more rubbish, tatty buildings and God knows what else. We need to make Crews Hill as nice as The Ridgeway or Waggon Road, with agriculture on one side and nice housing on the other.' He said the idea was to offer a 'juicy carrot' to the owners of problem sites, so that if the businesses could see a financial incentive, they might consider selling to a developer who would build homes within council guidelines. The packed meeting would have none of it, and voted unanimously to keep Crews Hill in the green belt, with a recommendation that the council should use its existing powers to curb unauthorised activities. After the vote, Councillor Course promised to abide by the decision. Enfield Councillor John Yates told the *Enfield Independent*: 'This is a great decision for local residents and a victory for people power'.

A further unexpected threat to the green belt occurred in February 1995 when Enfield Community Care Trust announced plans to build in the thickly wooded grounds of Wolverton, a nursing home in Hadley Road, just off The Ridgeway. In the EPS newsletter for spring 1995 Colin Pointer, the Preservation Society's chairman, commented: 'This vital part of the green belt off The Ridgeway falls away sharply and provides a fine green view as one approaches from the west. The whole open space corridor between the developed western side of The Ridgeway and the farmland would be under threat if this planning application were to succeed, not to mention the disastrous effect on wildlife which at present enjoys an undisturbed, fine natural habitat'. His remarks echoed those of a government Inspector who, following a local planning inquiry in 1975, had commented that the trees on this ridge made 'a significant contribution to the rural character of the area to the west of The Ridgeway'. The Inspector recommended that Enfield Council 'should endeavour to preserve the woodland feature which now enhances the rural outskirts of Enfield'.

The Community Care Trust stated that the new nursing home was needed to rehouse patients with Alzheimer's disease who would be evicted from a unit called The Oaks when the Highlands Hospital site was redeveloped. The trust claimed it was forced to build in the green belt because no alternative site was available. This emotive but somewhat dishonest pleading was exploited to the full by the Community Care Trust in a highly-charged campaign. The local press carried impassioned pleas from the families of patients

190. The frontage of Whitewebbs House, showing the canopied carriage entrance which will no doubt be used by the public when the building reopens as a country house restaurant.

in The Oaks, worried about their relatives' future care. Enfield Preservation Society, and others opposing the plan to build in the green belt, pointed out that the Community Care Trust was currently disposing of land inside St Michael's Hospital, Chase Side, which could have been used for the new nursing home. Instead, the trust expected to make £2million by selling three plots in St Michael's for housing, leaving a much reduced area for health service activity. The EPS newsletter for summer 1995 criticised this short-sighted policy and warned that with Highlands and the War Memorial Hospital both gone, it would be difficult to find sites for additional health care facilities in the future. The prophesy was fulfilled almost immediately, when the Community Care Trust began discussing the possibility of building on St Michael's Green.

Following receipt of more than 60 letters of objection from residents, a 290-name petition and letters from the Preservation Society and other organisations, Enfield Council refused permission for the Wolverton development in June. The following month, it reluctantly gave the go-ahead for housing development within the grounds of St Michael's Hospital, but this planning permission was granted only after a written undertaking from the Community Care Trust that it would make no further claims to St Michael's Green, which was to remain a permanent open space. As anticipated, the trust later lodged an appeal against the council's refusal to allow a new nursing home in the grounds of Wolverton. Despite the widespread controversy aroused by the proposal, the Department of the Environment decided to give its verdict after receiving written representations instead of holding a public inquiry. It was, however, agreed that the final decision on the application would be made by the minister. Enfield Preservation Society submitted 12 pages of evidence. In the meantime Enfield Council, which had been doing its best to suggest alternative sites for the nursing home, gave permission for land in Bury Road West to be used, thus depriving the Community Care Trust of its claim that no alternative to the green belt location was available.

Chapter 17
Broomfield & Other Battles

Concern about the fate of Enfield's historic buildings continued to exercise the Preservation Society as the 1980s wore on. One of the most keenly fought battles was over the restoration of Broomfield House, which had been badly damaged by fire in 1984. The house, in Broomfield Park, Palmers Green, was held in great affection by local people. Originally a modest farmhouse, it had been transformed by more than 400 years of alterations and extensions into a fine, if rambling, mansion. Some rooms were embellished with intricately carved panelling, but the outstanding feature was a magnificent early 18th century staircase with baroque mural paintings, dated 1726, by Gerard Lanscroon. Broomfield House and 54 acres of its grounds were bought for £25,000 by Southgate Urban District Council in 1902. Since then, it had undergone a variety of uses including a school, maternity centre, dental clinic and, after the Second World War, a health centre. In

191. Broomfield House, in Broomfield Park, Palmers Green, contained one of the most popular museums outside central London. The 400-year-old mansion was used and enjoyed by a wide local community following its purchase by Southgate Urban District Council in 1902. When Broomfield House was partly destroyed by fire in 1984, Enfield Preservation Society played a leading part in the long battle to have the building restored.

1925 part of the house was opened as Broomfield Museum. With a changing series of local exhibitions and permanent collections of stuffed animals and birds, this became one of the most popular museums outside the central London area. A cafe on the ground floor, serving visitors to the house and park, added to the attractions of a cherished listed building which for many years had been used and enjoyed by the whole community.

Soon after the fire it became evident that few, if any, councillors were in favour of rebuilding Broomfield House. Influential spokesmen began making ominous statements hinting that the building might have to be demolished. It was claimed that the borough architect's confidential report to Enfield Council had condemned the remains of the building as structurally unsound and incapable of being restored. The EPS newsletter for winter 1984 urged that before any decision was taken, the report should be made public and a second opinion sought. The costs of all the options, including details of insurance monies and likely grants, should then be set out for all to see. Others took up the call and in January 1985 an acrimonious public meeting took place in Southgate Town Hall. With the exception of a spokesman from FERAA (who thought it a waste of money), the delegates who packed the hall were unanimous in demanding that Broomfield House should be restored. In the face of what the *Enfield Independent* later described as 'impassioned pleas from Enfield Preservation Society and local people', the council commissioned a survey from an independent firm of architects and planning consultants. This report was suppressed for several months because, to the council's consternation, it stated: 'We have no hesitation in confirming that the house should be readily capable of virtually complete restoration. ... Broomfield House is an historic building whose architectural and historic interest becomes more apparent the longer one studies the fabric ... Restoration is a challenge we would like to see the Borough of Enfield accept'.

The *Enfield Gazette*, which had received a leaked copy of the report, devoted a whole page to Broomfield on 12 December 1985. Councillor Clive Goldwater, chairman of the council's leisure and amenities committee, was quoted as saying that the cost of total repair would be 'something like £1 million'. Insurance would probably cover only one-fifth of the bill for restoration and in the meantime protective scaffolding round the building was costing £50,000 a year to hire. Councillor Goldwater said that architects were currently designing a suitable replacement. He promised that the eighteenth century staircase and murals, which had been salvaged after the fire, would be incorporated into the new building. The EPS (described by the *Gazette* as 'the borough's environmental watchdogs') was unimpressed. Its chairman, Valerie Carter, complained that while the council had been sitting on the consultants' report the building had been deteriorating, and valuable time which should have been used to obtain restoration grants had been wasted.

Plans for the 'suitable replacement' were unveiled in March 1986. The Preservation Society was not alone in raising its hands in horror at the modern glass and steel structure proposed by the leisure and amenities committee. The Friends of Enfield Museums welcomed the prospect of rehousing the collections which had been rescued from the fire, but theirs was a lone supporting voice. Ken Powell, national secretary of Save Britain's Heritage, agreed that the replacement resembled a 'crude factory shed'. Local residents and organisations were outspoken in criticising the angular building, which would have looked utterly incongruous in such a leafy and historic setting. Their verdict was shared by officers in Enfield Council's own parks department, who refused to give their approval, and the scheme was abandoned. The following month, just two years after the fire, councillors decided it would be prudent to purchase the scaffolding, but few could have anticipated how long it would remain in position round the ill-fated building.

192. Members of the EPS footpaths group admire the lake in Broomfield Park on a mid-week walk through local parks in February 1994. The grounds of Broomfield House, which are listed Grade II in the national register of historic parks and gardens, contain features which have survived from the early 18th century.

Another small fire, probably started by vandals, caused minor damage early in 1988, but the future of the house seemed more hopeful. Len Keeble, leader of the EPS historic buildings group, reported in the spring newsletter that the council had finally announced that Broomfield House would be restored. Tenders would be invited in May and it was anticipated the work would take 21 months — but he added, with some caution, that the Preservation Society had not yet seen details of the plans. It soon became clear that councillors had been clutching at straws in an effort to find a solution to the problem. Having announced that it had no intention of funding the restoration, the council had offered the house to Chicken Shed, a children's theatre company. The EPS, in its winter newsletter, attacked the council for abandoning its obligations and for trying to pass on the responsibility to a group which had probably not appreciated the financial and other implications of restoring a Grade II* listed building. Inevitably, Chicken Shed had second thoughts and found a more suitable site for its activities. The charred remains of Broomfield House settled down under the flimsy tarpaulin for yet another winter.

The following year delegates attending the annual meeting of FERAA recommended to Enfield Council that Broomfield House should be demolished and 'a single-storey unit' built in its place. This must have encouraged the councillors, who set up a Broomfield House Panel to recommend future action. The panel's tactics provoked a furious reaction. Writing in the EPS newsletter for autumn 1991 Len Keeble complained that a cynical and philistine attitude to conservation and the protection of historic buildings was developing among local councillors. Although recent consultations had shown overwhelming support for the house to be restored (as had consultations immediately after the fire) the public's views had been ignored and the Broomfield House Panel had decided to put

193. Broomfield House in 1991, shrouded in scaffolding and tarpaulin.

the building up for sale. This was a necessary first step before the council could apply to the Department of the Environment for permission to demolish Broomfield and erect a new building. It was time to make a stand, and Enfield Preservation Society, Southgate Civic Trust, Enfield Archaeological Society and Edmonton Hundred Historical Society formed a joint committee to fight for the restoration of the building.

In November it was confirmed that Broomfield House would be put on the market with the offer of a 125-year lease. Councillor Goldwater, chairman of the Broomfield House Panel, told the *Enfield Advertiser* that it was hoped to attract 'a suitable developer or building trust' to take on the renovation. Interested parties would be given 12 weeks to submit conditional offers. The news galvanised the Broomfield restoration committee into action. It decided to play the council at its own game: if the council wanted to sell to a trust, so be it. In a remarkably short time, legal documents were drawn up to form the Broomfield Historic Buildings Trust. The aim was to acquire an interest in Broomfield House and restore it as a local museum, specialist museum, cafe and meeting room, for the benefit of the community. It was hoped that a major exhibit in the specialist museum would be the world famous Silver Studio Collection of 40,000 designs and pattern books made by the Silver family of north London in the late 19th and early 20th century. The collection, which has been used extensively for wallpaper and fabrics, was currently being stored by Middlesex University. Members of the trust visited Broomfield in autumn 1991 and Len Keeble told the Preservation Society they were impressed by the state of preservation. Despite the appalling neglect, three-quarters of the building remained in good condition and the house was 'perfectly capable of being restored without in any way being a replica or pastiche'. Early in spring 1992 the EPS newsletter announced that following an encouraging meeting with councillors and council officers, the trust had commissioned Donald Insall Associates (who had made the original independent report on Broomfield for Enfield Council) to prepare a feasibility study on restoration.

However, hopes of smooth progress were soon dashed. No other offers for the purchase of Broomfield having been received by the closing date (6 March 1992) the trust asked the council to accept or reject its bid by 20 March so that it could go ahead with plans. The council dragged its feet, insisting with some scepticism that it must vet the trust's financial plans before agreeing the sale. On 25 June the *Enfield Gazette* reported that the council had given the trust one year to raise the money to restore the house, but at the same time had decided to apply to English Heritage for permission to demolish the building. The trust felt this application would seriously undermine its ability to raise funds and trust secretary Colin Pointer complained in the *Enfield Gazette*: 'The council has given us the all-clear, but has tied our hands and feet'. Months of wrangling followed and it was not until the spring of 1993 that the EPS newsletter could announce that Enfield Council had agreed to rescind its decision to apply for demolition consent. The council had also confirmed that, subject to the trust conforming to a realistic timetable, it would grant an agreement for a lease of Broomfield House.

Encouraged by this assurance, and supported by a £3,000 loan from Enfield Preservation Society, the trust commissioned Redmond Mullin Ltd to make a fund-raising feasibility study. The firm's report was optimistic. It stated that the appeal should be successful and recommended that it should be made for 'The National Decorative Design Museum at Broomfield House, in association with Middlesex University'. In 1993 Len Keeble confidently announced in the EPS summer newsletter that the trust was poised to start fund raising as soon as a chairman and committee had been appointed for the appeal. He added that a local campaign would be launched after the bulk of the money had been raised from national and regional sources. EPS members, in response to an earlier appeal in the newsletter, had already made individual pledges of more than £2,700. The trust had persuaded English Heritage to promise a substantial amount and had been offered a sizeable loan from the Architectural Heritage Fund. However, it had failed to find an appeal chairman with the necessary commitment and status, and things began to go wrong. The national appeal had still not got off the ground when, just before Christmas 1993, Broomfield suffered the first of a new series of fire attacks culminating in a serious blaze on 14 February 1994. This caused such severe damage that a police spokesman considered it could have been deliberate arson, set to destroy the building. Most of the first floor was lost, together with much of the 1550s timber framing.

Enfield Council — which had continued to procrastinate over drawing up a lease and legal agreements for the trust — was quick to serve a Dangerous Structure Notice. Fortunately, the council was swiftly disabused by English Heritage of the notion that it would then be permitted to raze the building to the ground. Instead, with the involvement of the Broomfield Trust, English Heritage supervised the methodical demolition and storage of dangerous parts of the house, and informed the council that full demolition would require listed building consent. The following month, in March 1994, round-the-clock security was installed at Broomfield House. At this point, the Broomfield Trust pulled out. But though no longer prepared to take responsibility for restoring the now devastated house, the trust continued trying throughout 1994 and the following months to find possible users for the house.

The next episode in this sorry story of procrastination and prevarication occurred in February 1995. Under the heading 'What a waste' the *Enfield Advertiser* reported that £60,000 a year was being spent on security at Broomfield. It was claimed that the decision to employ security guards had been taken by council officers without the knowledge of councillors. The guards were removed. Broomfield was becoming an increasing embarrassment to the new Labour council and on 23 February Jeff Rodin, the council leader, told the *Enfield Gazette*: 'I think we should bring this matter to a conclusion very soon because that building has been a drain on the council's resources for many years now'. Councillor Richard Course made no secret of his feelings. In his regular column in the *Advertiser* he referred to the derelict house as 'a pile of rubble'. Consultations were held with various bodies interested in finding a use for the building and at the end of June 1995 the council put an advertisement in the London *Evening Standard* and other national publications offering Broomfield House for sale either on a long lease or with the freehold. The response was, up to a point, encouraging. Two brewery chains expressed interest in converting the house into a 'themed' restaurant, and began negotiating with the council. Enfield Preservation Society and the Broomfield Trust agreed that this could be an acceptable solution, provided the restoration was sympathetic, that it included the reinstatement of the staircase and murals, and that the setting of the house in the parkland was respected. The following April Enfield Council accepted an offer from Whitbreads to reinstate the historic features and convert Broomfield House into a restaurant, with a cafe and rooms for community use on the first floor. The separately listed stable block was not included in the deal.

Thus, in the spring of 1996, there were hopes that within a year or two a restored Broomfield House could open its doors to the public. On at least two occasions during the eleven-year saga, there were well justified fears that Enfield Council was on the brink of applying for permission to demolish the house. There can be little doubt that had it not been for the tenacity of Enfield Preservation Society and Southgate Civic Trust, campaigning both separately and through the Broomfield Trust, Broomfield House would have been lost. The trust subsequently announced its intention to find another project for restoration — albeit on a much smaller scale. Another positive outcome was that Middlesex University seemed to gain a new appreciation of the importance of the Silver Studio design collection. In December 1995 it was announced that the collection would be a main exhibit in a museum of decorative art to be set up by Middlesex University at its campus at Cat Hill, Southgate.

The battle for Broomfield was among the most protracted campaigns fought by Enfield Preservation Society, but it was by no means unique. The Preservation Society's valiant efforts to save the best buildings and trees on the Highlands Hospital site proved equally long drawn out.

It was precisely the archaic charm of Highlands, with its Victorian hospital pavilions scattered in green grounds, that made it an obvious candidate for development. The idea of centralising Enfield's hospital facilities had first surfaced in the 1960s but it was not until January 1986 that Enfield Health Authority announced it was submitting plans to the Health Department for a £28,700,000 'hospital of the future' at Chase Farm, with 45 acres of new buildings. To help finance the development, the authority intended to close Highlands Hospital and hoped to raise at least £19million from the sale of the 56-acre site covered by Highlands and the adjacent South Lodge Hospital. Enfield Preservation Society, having realised that the hospital's days were numbered and that there was an urgent need to safeguard its special character, had suggested in 1984 that Highlands should be designated a conservation area. In October that year, following a decision by Enfield Health Authority to demolish four of the pavilions, Christopher Jephcott told the *Enfield Gazette*: 'Here we have a group of very good 19th century buildings, set among fine trees, which we are likely to lose completely, just when the merits of this type of building are being appreciated'. On 22 November the *Gazette* reported that Enfield Council's environment and land committee had agreed to the Preservation Society's request for conservation area status. Bill Issitt, the borough planning officer, supporting the request, had told the committee: 'The Victorian buildings, arranged in an attractively planned layout in a mature park landscape, form one of the most distinguished and distinctive areas of development within the borough'.

Despite his recommendation the council dithered, and twice put off making a decision. The Preservation Society's fears were reinforced when, less than a week after the Health Authority's announcement in January 1986, contractors began felling trees in the grounds. The Society made a final, urgent request to the GLC, which — in one of its last

194. *Aerial view of Chase Farm Hospital in about 1952, with green fields on three sides and Rendelsham Viaduct in the background.*

195. Highlands Hospital administration block, described as 'a fine specimen of masonry' when it was opened in 1885.

acts before dissolution — gave Highlands the protection it needed. The decision did not please the Enfield Health Authority, which had been looking forward to offering a vast development site unencumbered by buildings or other restrictions. In addition to its planning application for houses, it now sought consent to demolish buildings. EPS representatives met the health authority to promote the Preservation Society's views, which were set out two weeks later by Christopher Jephcott in the *Enfield Independent.* He explained that the EPS had been pressing for the conservation area for 18 months, ever since it had become clear that the health authority had no intention of caring properly for its heritage at Highlands. 'The physical environment of Highlands is of a quality matched by very little else in Enfield' wrote Dr Jephcott.

Patients at Highlands, which was founded in 1885 as the Northern Hospital, were originally housed in seventeen brick pavilions. This was a convalescent fever hospital and the buildings were well spaced on the elevated parkland site, parts of which commanded striking views. When it was opened, the *Enfield Observer* described the main entrance of the administration department as 'a fine specimen of masonry', and many of the pavilions were also good examples of fine Victorian craftsmanship. The Preservation Society was anxious that those which could be converted should form part of the new housing development. Outline planning permission was granted by the council in 1986 and over the next few years members of the EPS architecture & planning group spent many hours examining and commenting on an avalanche of plans and drawings for this vast housing complex. Eventually a scheme was drawn up which satisfied the developers, Enfield Council and the Preservation Society. But these were extremely difficult times for the property market. Land prices had plummetted, the developers pulled out, and the EPS newsletter for summer 1990 reported that plans to redevelop the site were stalled, with no sign of when negotiations would be resumed. Meanwhile, hospital activity at Highlands was being reduced and rubbish was accumulating round the derelict buildings.

Efforts to salvage the deal were unsuccessful and in the EPS newsletter for winter 1992 Christopher Jephcott confirmed that the scheme had fallen apart and that the whole matter was being sorted out from scratch all over again. 'This time, however, it is not even clear what the new proposals are', he complained 'since all the discussions have been behind closed doors'. It did, however, seem clear that the Victorian buildings on the site were once again under threat because the health authority wanted most of the prior conditions removed to give it a free hand. 'The EPS believes that the democratic process of public consultation, on proposals which will change the face of one of the borough's major conservation areas, cannot be brushed aside in this way', wrote Dr Jephcott, 'and we will be considering whether legal steps need to be taken to make this clear'. This issue of the newsletter contained so many depressing reports that he added the gloomy comment: 'Major threats to the borough's heritage of open spaces and fine buildings have come so thick and fast in recent weeks that it is difficult to avoid a feeling of embattled hopelessness.'

The long-awaited master plan for the new Highlands Village, comprising a total of 1,000 homes to be built by various contractors, was released for public consultation early in 1994. The Preservation Society was disappointed by the standard of the Barrett housing which would eventually cover much of the site. It reported that the first tranche consisted of 'bottom-end of the market, off-the-peg designs, which is what the developers feel are appropriate in the locality'. The EPS architecture & planning group made a number of detailed suggestions, some of which were taken on board, and stressed the need for the plans to include a community hall, which was ignored. Within months the developer had sought, and been granted by the Department of National Heritage, a certificate of immunity from the listing of the remaining Victorian hospital buildings. The absence of listing would make it simpler to obtain permission for unsympathetic alterations or demolition, although conservation area consent would still be required. The Preservation Society, unhappy with this situation, continued to make strenuous efforts to ensure that the unique character of the site was maintained.

In a bitter attack in the EPS newsletter for spring 1995, Christopher Jephcott complained that the council's planning sub-committee had approved the developer's scheme for the second stage of Highlands Village without a single alteration, although the plans (for social housing) involved an unsatisfactory layout and the demolition of a unique original pavilion. The EPS architecture & planning group had spent a great deal of time and thought giving prolonged scrutiny to the plans, before making lengthy comments and positive suggestions. Southgate Civic Trust, the council's Conservation Advisory Group and local residents' groups had also criticised the plans. The borough planning officer, in a long report, had detailed many deficiencies in the scheme and English Heritage was concerned at the demolition of the pavilion. Yet the committee had ignored all these

196. Substantial Victorian pavilions and mature trees help to give the Highlands Conservation Area its special character. Picture shows one of the pavilions being demolished. Will the tree survive?

197. The so-called Highlands Village takes shape. The standard of housing on the site has so far disappointed Enfield Preservation Society.

considerations. 'We have grave doubts as to whether it was acting within its powers in so doing', wrote Dr Jephcott. 'Certainly it made a mockery of the effort that had gone into thinking about and commenting on the scheme, and demonstrated in no uncertain terms just how much the committee values public comment when it clashes with a perceived political objective. We have to ask: what is the value of the consultation process on which so much store was placed a few short months ago [when Labour took control of the Council]? What is the point of a planning officer's team with all its expertise? What is the point of the DoE issuing rules on conservation? Despite the many reservations of the planning officer, the chairman declared he was satisfied with the plans as they stood. This view was seconded by Councillor Smythe, the sub-committee approved the application and that was that.' But the controversy was far from over. In autumn 1995 the EPS newsletter revealed that the Highlands development was once again back in the melting pot because applications for a massive new housing block and a resited access road meant that the master plan for the whole site would have to be renegotiated. Applications had also been made for the demolition of eight more of the original Highlands buildings and all of the buildings on the South Lodge site. The Preservation Society joined other amenity associations in asking the Secretary of State to stop the demolitions, but he refused to intervene and the buildings were flattened.

The first phase of the Highlands Village development was officially opened by Michael Portillo MP, Secretary of State for Defence, at a glitzy reception on 15 September 1995. According to the *Enfield Advertiser* 'wine glasses clinked and an orchestra serenaded the guest of honour' who toured the site in a golf buggy before planting a tree (which was later due to be moved to make way for a car park). A Barrett spokesman was elated. 'It's a superb location' he told the *Advertiser*. 'Developments like this inside the M25 are very rare indeed.' Fifty of the private sector houses had been sold before the opening. Mr Portillo, perhaps unaware of the controversy surrounding the pavilions, told the newspaper: 'I very much like the way in which the new apartment buildings are in sympathy with the old buildings. We are going for different sorts of building and different sorts of people mixing together.' Weeks after the opening, Enfield councillors were still arguing about the right mix of people for Highlands Village. Work had already begun on converting some of the remaining Victorian pavilions into flats and on building new houses and flats to be managed by a housing association. The original plan had envisaged 15 per cent social housing in the village. The Labour majority eventually increased the proportion to 25 per cent, although Conservative councillors warned that this would result in property prices both in and around Highlands being devalued. Ironically, the same argument had been used more than 100 years before by those who opposed the building of Highlands in the first place; after the foundation stone was laid in 1885 it was claimed that rents of nearby houses in Winchmore Hill had fallen to half their former value.

Yet another crunch point in the Highlands development occurred as 1995 wore on. Christopher Jephcott reported in the EPS newsletter for spring 1996 that the developers had submitted revised plans which included the demolition of 13 of the remaining 30 pavilions on the site. The council had been set to approve the demolitions, once again ignoring government guidelines and local opposition. However, Enfield Preservation Society and other amenity groups had alerted English Heritage, which had advised Evironment Secretary John Gummer to place a Holding Direction on the application to ensure that no buildings of conservation interest were lost.

Enfield Council was forbidden to take any action until the minister had examined the site plans and decided whether to hold a public inquiry. Councillors were dismayed at this setback. Richard Course, environment committee chairman, singled out the Preservation Society as target for his frustration, criticising the EPS in the local press as 'liberal-dominated nimbys' and 'a bunch of middle-class whingers who want to preserve ugly buildings'. These and other abusive comments drew protests from Labour councillors (many of them EPS members) as well as rebukes from uncommitted readers of all four local newspapers. Christopher Jephcott, on behalf of the Preservation Society, replied to Councillor Course's outburst and refuted the implication of political bias. He criticised the council's handling of the Highlands situation, pointing out that it had ignored planning procedure, advice and objections to its plan. Dr Jephcott told the *Enfield Independent* (27 March 1996): 'For the Secretary of State to "call in" applications in this way is very, very rare and only done in cases where local councils have shown a flagrant disregard for normal planning processes'. The Department of the Environment announced that a public inquiry would be held in January 1997, but within a month, the developers had produced revised plans which (with the approval of English Heritage) preserved many of the pavilions, as well as revising the access road to make it less obtrusive. Regretting that some significant buildings would not be saved, Enfield Preservation Society did not withdraw its objection but relectantly had to agree to the compromise approved by English Heritage.

Highlands was not the only site on which councillors were prepared to sacrifice conservation to commercial interests. The Preservation Society also fought a frustrating campaign to prevent the demolition of important 19th century buildings at the Royal Small Arms Factory at Enfield Lock. In the words of Len Keeble: 'The importance of this rare, historic industrial site cannot be overemphasized. It took the name of Enfield across the world with the Lee Enfield rifle.' The Royal Small Arms Factory had been unique as a self-contained, government-owned factory. It had its own school, church, theatre and mechanics' institute. Its own housing dated back to the establishment of the factory in 1816. Around the works after the great expansion of 1850 there grew up a considerable work-

198. The main machine shop, Royal Small Arms Factory, Enfield Lock. Up to 1,000 new homes are due to be built on the factory site. After years of wrangling with successive developers, there are hopes that this listed building will be preserved and the basin reinstated, so that the finely detailed brickwork will once more be reflected in the water.

ing-class community which had a character of its own and was entirely dependent on the manufacture of small arms. But in the autumn of 1987 Royal Ordnance plc announced that the factory would be closed by the end of the following year — thus placing another piece of Enfield's heritage in peril.

Enfield Preservation Society at once urged that the best buildings on the so-called Island Site should be listed and saved. The EPS was particularly concerned that the Pattern Room, which contained an unrivalled collection of small arms from countries all over the world, should remain intact. It was suggested it could form the basis of an army museum, but the Ministry of Defence, which still owned the room, decided to relocate it in Nottingham. Early in 1989 the main machine shop and some adjoining buildings on the RSAF site were given Grade II listing, However, it soon became clear that the pressures for development would be hard to resist. The EPS newsletter for autumn 1991 reported that Enfield Council had turned down a request from the Preservation Society, supported by English Heritage and others, that the RSAF should be included in the Enfield Lock Conservation Area.

Enfield Council's own planning department had urged that the Victorian buildings on the vast RSAF site should be retained, but the developers wanted to flatten the lot. They had the support of many councillors who considered, contrary to the advice of all the experts, that the buildings had no architectural or historic merit. The EPS newsletter for winter 1992 glumly reported that at a recent meeting of the council's environment committee, the prospective developers had been tacitly given the green light for a scheme that would leave half of the main machine shop as the only tangible reminder of the long history of the RSAF.

As borough planning officer Martin Jewell commented in his 1994 annual report, Highlands and the RSAF presented Enfield Council with two of the largest and most complex development proposals within the Greater London area. The council thought the RSAF site suitable for a mixed scheme of housing, business, open space and tourist/heritage attractions which made full use of the adjacent river and canal (which had been the reason for siting the factory at Enfield). The report confirmed that a scheme had been drawn up for 1,100 homes on the Island Site, with the option of providing a hotel, and that it was intended that a museum should be incorporated into the listed Victorian machine shop. English Heritage, alerted by local organisations, became involved in lengthy negotiations about the future of historic buildings on the site, but there were other stumbling blocks. Details concerning road access to this new community in Enfield Lock, environmental features, new schools and the level of social housing were not settled until shortly before the 1994 local elections. Within a month, the new Labour administration had rescinded the agreed plan, demanding more social housing. After locking horns with the developers for more than a year, the council — too late — approved an amended scheme. The borough planning officer's report for 1995 revealed that Trafalgar House, the developers, had appealed to the Secretary of State against the council's failure to announce a prompt decision. In the meantime, Enfield Preservation Society had written to the Secretary of State asking him to call in the application. Christopher Jephcott explained in the EPS newsletter for autumn 1995 that the request was prompted by the extremely low priority given to amenity considerations in the revised scheme. There was general relief when it was subsequently announced that the Government Office for London had issued a Holding Direction, to allow more time to consider whether the application should be called in for the Secretary of State's own decision, but by the spring of 1996 the situation had changed yet again. In April it was announced that Trafalgar House had sold the site to local developers Fairview Estates, and that Enfield Council had set up a joint panel, under the chairmanship of Councillor John Jackson, to work out proposals for developments in some of the old buildings.

Occasionally the Preservation Society's pronouncements showed its extreme frustration, an understandable reaction after months — sometimes years — of fruitless attempts to persuade Enfield Council to care for some of the finest buildings in the borough. The Society's patience snapped in 1989 when it learned that the council had recklessly demolished a fine, listed brick wall at Millfield House in Silver Street, Edmonton, a part of the borough which could ill afford to lose one of its last remnants of historic beauty. The wall, standing more than six feet high, was probably contemporary with Millfield House, first mentioned as the residence of 'the imperial ambassador' in the minutes of the Edmonton Vestry, 1796. In the mid-nineteenth century the house (at that time with two meadows, a few acres of cultivated land, a herd of cows and some pigs) was used as a school for workhouse children from inner London. It housed Belgian refugees at the outbreak of the First World War, but was converted to a hospital in 1915, retaining that use until it was closed in 1971. Opened by the London Borough of Enfield as an Arts Centre in 1979, Millfield House stood, a small but beautiful oasis, within yards of the noisy North Circular Road. In the EPS newsletter for spring 1989 Christopher Jephcott complained that the wall had been demolished, and a replacement 'of unsatisfactory design' swiftly erected, without waiting for the approval of the Secretary of State for the Environment, and without consulting local bodies. The official excuse was that the wall had suddenly become unsafe, but Dr Jephcott was sure this could have been dealt with in other ways. 'By its action the council has made a farce of established public consultation procedures and has descended to the level of the worst type of cowboy developer' he wrote, 'but perhaps this is not surprising when one considers the enthusiasm with which it has pursued the demolition of Edmonton's Town Hall.'

The local press frequently followed up reports in the EPS newsletter and in June 1990, prompted by a newsletter item exhorting 'New council must protect our heritage' the *Enfield Advertiser* published an interview with Len Keeble under the heading 'Heritage sell-off scandal'. Mr Keeble was quoted as saying: 'The council's record on care, maintenance and attitude to our historic buildings is not reassuring'. He cited the demolition of Edmonton Town Hall, the failure to restore Broomfield House, the neglect of barns round the reception suite at Forty Hall, the possibility that the 'exquisite' stable block at Capel Manor would be converted into a cafe and the threat that the council would sell Salisbury House on Bury Street 'in preference to repairing its serious structural problems'.

Salisbury House, a fine, timber-framed, late sixteenth century building and one of the oldest dwellings in the borough, listed Grade II*, was a popular meeting place. The numerous local organisations who used it, shared the Preservation Society's dismay that the house might be sold. The publicity that followed the newsletter item may have nudged the council to reach the right decision because, happily, the fears for Salisbury House proved unfounded. The EPS newsletter for winter 1992 reported that the building, which had been closed for eight months, had been meticulously restored, renovated and redecorated using traditional building techniques and materials. Full credit was given to Enfield Council, which had funded and supervised the work. The house and grounds had been bought by Edmonton Council for £4,500 in 1935. Long before that, in 1907, some fine panelling, a splendid carved chimney-piece and a window from an upper room had been ripped out and sold to the Royal Scottish Museum in Edinburgh. To complete the restoration of Salisbury House the museum generously returned the items on an annual renewable lease. In 1993, when the chimney-piece was reinstated in the newly-named Edin-

199. Salisbury House, Bury Street, one of the borough's oldest buildings, after being finely restored by Enfield Council in 1992.

200. Capel Manor, Bullsmoor Lane, as it appeared in 1956 when the house was owned by Colonel Sydney Medcalf, a famous breeder of Clydesdale cart-horses. Vehicles are now allowed to park in front of the house, which is the headquarters of Capel Manor Horticultural and Environmental Centre. The stable block, with a weather-vane in the shape of a Clydesdsale, is on the right.

burgh Room on the first floor, the remains of a rare decorative painting dating from 1620-39 were uncovered.

Concern about the stables at Capel Manor first surfaced in 1988. The stables had been well used by the last private owner of the house, Colonel Sydney Medcalf, an internationally famous breeder of Clydesdale heavy draught-horses, who died in 1958. In 1963 the stables and 12 acres were leased to the Horses and Ponies Protection Association (HAPPA) whose charitable efforts to provide homes for neglected and mistreated animals continued undisturbed when Enfield Council acquired the house and grounds in 1966 and subsequently established the Capel Manor horticultural institute and environmental centre. From modest beginnings the institute rapidly expanded its range of educational courses and launched other ambitious activities. These engulfed not only the Capel Manor grounds, but extended into the estate surrounding the nearby Theobalds House. In June 1988 Enfield Preservation Society learnt that HAPPA had been given notice to quit. To safeguard the fine Victorian stables, which had their magnificent original fittings intact, the Preservation Society immediately asked the Department of the Environment to list them. The stable block and coach house were duly listed Grade II early in 1990, but in the meantime Capel Manor and Enfield Council had provoked universal antagonism with a plan to convert the stables into a students' canteen as part of huge expansion proposals, including a new Heritage Centre. The Preservation Society's protests were taken up by local and national conservation bodies, animal welfare societies and concerned individuals, but in the EPS newsletter for spring 1990 Christopher Jephcott reported that despite these widespread objections Enfield Council was pressing ahead with the development, involving the construction of massive coach and car parking areas. With some irony he pointed out that the Heritage Centre would wipe out a valuable and very rare part of London's genuine heritage, namely the working Victorian stables occupied by HAPPA. Plans for the conversion were drawn up, rejected and amended while Enfield Council tried to find alternative accommodation for HAPPA, and Capel Manor Centre loudly complained that its student intake would suffer unless it could offer better facilities. The impasse dragged on for months. HAPPA eventually moved the horses and ponies to the charity's original site in the Midlands, leaving the stables empty. But behind the scenes negotiations were taking place which would allow Capel Manor to extend its activities into other areas of the nearby countryside.

In 1992 Enfield Preservation Society learnt that covert discussions with Enfield Council were in progress which could result in Capel Manor Centre having control of some of the farm buildings at Forty Hall with the use of part of the park and woodland. No mention of these possible changes had appeared in the council minutes and some councillors were completely in the dark until enlightened by the Preservation Society. EPS members were given the news in their spring 1993 newsletter, which explained that the negotiations had been triggered by the Further and Higher Education Act 1992 under which Capel Manor Centre and similar institutions would become incorporated (i.e. independent) in April 1993.

In addition to using the gardens at Capel Manor, the centre ran an environmental unit and demonstration farm, both well patronised by local schools, in the grounds of Theobalds House. These activities presented a problem because Enfield Council wanted to sell Theobalds, and the imposing mansion would obviously be more attractive to prospective purchasers if its sizeable grounds were included. Under the new Act, Capel Manor was entitled to claim replacement land and property rights to enable it to carry on its activities. Hence the secret discussions, which had centred on Capel Manor transferring parts of its farm and environmental unit into Forty Hall, with a long lease on 14 acres of the park and the use of some woodland for student tuition. Had it not been for the Preservation Society, these negotiations would have been concluded in secret. In the event a package deal was agreed, despite a last-minute attempt by some councillors who protested at the heavy financial commitment (reportedly £1.25million) at a time when council expenditure was being severely cut back. Dr Steven Dowbiggin, principal of Capel Manor, gave an assurance in the EPS summer newsletter that he was committed to enhancing, not damaging, the Forty Hall estate. Over the next few years Capel intended to restore some of the derelict farm buildings to create a Farming and Countryside Centre, he said. The schools operation would also be transferred from Theobalds to Forty Hall. Proposals for this enterprise, which would be open to the paying public, seemed vague. 'Our working plan is to use this site to preserve and display much of the history of the rural Enfield Chase community' said Dr Dowbiggin. In an attempt to allay public disquiet, Capel Manor invited local organisations to sit on an advisory forum, with the promise that this body would monitor future developments. The Preservation Society participated in good faith and at its first meeting the forum elected Colin Pointer as chairman, but hopes that this would be something more than a window-dressing exercise soon evaporated.

Although deeply apprehensive about the impact which a thrusting commercial corporation like Capel Manor could have on the peaceful surroundings and fragile ecology of Forty Hall park, the Preservation Society welcomed one aspect of the deal. As part of the package, the listed 17th century barns adjoining the Forty Hall reception suite were to be restored under the supervision of English Heritage. These once fine buildings had caused problems even when the Forty Hall estate was owned by Sir Henry Bowles. In February 1936 the *Enfield Gazette* reported a speech made by Sir Henry to the Rotary Club of Enfield. Speaking as a landowner, he had complained: 'Rates are increasing and it is more and more difficult to maintain open spaces in a manner which one would like. Barns, for instance, though much admired by people from overseas as being typical of the English countryside, are no longer useful since the coming of the modern threshing machines, and it is becoming an expensive matter to maintain these barns as objects of beauty because, as buildings, they are taxed.' The Preservation Society had first become seriously concerned about the state of the barns in the 1980s, but repairs had been low on the council's list of priorities. The situation went from bad to disastrous when, early in 1990, gales took hold of the already damaged roof of the largest barn flanking the courtyard. Under the heading 'More council neglect' the building was pictured in the EPS newsletter for spring 1991. The photograph, which showed the barn in a disgraceful state of dilapidation, was accompanied by a statement from the borough planning officer that there were no current plans to repair or restore the Forty Hall outbuildings. The Preservation Society informed English Heritage and urged EPS members to protest. Some basic repair work was done but no restoration was carried out.

Activities on and near Capel Manor's home site had meanwhile continued to multiply to such an extent that some feared the centre was in danger of threatening the environment to which it was dedicated. The student intake had increased, and there had been mixed reactions to the announcement in 1994 that the college was to run a BTEC course in horse studies. The Preservation Society, while rejoicing that the listed stables would once again be used for their proper purpose, had considerable sympathy with HAPPA,

201. This picture of one of the ancient barns flanking the courtyard at Forty Hall appeared in the EPS newsletter for autumn 1991 under the heading 'More council neglect'. The roof has since been patched up, but for several years the Forty Hall barns have been included in the English Heritage register of buildings at risk.

whose representative complained in a bitter letter to the *Enfield Independent* that the horse rescue charity had been thrown out of Capel Manor 'on the spurious excuse that the college absolutely had to have the stables to convert into a cafeteria'.

The Preservation Society once again leapt to the defence of Forty Hall when it learnt that Enfield Council, as part of its leisure and tourism programme, intended to stage a Civil War battle re-enactment in the grounds over the 1994 Easter weekend. The EPS protested that this informal park and woodland was totally unsuitable for large commercial events. Other organisations added their objections, but the council, determined to make a quick profit whatever the long-term consequences, brushed all opposition aside and went ahead. Plans were made for 900 players from the Sealed Knot company to camp in the park, complete with horses, cannons and full battle paraphernalia. Space for 3,000 cars was allocated on the meadow for spectators. The event, which made a heavy financial loss, was a disaster. Torrential rain before and during the weekend turned Forty Hall meadow into a quagmire, trapping vehicles axle-deep and leaving deep ruts which made the field hazardous to walkers for months afterwards. In June 1994 the council, by now with a Labour majority, appointed a special panel to investigate the way the event had been organised and hear public comments. The panel was informed by Irene Smith that English Heritage had noted the tyre damage and that because the remains of the 15th century Elsynge House were buried under the meadow, the council should have obtained scheduled monument consent before going ahead. The panel recommended that in order to preserve Forty Hall

202. The cobbled yard and Victorian stables at Capel Manor.

203. Clear traces of terracing can be seen on Forty Hall meadow, photographed here in 1970. The remains of the 15th century Elsynge House, scheduled as an ancient monument, lie under the field.

and its environs for the benefit of future generations, it should only be used as a countryside and nature park. As a result, Enfield Council decided that in future no large commercial events would be staged in Forty Hall, a policy welcomed by the EPS.

By the end of 1995, despite a plethora of planning applications, work had still not begun on restoring the barns or moving some of Capel Manor's activities into Forty Hall. One of the main difficulties was the requirement that additional car parks should be provided. A suggestion that the Forty Hall car park should be extended into the meadow had been fiercely resisted by the Preservation Society and others. During the ensuing deadlock, Capel Manor had second thoughts about the commercial viability of establishing a historic farm in Forty Hall and the college began considering other ways of using the buildings and land it had been allocated. Towards the end of March 1996 it became known that negotiations were almost completed to allow Capel Manor to take over the lease of the 140-acre Forty Hall Farm and establish an equestrian centre and Museum of the Horse in the park. Many aspects of the plan, announced less than a month before the council was due to decide whether to assign the farm lease, worried the Preservation Society, which protested that it was being rushed through without adequate consultation. As a result, a public meeting was held in Forty Hall, attended by some 250 people, all of them hostile to what they perceived as a plan to establish a commercial enterprise in a favourite country park.

More than 560 letters of objection and a protest petition with 4,000 signatures were received by the council. Ignoring this convincing display of public opinion, councillors agreed in July 1996 that Capel Manor could take over the farm lease.

Chapter 18
Threat of the Superstores

The problems facing Enfield Town in the early 1980s were drearily familiar and horribly hard to solve. How to keep the traffic moving, find space to park all the cars, run decent public transport and still leave enough room for more offices and more shopping space — without, of course, wrecking the entire character of the Town. It had foxed the last Labour administration in the 1960s and their Tory successors were finding the struggle equally intimidating. When it prepared the Borough Development Plan that was adopted in September 1983, the council decided the Town needed a separate, more detailed Inset Plan. When this was published towards the end of 1986 the Preservation Society found it, like the curate's egg, to be good in parts.

The EPS winter newsletter welcomed several aspects of the plan, including a new link road from Genotin Road to Cecil Road. But a proposal to knock down a group of attractive Victorian houses in Sydney Road, Raleigh Road and Cecil Road to make way for a car park, so that the shopping precinct could be extended onto the car park behind Wool-

204. In 1987 the EPS successfully campaigned against a proposal by Enfield Council to pull down a group of Victorian houses in Sydney Road, Cecil Road and Raleigh Road to make way for a car park. This well-built house of yellow stock brick, under a natural slate roof, is one of the properties in Sydney Road which was threatened with demolition.

worth's, was condemned as 'turning back the clock to the bad old days of the 1960s'. The Preservation Society, anxious that its members and the general public should be fully informed, organised a meeting at the Civic Centre in January 1987. Councillor Frank Nellis, chairman of the environment and land committee, who had been invited to explain the proposals to the audience of more than 200, did not have an easy time. A heated debate was dominated by insistent demands that the houses must be saved and that the Genotin Road link should be realigned to avoid the demolition of four shops in London Road. Two of these shops (Hammond opticians and Furncrafts) were family businesses which had been in Enfield Town for over 50 years, and their owners claimed it would be impossible to relocate and said they would be forced to leave the area. The *Enfield Advertiser*, in its report of the meeting, quoted Christopher Jephcott as saying: 'Under no account have we got to start knocking down houses in 1987 to accommodate car parking. If this is a consequence of developing the site, then the Preservation Society says forget about extending the precinct. Surface car parks in a centre like Enfield Town are wasteful and unsightly. I don't know why we can't make an attractive multi-storey car park.' The Preservation Society had fought, and won, a similar battle in 1971 when the council had proposed demolishing several houses so that the Sydney Road car park could be extended. The Society had opposed the plan, suggesting that the council should instead look for a site in the Genotin Road area — which it did, resulting in the busy car park at the end of that road.

As usual, the Preservation Society's official comments (which filled eleven closely typed pages) were detailed and constructive. Numerous objections to the scheme were received by the council, and the planners were asked to try again. The result, in October 1987 was a revised Inset Plan which was welcomed in the EPS winter newsletter as being far more in line with the Society's thinking. The Genotin Road extension had been realigned to link more smoothly with Cecil Road. No small shops would have to be pulled down; instead, the new road would cut through the Townhouse and a branch of the Trustee Savings Bank. It was envisaged that the shopping centre would be extended onto the car park adjoining Sydney Road and Cecil Road, with a multi-storey car park and offices on the London Road surface car park.

The problem of finding alternative car parking space while the transformation took place had been solved by a smart piece of lateral thinking. Over the previous two years a property company had been buying up houses in Cecil Road intending to demolish them and build flats. An application for a four-storey block on the site of nos. 59-67 Cecil Road, strongly opposed by the Preservation Society, had been turned down by the council. Borough planning officer Martin Jewell now proposed the council should buy the properties and use the site as a temporary car park, after which it would be redeveloped for sheltered housing. (When it became evident that, because of the national recession, the expansion of the town centre would be delayed for a good many years, the houses were demolished and the site was laid out as part of the Town Park.) The revised Inset Plan also contained what Christopher Jephcott described as 'a somewhat improved policy' relating to the borough's last remaining cinema, the Cannon in Southbury Road. It suggested the possible retention of the facade and the certain incorporation of a cinema in any new development. However, apart from these major changes Dr Jephcott was disappointed that the document was virtually word for word the same as its predecessor. 'The numerous comments the EPS (and others) made on points of detail appear to have been ignored and all the scrutiny and thought involved, a wasted effort' he wrote. In any case, he added, it was a reminder of the limited value of such plans that the council had already abandoned a fairly major item and had given permission for a sizeable office block and

205. The Cannon, Enfield's last remaining cinema, provides a perfect stop to the vista down Willow Road.

high density car parking on the site at 100 Church Street which had been scheduled for sheltered housing. The site, between the New River Loop and St Paul's Church, is now occupied by the stylish, well-designed offices of Data Connection.

Changes in local government procedure meant that the revised Inset Plan was never adopted, but much of its content was incorporated within the new Unitary Development Plan which Enfield began to prepare in 1989. Even then, Dr Jephcott's words of warning were to prove characteristically far-sighted. Development in Enfield had a habit of ignoring the council's grand designs.

In the mid-1980s the Town was still trying to recover its equilibrium after the upheaval which had followed the opening of the Palace Gardens shopping precinct in 1982. Several established retailers had eagerly moved into the precinct, leaving large shops vacant in Church Street and elsewhere. Enfield Council had done its best to keep the town's shopping streets alive by ruling that non-retail uses would be barred in shops situated in a 'core frontage' at the heart of the Town. Nevertheless there had been a steady loss of retailers, particularly small food shops, in the town centre and national concerns were casting predatory eyes over the vacant premises. Pressure from building societies was particularly intense and when Burtons moved out of the imposing building on the corner of the Market Place, the EPS strongly supported the council's refusal to let the Bradford & Bingley Building Society take over these important premises within the core frontage. The council's policy suffered a setback when the building society moved in after winning an appeal. The precinct itself was now well established and was attracting crowds of shoppers into the Town, but in July 1987 the *Enfield Gazette* reported a comment by Roger Lynch, president of Enfield Chamber of Commerce, that Palace Gardens was 'booming' at the expense of other centres like Southgate and Waltham Cross. Mr Lynch added that Enfield could suffer later from out-of-town developments such as the giant Tesco and Marks & Spencer stores which were taking shape on the A10 at Cheshunt. The warning was timely. Shopping patterns were changing rapidly, mainly because the continued growth in car ownership meant that families were no longer tied to their nearest shops. Even in 1985, two years before Mr Lynch's remarks, 65% of households in Enfield had the regular use of a car, compared with 41% in 1965.

Enfield Preservation Society watched with mounting concern as a succession of building societies, estate agents, fast food take-aways and cheapjack 'bargain' merchants gradually replaced many of the speciality shops that once lined Church Street. The council had only limited powers to restrict changes in the use of shop premises outside the core frontage, but because Church Street was part of Enfield Town Conservation Area it was able to exert some control over the design of new shop-fronts. When changes were planned the

206. Aerial view of Enfield Town, 1989. Massive new buildings dominate the Grammar School grounds, while the Palace Gardens shopping precinct dwarfs the shops in Church Street. The ubiquitous motor vehicle has taken over every open space except the Library Green (right), and the banks of the New River Loop (foreground).

EPS architecture & planning group made frequent recommendations about styles, colours and lighting as part of the Preservation Society's efforts to improve the general appearance of Enfield Town. An opportunity to take stronger action came early in 1991 when Rank Leisure applied for planning permission to convert a double-fronted shop at 47/49 Church Street into an amusement arcade. As soon as the application was published, there was a storm of protest. EPS secretary Irene Smith spent hours on the telephone assuring anxious members that the Preservation Society would oppose the application. She told the *Enfield Advertiser* in March: 'My phone hasn't stopped ringing about this. Members want to

207. The busy stalls in Enfield's Market Place are a colourful sight every Thursday, Friday and Saturday. The awnings, once drab tarpaulin, were replaced with striped canvas at the suggestion of the Preservation Society.

know how we can stop it going ahead'. Within weeks, the EPS had received so many complaints that it published an information sheet for concerned residents, outlining the planning situation. Christopher Jephcott, in a letter to the borough planning officer, registered the Preservation Society's strong objection and stated that Rank's planning application had attracted more attention from EPS members, all of it hostile, than any other application the Society could remember. He pointed out that Church Street was within the Enfield Town Conservation Area which had, on the whole, retained its special character as an individual market town. There was already quite a problem of anti-social behaviour in the Town during the evening, which had serious consequences from time to time, and Preservation Society members strongly opposed any changes that would worsen the situation. An amusement arcade would, he concluded, add to the traffic problems that existed in Church Street when daytime parking restrictions were not in force.

Local police, schools, churches and shopkeepers were united in their opposition to the amusement arcade. In May, Enfield councillors, in a rare display of unanimity, refused permission for Rank's application. The company immediately lodged an appeal and on 6 June the *Enfield Gazette* reported that Rank had told the council that hundreds of similar applications 'which catered mainly for the adult, female shopper' had been granted on appeal. But although it had received 334 letters objecting to the plan and eight petitions with more than 500 signatures, the council was on shaky ground when it refused the application. The government's planning policy guidance made it clear that applications for amusement centres should be judged on strict planning criteria only. Factors such as parking problems or the possible disturbance to nearby property could be taken into account, but however overwhelming the local opposition, moral and social considerations like proximity to schools and churches had to be disregarded. Local authorities ignored these guidelines at their peril because, as a result of a recent government Bill, they could become liable for costs if a refusal to grant planning permission was overturned on appeal. Rank's appeal was heard at a two-day public inquiry in October 1991. Irene Smith (on behalf of EPS) and Beryl Dorrington (for the London Road & District Residents' Association) both gave evidence, stressing the noise and disturbance the arcade could bring to the conservation area. Within two months it was announced that the Secretary of State had allowed Rank's appeal, although the Inspector had refused to make the council pay Rank's costs. He also ruled that the arcade must remain closed after 6pm on weekdays and all day on Sundays (Rank wanted to open from 9am — 10pm on weekdays and from noon until 8pm on Sundays). However, that was not the end of the story, for the real battle was about to begin.

Although Rank Leisure had won the necessary planning permission, it would not be able to operate an amusement arcade without a gaming permit, which had to be granted by the local licensing panel. There was general agreement in Enfield Town that the application for a gaming permit must be opposed by every possible means. To unite and mobilise public opinion, Enfield Preservation Society, again with the London Road & District Residents' Association, organised a public meeting at Enfield Grammar School on 16 January 1992. More than 400 people crowded into the hall. Tory and Labour councillors sat side by side among an enthusiastic audience which included church leaders and representatives from local schools. An action committee was set up to lead a campaign under the acronym RAGE — Residents Against Gaming in Enfield. It was explained that if the licensing panel refused to grant a gaming permit, Rank was likely to appeal to the Crown Court, in which case the London Borough of Enfield would be represented by counsel. The overwhelming feeling of the meeting was that RAGE should instruct a barrister to represent the community at any appeal, in order to demonstrate the strength of public opposition to an amusement centre in Church Street. The campaign got off to a flying start when £555 was donated on the spot to start a fighting fund. Beryl Dorrington, who had chaired the meeting and had been elected chairman of RAGE, now began a vigorous campaign to raise more money.

So many objectors turned up at the Civic Centre to speak at the licensing panel in March that the hearing had to be adjourned. Head teachers from Enfield Grammar School and Enfield County School were among those who gave evidence, claiming that the amusement centre would attract schoolchildren and become a focus for crime and disturbance. The RAGE campaign had set out to prove that women did not want an amusement arcade in the town centre. Leaflets had been distributed to female shoppers, inviting them to write to Councillor Audrey Thacker (a representative for Town ward) who presented a pile of petitions and letters to the panel. She said she had received 1,000 letters from women aged from 14 to 80 expressing total opposition, which made nonsense of Rank's claim that it was catering to the demand of female shoppers. Tim Eggar MP, who spoke forcefully in support of the protestors at the reconvened hearing in April, said it was one of the largest displays of public opposition he had known in 13 years as a local MP. After listening to 15 hours of evidence the panel refused to grant the necessary gaming licences.

As expected, Rank lodged an appeal. Thanks to an energetic programme of concerts, quiz nights and jumble sales, the RAGE fighting fund had reached £6,000 and the campaign instructed its solicitor to brief a barrister for the appeal, which was held at Wood Green Crown Court in January 1993. After a three-day hearing, a judge and four magistrates killed off Rank's plans. Upholding Enfield Council's refusal to grant a fruit machine licence and a bingo licence, Judge Kenneth Zucker QC said the ruling was based on the lack of demand for an amusement centre, the proximity of two schools, and public opposition. Rank was ordered to pay the council's costs, estimated at £30,000. A spokesman for

Rank, which had leased the premises in Church Street conditionally, told the *Enfield Advertiser*: 'We will certainly not be trying to move back into Enfield in the forseeable future'. It was a resounding victory, and was the first time in 109 applications for amusement centres throughout the UK that Rank had been defeated at this stage. RAGE was disbanded and the substantial balance left in the fighting fund was transferred (as had been agreed at the first public meeting) to the Save Enfield Fund administered by the Preservation Society.

The two-year campaign against the amusement centre, which had brought together a unique alliance of residents, police, councillors and planning staff, achieved results which were felt far beyond Enfield. Early in the campaign Beryl Dorrington had told the *Enfield Gazette*: 'We are not just representing ourselves here, we're standing up for people all over the country who may face having their towns ruined by amusement centres'. When the council's refusal to grant planning permission was overturned on appeal, local Members of Parliament agreed that the government's planning policy guidance was inadequate. In March 1992 Edmonton MP Dr Ian Twinn arranged a meeting at the House of Commons with Sir George North, Minister of State for Housing and Planning. Those attending were Councillor Terence Neville (chairman of Enfield Council's environment committee), Councillor Audrey Thacker and Beryl Dorrington (RAGE) with Enfield North MP Tim Eggar and Enfield Southgate MP Michael Portillo as observers. Officials from both the Planning Directorate and the Home Office were also present because Sir George said he had been unable to differentiate between the planning implications and the moral and social issues in the Enfield case.

The outcome was that Councillor Terry Neville, who had opposed Rank's application from the start, was asked to draft an amendment to the relevant planning guidelines. His amendment, which was accepted, included the following advice to help local authorities resist unsuitable applications: 'Amusement centres are most appropriately sited in secondary shopping areas, or areas of mixed commercial development. They are unlikely to be acceptable in primary shopping areas, close to housing or near schools, churches, hospitals and hotels and will be out of place in conservation areas.' Enfield's victory gave heart to other areas trying to resist amusement arcades in their town centres. In 1995 the RAGE campaign was used as a blueprint in the neighbouring borough of Barnet where Residents Against Gambling in Golders Green (RAGG) routed an application by Family Leisure Ltd.

A government policy guidance note on major retail developments, published in 1988, had been followed by a marked increase all over the country of appeal decisions in favour of out-of-town superstores. The effects soon began to be felt in Enfield. The borough planning officer's report for 1989 commented that his major concerns included the growing number of applications for change to the non-retail use of premises within shopping centres, and increasing pressure for new retail developments, particularly outside shopping centres. The government made a feeble attempt to stop the decline of established town and neighbourhood centres by publishing revised planning guidelines in 1993. These put forward the view that in-town and out-of-town retail developments should complement each other, but the advice was so general that instead of clarifying the issue it added to the confusion. In any case, the guidelines came too late to influence the unsettling developments which were taking place on the A10 Great Cambridge Road near the outskirts of Enfield Town, where superstores and so-called retail parks were replacing factories that had been household names for generations. Application was made in 1991 for the largest of these developments, on the site of the former Schlumberger factory. This was to be a Sainsbury superstore of 7,060 square metres with 650 parking spaces, a petrol filling station and adjoining space for seven large retail units (later occupied by Homebase, Comet,

208. Industry in decay: the dismal remains of the Thorn EMI building on the A10 tells the story of other companies which once lined the Great Cambridge Road and Southbury Road, providing many thousands of jobs. This picture was published in the Enfield Advertiser *in October 1995.*

Halfords, Olympus, Currys and Toys 'R' Us). Christopher Jephcott pointed out in the EPS newsletter for summer 1991 that the policies in the council's Unitary Development Plan should clearly have ruled out this shopping complex as being likely to undermine the viability and vitality of Enfield Town, yet it had been approved in principle. The policies were supposed to guide development within the borough over the ensuing ten years, he complained, but a plan was only as good as the way it was implemented. Even before it had been finalised, its guidelines had been overturned.

The following year the council gave approval for a 6,338 square metres Safeway store with 568 car parking spaces and a petrol filling station at the junction of Southbury Road and the A10, where Thorn's factory had been a familiar landmark. The Preservation Society again expressed fears about the effect the new store would have on Enfield Town, and predicted that there would be traffic problems at this already busy junction. Adjoining Safeways was another large site, but the council turned down a plan for retail development there because of the loss of industrial land and the impact on nearby shopping centres. However, following a public inquiry in November 1993, the application for shops was allowed. In his report the Inspector considered there was little prospect of the site being developed for industry for some years. As regards retail impact, he felt that the results would be noticed in Enfield Town, but given that centre's underlying strengths, its overall vitality and viability would not be significantly undermined by this one further out-of-town scheme. By 1995 the four large units covering this A10 site, now known as Mandeville Gate, had been let to PC World, World of Leather, Carpet Right and Furniture Works. In 1994, adding to the upheaval on this section of the A10, Pickfords decided to transfer its depot and offices from the A10 onto the vast area in Southbury Road formerly occupied by Belling & Co. The council subsequently gave permission for the old Pickfords site to be developed as a B & Q store and garden centre with part of the area set

209 (opposite). The A10 Great Cambridge Road in the 1950s, showing the junction with Southbury Road. Kingsmead School was later built on the site in the centre foreground, opposite the 1930s housing on the other corner of Southbury Road. Among the factories fronting the east side of the A10, Pickfords depot and the well-designed Thorn EMI building, with fountain and landscaped forecourt, form a stylish pair on either side of Southbury Road, while the extensive Belling works stretch down Southbury Road to the railway.

210. Pickfords' original depot on the A10

211. In its heyday in the 1960s the Belling factory at Bridge Works, Southbury Road, was one of the largest factories in the world devoted solely to producing domestic electric cookers. The 86 vehicles in the transport fleet, shown parked in front of the main administrative block in 1963, made deliveries to all major towns at least twice a week.

aside for a restaurant, bingo hall, discotheque, or other leisure uses.

Besides their implications for the survival of Enfield Town, this welter of developments raised another issue of great concern to the Preservation Society. Bluntly put, it was beginning to appear that, as a result of government policy, planning permission could be 'bought' on sensitive sites. For a long while it had been usual to ask developers to provide some improvement that would outweigh the disadvantages of a particular proposal, such as meeting the cost of highway improvements that would be needed as a result of a development scheme. This came to be known as 'planning gain'. In 1993, because of the obvious danger that authorities would be tempted to approve otherwise unsuitable schemes, the practice had been more clearly defined and regularised in government circulars under the heading of 'planning obligations'. At the same time the link between disadvantage and the improvement offered had become more tenuous and the scale of the operation much larger. Christopher Jephcott raised the alarm in the EPS newsletter for winter 1993. 'Where large schemes are involved', he wrote, 'it is difficult not to feel that the recompense may be inadequate and that long-term harm may be permitted for only short-term benefit.' He quoted three recent examples:

1 • Tesco Store, Gothic Works, Angel Road, Edmonton.
Planning permission was granted in March 1991 subject to a payment of £1,000,000 to fund improvements to the Upper Edmonton Shopping Centre.

2 • Sainsbury Superstore, Great Cambridge Road, Enfield.
For removal of conditions restricting the type of goods to be on sale, payment of £150,000 towards Enfield Council's enhancement scheme for Enfield Town.

3 • Safeway Superstore, Great Cambridge Road/Southbury Road, Enfield.
Payment of £500,000 to be used to address concerns arising out of the permission. This was being allocated under four headings:
i Improvements to street lighting;
ii Upgrading the retail centres in Ponders End and Enfield Town;
iii The establishment and development of facilities within the borough to provide advice and premises for business use;
iv Provision of nursery and creche facilities for customers to the superstore.

Referring to the Safeway development, Dr Jephcott commented: 'The relevance of i) is difficult to detect, and one would have expected a developer to provide creche facilities in a scheme on this scale.' His comments were a somewhat bland interpretation of the scathing comments that had been made by the EPS council of management at its August meeting. The Preservation Society had learnt that the council had set up a borough officers' working group with the specific task of assessing whether proposed developments should be accompanied by a planning obligation. The group would consider if a development was likely to have a harmful effect on features such as the green belt, conservation areas, and listed buildings, and whether this harm could be mitigated by the imposition of a planning obligation. Some members of the EPS council of management interpreted this as meaning that planning permission could be obtained by what were little better than bribes and could be 'bought' on sensitive sites. The EPS minute book records: 'Council of management members expressed very grave concern, the consensus being that this was totally amoral and implied that given enough money, anything was possible.' It was agreed to lobby local MPs about the practice, but government policy has remained unchanged.

The determined fight to save the town's one surviving cinema — the Cannon in Southbury Road — intensified in 1990. It had been known for some time that the site, which included other buildings and allotments at the rear, was to be redeveloped and the council's revised Inset Plan had envisaged a replacement cinema. There was widespread dismay when Frogmore Developments, owners of the site, made it clear there was no intention of including a cinema in any new scheme. The *Enfield Advertiser* reported that Enfield Preservation Society was 'fiercely opposed' to the Cannon's closure, particularly as there were already few enough leisure facilities for young people in the Town. The Preservation Society was also unhappy because the loss of the cinema would leave a gap in the vista down Willow Road where the 1930s building had provided such an appropriate backdrop. Councillors were loath to sign the cinema's death knell and the council dragged its feet for as long as it dared. Frogmore Estates was refused planning permission to build offices at the rear of the cinema site but the firm made a successful appeal and damages, described by the *Enfield Independent* as 'punitive', were awarded against the council.

The complicated planning dilemma dragged on until 1994 when Frogmore Invest-

212. Sainsbury's began trading in Enfield in 1896 at 16 Church Street. This display of poultry shows the shop in about 1900.

213. The decorative tiled walls which distinguished Sainsbury's high street shops are just visible inside the windows of these branches on Windmill Hill. The butcher's shop at no.41 was trading only from 1919 to 1929, but the larger grocery shop at no.43 remained open from 1908 until September 1973.

214. Pushchairs had to be left outside the busy Church Street shop in the 1950s. It was closed in September 1973.

215. The combined floorspace of both the old shops would take up only a fraction of the area occupied by the vast Sainsbury superstore which opened on the A10 Great Cambridge Road in September 1993. This was the first in a series of new shopping developments on the outskirts of Enfield Town.

ments put forward a scheme for a fast food and shopping complex with a sizeable hall for 'leisure purposes'. The council stalled again, with the result that the developers appealed to the Department of the Environment because the council had failed to give a decision within the statutory eight weeks. A public inquiry was fixed for September, raising the possibility that damages would again be levied against the council if the appeal was successful. However, the developers sent a duplicate application to the council, promising that if the scheme was approved the consortium would withdraw its appeal and give the council £50,000 for 'reprovision of leisure facilities'. Christopher Jephcott reported in the EPS newsletter for autumn 1994 that councillors had dismissed the offer and had asked council officers to negotiate better terms. They were not successful and in March 1995 the planning committee reluctantly gave Frogmore Investments permission to demolish the cinema when its lease expired in the year 2000. In November 1996 Tesco was given the go-ahead to build a supermarket on the site.

Complicated negotiations were also taking place during 1994 concerning another Southbury Road landmark which, like the cinema, held fond memories for thousands of local families. The open-air swimming pool in Southbury Road, which was the largest freshwater pool in the country when it was built for Enfield Council in 1932, had been drained and closed in 1991. The council was anxious to make the most of this extensive site. Schemes incorporating leisure facilities were invited and talks were held with several likely firms before a front runner emerged. In the EPS newsletter for autumn 1994 Christopher Jephcott reported that a large leisure development planned for Southbury Road between Bryn-y-Mawr Road and the A10 had been discussed at a well-attended public consultation meeting at the Civic Centre. But he added: 'The proposals were generally not well received — too intensive, generating too much traffic and taking over part of the King George V Playing Field'. The Preservation Society lodged an objection to the development, principally because of the loss of playing fields. By October 1995 the scheme had been altered and the council had chosen developers Berkeley Cap as its 'preferred partners' to build a giant complex that would include a multi-screen cinema, theme restaurants, a football pitch, two swimming pools and a sports hall. A year later, no detailed plans had been submitted. On 19 September 1996 the *Enfield Gazette* reported that one of the backers had pulled out of the Berkeley Cap partnership, giving rise to fears that the £10 million development for the pool site could be delayed.

Welcoming the council's decision to accept the scheme, Berkeley Cap chairman Ronald Nathan had told the *Enfield Gazette* in October 1995: 'This development will anchor the Southbury Road area, with shopping at the nearby retail park during the day and leisure at night'. This was one aspect of the scheme that worried the Preservation Society, concerned as always that Enfield Town should remain a viable shopping centre. The EPS architecture & planning group had already expressed concern at the eastwards shift of the town's centre of gravity that would result from the developments on the Southbury Pool and Cannon Cinema sites, coupled with the huge clusters of new shops (all with free parking) along the Great Cambridge Road. However, although it was still suffering from the general downturn in retail trading, the situation in Enfield Town was gradually improving. In April 1992 the Standard Life Assurance Company had felt sufficient confidence in the town's future to buy the Palace Gardens shopping centre from Norwich Union for £39.5 million. When the deal was announced Robert Allan, Standard Life's assistant property manager, told the *Enfield Gazette* that his firm saw Palace Gardens as 'a good long-term investment in a populous London suburb, despite the present recession'. From 1993 onwards applications for the non-retail use of shops had shown a steady decline. In February 1993 the council

216. When Southbury Road swimming pool opened in 1932 it was advertised in a contemporary brochure as 'the largest open-air baths in the London area ... with room for 1,000 bathers at any one time'. The description added: 'At each end of the swimming bath there is a sun-bathing beach, approximately forty feet by eighty feet, the shingle for which was obtained from Folkestone beach.'

had begun to widen the pavements in Church Street and this improvement, together with stylish street furniture and distinctive surfacing (as advocated by the EPS as long ago as 1969) was adding to the attraction of the shopping centre, though car parking remained a bugbear. By July 1995 only 5.5% of shops in the Town were vacant, a far lower proportion than in any of the borough's other major shopping centres. But competition from the increasing number of new and proposed shopping developments on the fringe of the Town meant there was an urgent need to find an answer to the question that had remained unanswered for more than 30 years: could Enfield Town rest on its laurels or must it expand (and if so, how) to survive into the 21st century?

In September 1993 the council commissioned Donaldsons to advise on a strategy for Enfield Town for the ensuing ten years. The consultants' report, published the following autumn after extensive background research, was basically reassuring. It revealed that although Enfield Town drew its shoppers from a fairly small area, it still traded very profitably for both food and non-food retailing. Most shoppers (39%) travelled to the Town by car, 29% went by bus and 28% on foot, although 33% went home by bus. It also noted that there was currently very little demand for office floorspace. Outlining the report in the EPS newsletter for winter 1994 Christopher Jephcott said that most of the arguments had already been rehearsed many times over the years. The study came up with three options for a development strategy:

1 • A 'do nothing' approach.
2 • Promote Enfield Town as a strategic centre involving major expansion.
3 • A pro-active approach to protect and enhance the town's existing role.

In essence, the third option was an expanded and more imaginative version of pro-

217. The Post Office in Church Street, 1976. As part of a series of welcome improvements to Enfield Town, the pavement outside the Post Office was widened in 1993, eliminating what was often a bottleneck for pedestrians.

posals in the revised Enfield Town Inset Plan which, because of the recession, had been kept on ice. It would aim to broaden the range of multiple retailers in the town centre by including more food and general shopping and if possible a variety store such as BHS, and would involve environmental improvements including pedestrianisation. Sydney Road would be closed, the Genotin Road link would be revived, there would be two-way traffic in Cecil Road and probably east-west bus traffic in the pedestrianised Church Street.

The council adopted the third option as a basis for further discussion and deposited the weighty report in local public libraries. The Preservation Society spent £20 on its own copy and members of the EPS council of management endured a long evening discussing its proposals with the architecture & planning group. The unanimous decision was that options one and two were unacceptable but that the Preservation Society would give support, in part, to the third option. There were, however, several crucial recommendations which the EPS could not endorse. Although no formal consultation procedure had been launched, Christopher Jephcott was asked to write immediately to the borough planning officer.

The Preservation Society's quick response made an immediate impact. Alongside the many worthy proposals in the Donaldsons report was a suggestion that Church Street should be wholly or partly pedestrianised. This, explained Dr Jephcott in his letter, was where the Preservation Society parted company with Option 3. Members were unhappy that one bus every minute would pass through the pedestrianised street, and they also feared it could become a 'no go' area for pedestrians at night. But the Preservation Society's major sticking point was the consequence of reintroducing two-way traffic into Cecil Road, because it was clear this would reduce the Library Green to a travesty of its current

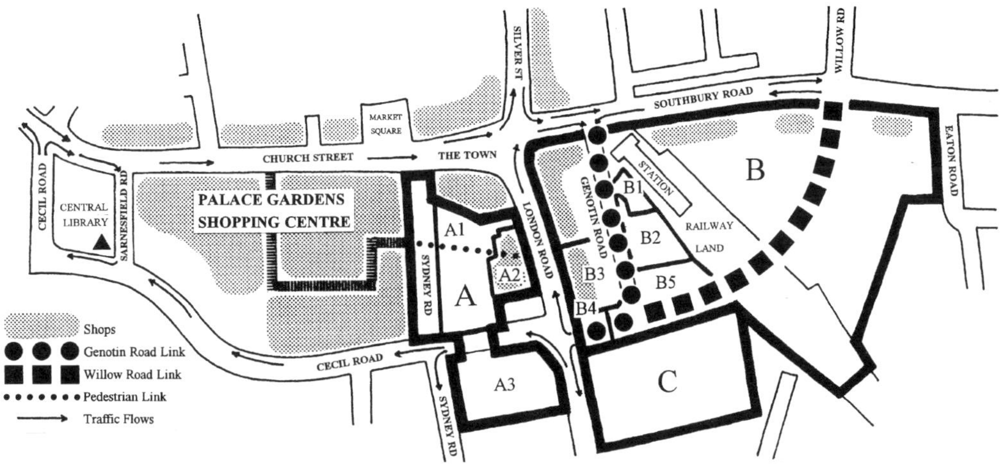

Enfield Town: a plan for the future? The question was put by Enfield Council in a questionnaire accompanying this plan, based on Option 3 of the Donaldsons report. Area A would be developed as a second phase of the Palace Gardens shopping precinct. Area B is seen as 'an area of opportunity' and Area C would be developed only if St Anne's Catholic High School (the present occupants) vacate the site.

status. The Preservation Society was still fiercely determined to safeguard the beautiful little green that had been described by its founder-chairman as 'one of the jewels of Enfield'. As Dr Jephcott pointed out, 'a threat to the Library Green was one of the things that brought this Society into being 58 years ago'. He also complained that other consequences of pedestrianisation would include a roundabout at the bottom of Windmill Hill, which would seriously damage the most attractive entry to Enfield Town, that some of the fine houses in Cecil Road would have their pavements narrowed to mere remnants and that the report did not even mention the mature plane trees in Cecil Road which had taken the best part of a century to reach their present size, and were thus irreplaceable.

The full text of Dr Jephcott's letter was included with reports considered at a special meeting of the council's environment committee in March 1995. Both Labour and Tory councillors agreed to launch a massive public consultation exercise on the suggestions in the Donaldsons report, but to abandon the pedestrianisation proposals. The *Enfield Advertiser* did not approve. Five-inch headlines on the front page on 1 February 1995 proclaimed 'U-turn coats' and complained that plans to pedestrianise Enfield Town centre had been dramatically dropped, although the council had promised 'just seven days ago' that the public would have their say. Environment committee chairman Richard Course said that although pedestrianisation had not been ruled out for ever, there were certain dangers. In some towns like Waltham Cross, he told the *Advertiser*, pedestrianisation 'had worked a treat', but in others like Hoddesdon it had been a total disaster. 'We are not going to do it, so we are not going to consult. My aim is to ensure Enfield remains vibrant. I am not going to gamble with its future' he said. He was quoted in the *Enfield Gazette* as warning that if all traffic had to by-pass the town centre 'it could make Enfield a ghost town'.

In November 7,000 leaflets and questionnaires were sent to businesses and residents in or near the town centre outlining the plan and asking: Enfield Town — Which way now? As the Preservation Society prepared to take part in these consultations on the future of Enfield Town, older members of the EPS council of management, some of whom were going through the process for at least the third time, sighed 'This is where we

218. H.H. Collier, proprietor of a menswear shop which began trading at 60 Church Street in 1912, was a founder member of the EPS council of management. Perhaps because of the shop's proximity to the Library Green, his was the sole dissenting voice when the Preservation Society opposed the sale of the green for a shopping development in 1936.

219. An art nouveau fascia, installed in the 1930s, distinguished the shop (then managed by Peter Collier) until it closed down in 1984.

came in' and felt a distinct sense of *deja vu*. The problems remain intractable, but casting scepticism aside the council of management as usual made a detailed, thoughtful and constructive response, in the hope that this time the consultations would lead to an exciting new phase in the development of the Town which, thanks largely to Enfield Preservation Society, has retained much of its distinctive character and charm.

Chapter 19
As Others See Us

O wad some Pow'r the giftie gie us
To see oursels as others see us!
It wad frae mony a blunder free us,
And foolish notion.
Robert Burns

One of the central dilemmas facing the Preservation Society has lain in its relationship with Enfield Council. At the same time as wanting to cultivate its links with the borough's planners and decision-makers, and to work with them in a spirit of friendly co-operation, the EPS has always been determined to retain its independence and avoid being drawn into too cosy an embrace. Perhaps the most fitting stance for the Preservation Society to adopt towards the council is one of constructive scepticism, or even benign mistrust.

In its early days Enfield Preservation Society fought for years, and with great persistence, to obtain council agenda papers. A clause in the Local Government Act ensured that from 1974 the public had the right of admission to all council and committee meetings and EPS representatives took full advantage of this. Agendas and background papers were available for perusal at the meetings but members of the public were not allowed to take them away — although council officials usually found that at the end of the proceedings they collected fewer documents than had been issued. With the passing of the Local Government (Access to Information) Act in 1985 the EPS was able to demand advance copies of all council agendas and committee papers by right. However, the Preservation Society soon became aware that it was missing informative documents on items of public concern, because these had been tabled at the last minute, or at unscheduled meetings.

The situation became particularly acute during the acrimonious Save Whitewebbs Campaign. No doubt to avoid the hostile reaction of campaigners who packed the public gallery on every possible occasion, the council began trying to slip decisions through at hastily arranged meetings which were often held at unexpected times of day. To make sure no important business was missed, EPS vice-president Stanley Smith began a daily routine of checking the notice-board at the Civic Centre, and the Society set up a rota of members to monitor the meetings of each main council committee and specially appointed panel. Thus, since the 1980s, an EPS representative has cast a beady eye over meetings of councillors open to the public, often sitting in conspicuous isolation as the only citizen with enough interest (and stamina) to keep watch on the borough's elected representatives.

Because the Preservation Society, in the steadfast pursuit of its aims and objects, has remained resolutely non-political throughout its existence, its relationship with the council has inevitably been ambivalent. One could say that the EPS has endeavoured to act as the council's conscience, trying to prevent it from damaging the borough's environmental assets for the sake of political or financial expediency. Over the years the Preservation Society has gladly seized the opportunity to co-operate with both Tory and Labour councils on numerous projects. When opposing the council or other bodies it has always tried to put forward reasoned and constructive arguments but it has consistently refused to compromise its ideals, notably on matters such as safeguarding the green belt and other open spaces. Although causing extreme irritation (or worse) to those who have been obliged to change or abandon their plans as a result, this inflexible attitude has earned the Preservation Society widespread respect.

Since the mid-1960s members of the EPS council of management have enjoyed a useful — and generally cordial — working relationship with Enfield Council officers. There have, as one would expect, been frequent 'full and frank' discussions, accompanied by a sharp exchange of correspondence, but these encounters have invariably been without rancour. Curious to learn what those at the receiving end felt about the Preservation Society's interventions, we asked three retired chief officers for their recollections.

Relations with the borough engineer's department had frequently become strained when the EPS criticised the design and siting of street furniture, or opposed road schemes that would damage trees and open spaces. John Little, who retired as borough engineer and surveyor in 1991, did not hesitate when asked to comment on his relationship with Enfield Preservation Society. 'It was a thorn in my side', was his immediate response. Later, after reflecting on his long association with the EPS (dating from 1965 when Southgate Borough Council, which he had joined in 1958, was incorporated into the London Borough of Enfield) Mr Little added: 'You must of course appreciate I am an engineer. That, by definition, makes me single-minded, somewhat blinkered in my approach and resistant to any attempt to delay, frustrate, stop or change things'. Although he considered the Preservation Society had sometimes been impractical 'and possibly more than a little fanciful and ever so slightly esoteric', it had a right to question and to complain. 'The borough needs societies and associations to put the brakes upon people like me', he said. 'It makes us think, which is no bad thing. Being on the receiving end, however, I confess to thinking, on occasions, that the EPS was an irritant I could well do without. Looking back from my position of comfortable retirement I now consider that much of what irritated me was due to my own impatience and the need to get things done — there were never enough hours in the day.' Summing up, he considered the Preservation Society's efforts had been well justified. 'You may not have always got it right', he said 'but my philosophy is that if one succeeds in getting it right 99% of the time, then one can live with the odd 1%. There is still a need for the Society. It does a first class job. It provides an alternative view on many topics and more than that, it represents grass roots opinion which it can express without fear of a ballot box reaction.'

Norman Stonard's professional relationship with the Preservation Society extended from the early 1960s, when he was chief planning assistant with the former Enfield Borough Council, until his retirement as borough planning officer in 1984. 'During that time we developed a healthy regard for our respective views on matters of common interest, even though we did not always reach agreement', he said. He paid credit to the Preservation Society for its involvement in the 1960s Save Enfield Campaign and acknowledged its key role in the setting up of the Gentleman's Row Study Group, whose success led to further study groups being established. Norman Stonard became borough planning officer in 1972 when the post was created by splitting the functions of the former architect/planner. During his 12-year tenure he fostered a positive attitude to conservation, setting up the council's conservation advisory group, which he regularly attended. 'The Preservation Society, through its representatives, made a valuable contribution to the group's discussions', he said. 'I would particularly single out the thorough and well set-out views and proposals submitted by Dr Jephcott, not only to the advisory group but on other matters.' Acknowledging that EPS had always been a passionate supporter of policies designed to preserve the green belt, Mr Stonard recalled that it was thanks to the Society that the GLC was persuaded to enter into a consultation procedure before felling further mature trees on the Hadley Road and The Ridgeway farmlands. He was in no doubt of the need for the Preservation Society to remain active and vigilant in the future, and he warned: 'I feel that increasing pressure to erode our attractive countryside will occur as land availability for housing diminishes. This will necessitate a keen watch on vulnerable land at the perimeter of the urban area.'

Bill Issitt, who had been Norman Stonard's deputy for some years, succeeded him as borough planning officer in 1984. A major cause of friction with the Preservation Society during Bill Issitt's term of office was the long-running dispute over development on the Brecon House site in Gentleman's Row. 'I thought the applications should be approved. Your Society objected, and on two separate occasions the Department of the Environment agreed with you and not with me', he recalled. He added: 'There were other planning applications where your strong lobbying resulted in certain councillors being more concerned with "ballot box clout" than with their genuine assessment of the town planning issues involved. As borough planning officer I accepted this as politics, but as a

220. Forceful comments in the quarterly EPS newsletter, while keeping members informed about the Society's policies and activities, have frequently irritated Enfield councillors and council officers. A frieze of newsletter covers formed part of the EPS Diamond Jubilee Exhibition in Forty Hall, and to mark the anniversary the spring 1996 edition carried two colour photographs.

professional officer I felt rather frustrated.' The forceful way in which the Preservation Society made its opinions known seems to have made a lasting impression on Bill Issitt. 'I recollect that certain of your representatives acted as if they had been elected to serve as additional councillors and I recall feeling a bit annoyed at this', he said. 'There were also times when your Society appeared to set itself up as an alternative planning authority and expressed surprise if its views were not automatically endorsed by the council's officers.' However, his overall recollection was that the Preservation Society had, by and large, been helpful to him and he looked back on his association with the EPS with affection rather than animosity.

It would be unrealistic to expect a serving chief officer to shrug off the Preservation Society's adverse comments with such benign detachment. We sought the opinion of Martin Jewell, who was appointed borough planning officer on Bill Issitt's retirement in 1987, having been his deputy for a number of years. Soon after he took office, Martin Jewell had obviously become increasingly irritated by a series of reproachful headlines in the EPS newsletter, but he decided to tackle the situation in a positive way. The critical headlines had included 'New council must protect our heritage', 'Do we want yet another superstore?', 'Unease over Enfield Town changes', 'Just lip service', and 'All protests ignored'. Martin Jewell said he had been disappointed to find very few newsletter headlines extolling any good work done by the council. But he appreciated that the comments on planning issues made by the EPS over the years had consistently been 'well thought out, well presented and in the main positive in their intent'. He also commended the Preservation Society's positive initiatives such as its footpath work, tree planting and litter clearance.

In 1989, following two particularly hostile newsletters complaining about 'Council's "cowboy" conduct' and 'The farce of "public consultation" ' Mr Jewell wrote to the newsletter editor expressing concern. 'It seems to me that in accordance with my general philosophy we should be working towards a more collaborative approach rather than one of suspicion and perhaps a little mistrust and antagonism', he said. Arising from that letter, representatives of the EPS council of management had what was to be the first of a series of regular meetings with Mr Jewell. The dialogue, which has been genuinely appreciated by the Preservation Society, has helped achieve a mutual understanding of each other's point of view. But although they have given the EPS a new insight into the complexities of today's planning process and the constraints placed on local government, these friendly encounters have not resulted in any softening of the Preservation Society's attitude on matters of policy or principle.

It was gratifying that all three retired chief officers had pleasant memories of their personal dealings with the Preservation Society. 'I enjoyed my many contacts with officers of the Society, even though we did not always reach agreement', said Norman Stonard. John Little described his numerous meetings with EPS representatives as 'a joy and never a chore' because the members had all been 'so helpful, understanding and friendly'. Bill Issitt was more specific. 'Any organisation must, of course, rely upon its individual members to reflect its image', he said. 'I recall that my meetings with your members were always carried out in a spirit of mutual helpfulness. There was Dr Jephcott, a town planner in disguise, whose views were always worth considering ... Mr Woodfield, who would appear to accept quite philosophically any disagreement I might have with him regarding preserved trees, and then quietly restate his original views ... And your secretary, Mrs Smith. One just couldn't hold a grudge against your Society, having met this lady. She had (and probably still has) the ability to smooth down any ruffled feathers.' He added: 'As borough planning officer I had no doubt that it was the aim of the Society's officers I

221. Irene Smith was presented with an engraved silver salver in 1994 to mark her 25 years of dedicated service as honorary secretary of Enfield Preservation Society. The Mayor, Councillor Rita Smythe (centre) made the presentation on behalf of the EPS, watched by chairman Colin Pointer.

dealt with, to help improve or at least retain the character of Enfield. The fact that their views and mine did not always coincide is not important. What is important is that as your Society is able to present to the council an informed public opinion on town planning matters, it continues to do so.'

Enfield Preservation Society has now been trying to fulfil that role for 60 years. January 1996 saw an auspicious start to its Diamond Jubilee year with the announcement that Irene Smith, the EPS honorary secretary, had been appointed MBE in the New Year Honours List. This timely and richly deserved award, officially made 'for services to the community in Enfield' was a fitting recognition that for more than a quarter of a century Irene Smith had been the dynamo at the heart of an organisation which had given unparalleled service to the borough. In 1994 the Preservation Society had presented Irene Smith with an engraved silver salver to mark her 25 years in office. On that occasion, EPS chairman Colin Pointer recalled that Irene's determination and dedication had helped to win many of the campaigns initiated by the Preservation Society. Since 1969 she had carried out the duties and responsibilities of honorary secretary with great skill, a firm hand and total commitment, and had even made time to take on additional roles. The EPS owed her a tremendous debt of gratitude, he said.

From the mid-1970s the Preservation Society was exceptionally fortunate in having long-serving officers in key positions. Two honorary treasurers — Gertrude (Trudy) Maunder, with six years service and Priscilla Lowen with 14 — were both qualified accountants and therefore undaunted by the complexity of managing the EPS finances. This is now no sinecure, involving day-to-day accounts, numerous publications, the hire and maintenance of Jubilee Hall, and the administration of trust funds. The EPS also owes a debt of gratitude to its auditors, now Moore Stephens, for their wise advice and help over many years. Since the Preservation Society's resurgence in 1959 a constant succession of individuals has emerged from the membership, prepared to devote a large part of their leisure to help run this large and busy organisation. Some of these activists have become well known to EPS members and to the general public because, as group leaders, they speak on specific aspects of the Preservation Society's work. Others, no less active, rarely hit the headlines, but the Society could not function without them. These members have been motivated by the determination, as enshrined in the EPS aims and objects, that all that is best in Enfield and its countryside must be safeguarded for future generations. Transcending narrow sectarian interests, they represent a concerned body of opinion that local politicians ignore at their peril.

An ambitious programme of special events was arranged to celebrate the Preservation Society's 60th anniversary, including illustrated talks at four of the borough's historic buildings: Salisbury House, Trent Park mansion, the Tudor Hall in Enfield Grammar School, and Capel Manor. The centrepiece of the jubilee programme was a retrospective exhibition — A Panorama of Preservation — seen by thousands of visitors to the gallery at Forty Hall Museum during six weeks in June and July. The event was brilliantly staged by Alan Skilton, who over many years had devised all the Preservation Society's major exhibitions. Drawing extensively on the EPS photographic archives, he skillfully arranged

222. The borough's three Members of Parliament (all EPS members) were among nearly one hundred guests who joined other members at the opening of the retrospective exhibition — A Panorama of Preservation — at Forty Hall in June 1996. A highlight of the exhibition was the wall hanging worked by the Enfield Branch of the Embroiderers' Guild. Here, Beryl Dorrington (chairman, EPS Diamond Jubilee committee) explains the scenes on the hangings to (left to right) Tim Eggar (Enfield North, Energy Minister), Michael Portillo (Enfield Southgate, Secretary of State for Defence) and Dr Ian Twinn (Edmonton).

panels showing the Society's campaigns, achievements and personalities above a panoramic frieze made from the covers of every EPS newsletter issued since 1963.

The exhibition was opened by Matthew Saunders, secretary of the Ancient Monuments Society, who gratefully acknowledged that he gained his first experience of conservation as a member of the EPS historic buildings group. Guests at the opening reception included MPs, councillors and representatives of local organisations with whom the Preservation Society had worked over the years. A high point of the evening was the unveiling of a wall hanging produced by 20 members of the Enfield and district branch of the Embroiderers' Guild. Measuring 5ft by 3ft and designed by Muriel Evans, the branch president, the hanging was made up of panels featuring Enfield Preservation Society activities from tree planting to publications, footpath creation to litter clearance and building preservation. Several EPS souvenir items were produced for members as more portable reminders of the year. These included local view paperweights and a booklet of postcards showing Enfield landmarks saved by the Preservation Society. A new rose was commissioned from local rose breeder Bill Bossom: cluster-flowered, in EPS red, it was patented in this country and registered with the American Rose Society under the name 'Preservation'.

In 1995 the EPS council of management decided that the Preservation Society's major Diamond Jubilee project would be an attempt to renovate the Enfield Loop of the New River. Announcing the news in his chairman's report to the annual general meeting in June 1995, Colin Pointer said that most of the loop — which in living memory had carried clean, clear water — was now choked with silt, algae, litter and decaying vegetation. He warned that there was a very real danger that unless drastic action was taken, it would deteriorate beyond recall. The Preservation Society hoped to launch a joint venture with Enfield Council to desilt the loop, repair the banks, improve public access and provide a pumped recirculatory system to maintain an adequate flow of water. He warned

223. The New River Loop, summer 1995. This typical stretch beside the path leading to the Crown & Horseshoes shows the shallow water thick with rotting vegetation, silt and algae. As its major Diamond Jubilee project, the Preservation Society decided to initiate a rescue plan for the New River Loop in co-operation with Enfield Council.

224. The lych-gate to St Stephen's Church, a prominent feature at the junction of Park Avenue and Village Road, Bush Hill Park. The lych-gate, which had fallen into disrepair, was restored and rededicated in 1991 to the memory of 'Spot' Ashton, a churchwarden at St Stephen's from 1938-1963. Mr Ashton was a founder member of the EPS council of management and for many years was one of the Society's vice-presidents. In memory of his long and loyal support, the Preservation Society made a donation to the restoration fund.

that the cost was likely to be so high that the work might have to be phased over a number of years. Enfield Council had made it clear that it would not contribute to the capital cost and the Preservation Society therefore intended to apply to the Heritage Lottery Fund for a substantial contribution. It would also ask for other grant aid, seek commercial sponsorship, raise a public appeal and make a sizeable donation from EPS funds. 'The scheme is an ambitious one' concluded Colin Pointer 'but the New River Loop has made a vital contribution to the character of the Town for nearly 400 years and the Preservation Society is determined to save it'. The news was received with delight by EPS members and approval by the general public. Enfield Council welcomed the proposal and promised full co-operation from council officers. By January 1996 arrangements had been made for a detailed survey by a professional team, including Thames Water engineers, to assess the extent of the loop's problems so that solutions, costings and a business plan could be prepared. The EPS summer newsletter announced that the flow of water in the loop had been increased and that there were hopes that, in advance of the major works, a central gutter could be cut in the silt to deepen the channel.

The plan to rescue the Enfield Loop was not the only long-term commitment entered into by the Preservation Society to commemorate its 60th anniversary. It also agreed to become actively involved in Enfield Council's efforts to produce what became known as the borough's Local Agenda 21. This was a brave attempt to draw up plans to stop the effects of environmental degradation and to promote sustainable development. The concept had taken several years to filter down to local level following the 1992 Earth Summit held in Rio, where the largest ever assembly of world leaders agreed to produce international, national and local plans to tackle environmental problems.

Enfield Preservation Society began its programme of jubilee events with a record membership of 2,254. Of the pioneers from the early years, only Robert Gowers was able to take part in the anniversary celebrations. Ernest ('Spot') Ashton, the last surviving member of the original council of management, had died in January 1990, aged 95. As a young man he ran four family grocer shops in Enfield, Bush Hill Park and Cheshunt and was one of the local businessmen who supported the formation of Enfield Preservation Society with great enthusiasm. Although invited, Spot Ashton had been unable to attend the inaugural meeting on 13 December 1935 but he was present when the EPS council of management met for the first time on 9 March 1936 and he remained an active supporter all his life.

Another link with the Preservation Society's formation had been severed in December 1989 with the death of Robert Dugdale Sykes, a partner in the local law firm Vanderpump & Sykes. Following the example of Frank Vanderpump, who had helped to set up the Preservation Society, Robert Sykes gave invaluable assistance during the 1960s Save Enfield Campaign. He later helped the Society in many practical ways, such as letting the EPS trees group establish a tree nursery in his large garden at Gough Park Cottage, Clay Hill. His professional colleagues were perhaps not best pleased when he later allowed the firm's offices in the Market Place to be used as a collecting point for EPS subscriptions. A special postbox was fixed to Vanderpump & Sykes's entrance door and EPS members were invited to drop their subscription envelopes into the box, but were asked not to go upstairs into the office. This convenient scheme continued smoothly for many years until, as a result of the Preservation Society's ever-growing numbers, members sometimes found the EPS box full to overflowing, which resulted in their dropping subscription envelopes into the normal letterbox or handing them to office staff. Tolerance snapped and the cosy arrangement came to an end.

Carinthia Arbuthnot Lane, who played such a dynamic part in shaping the Preservation Society when it was revived in 1959, died in January 1994. It was largely thanks to her ebullient personality that the reborn Society shed its somewhat staid pre-war image and began attracting a wider, younger membership in the early 1960s. Among many innovative schemes, Mrs Lane commissioned the EPS listed buildings plaques in 1964. Now prominently displayed on many of Enfield's most interesting and historic buildings, they are permanent memorials to her initiative. The first plaques, which cost the EPS a little over £3 each, were distributed as gifts from the Society. A charge was made for subsequent issues and the most recent castings, made in 1992 by a foundry in Waltham Abbey, were sold for £100 each to owners of local listed buildings.

Over the years, the Preservation Society's activities underwent a gradual change. By the 1980s Enfield Council's own volunteers (Groundforce) had taken over responsibility for most of the tree planting, footpath maintenance and countryside working parties formerly initiated by the Preservation Society. EPS working parties were left to cope with less glamorous tasks such as flower-bed maintenance and litter clearance in Enfield Town. The traditional pattern of set-piece meetings for EPS members in the spring, summer and autumn had also changed. A programme of less formal, fortnightly talks at Jubilee Hall had become so popular that monthly evening meetings were started at the EPS headquarters in January 1994 and the spring and autumn meetings were discontinued. However, a larger hall remained the chosen venue for the annual general meeting, major campaign events and special lectures such as the joint fixture each year with the Edmonton Hundred Historical Society. The Preservation Society continued to maintain a strong presence at major borough events, with displays promoting issues of current concern and a busy stand

225. Enfield Preservation Society has staged an exhibit at the Town Show — now known as the Autumn Show — almost every year since 1960. A notable exception was 1989 when, for the first time, the EPS boycotted the show as a protest at the steep rise in charges (from £42 to £80). Other environmental groups also stayed away, and charges were reduced the following year. Above, leaving nothing to chance, Tony Lane insisted on erecting the EPS stand in his garden and briefing helpers before the show each year; this was the 1963 exhibit.

226. The EPS tent and stand, with a display featuring tree planting and preservation, attracted a crowd of visitors at the 1980 show.

selling EPS publications. The EPS tent became a beacon for environmentalists at happenings such as the Autumn Show in the Town Park, the Steam & Country Fair in Trent Park, and Enfield Lock Village Fair, attracting many new members.

While the Preservation Society's outdoor pioneering activities were slowly declining, its committee and town planning work was increasing year by year. No invitation to serve on a body where the EPS aims could be promoted was ever refused. EPS representatives were (and still are) active on the London Green Belt Council, New River Action Group, Enfield Countryside Action Group, Myddelton House Gardens Advisory Group, London Forum, and Broomfield Historic Buildings Trust. The EPS is today (1996) represented on several London Borough of Enfield committees including the Conservation Advisory Group, Green Belt Forum, Enfield in Bloom, Forty Hall/Capel Manor Forum, and Local Agenda 21 working parties. For many years the EPS had representation on the Enfield Tidy Group, the Museum Steering Group (both now defunct) and the LBE Arts Council (now replaced by another organisation) In addition, representatives serve on the Enfield Town Study Group, Eastern Enfield Study Group and Trent Park Conservation Group. Thanks to the dedicated individuals who give so much of their time to these meetings, the EPS is uniquely placed to influence a wide spectrum of discussions and decisions affecting the borough's environment.

This crucial role was acknowledged in many of the messages received by the EPS on its 60th anniversary. Describing Enfield Preservation Society as 'one of the most active and consistently effective societies we have the pleasure of working with', Philip Venning, secretary of the Society for the Protection of Ancient Buildings, wrote: 'Whatever planning laws we have, there is no doubt that an alert and dedicated society that reflects the concerns of people in the area is far and away the best way of protecting the elements that give the place its special identity'. Lord Graham of Edmonton, who said he had admired the work of the Preservation Society for more than 40 years, said: 'Of course, there are ups and downs, very often to coincide with the intention of the planners — both private and public — to change the townscape. But the fact that so many individuals are willing to pay their subscriptions and, when demanded, turn up at a public meeting is a severe constraint on the planners' ability to get away with murder.'

The EPS was particularly pleased to receive a warm message from Matthew Saunders, who occupies an important place in the national conservation scene in his triple role of secretary of the Ancient Monuments Society, honorary director of Friends of Friendless Churches and secretary of the Joint Committee of National Amenity Societies. Born in Enfield, he pointed out that it was the buildings in the borough that first introduced him to the delights of architecture and the threats that it faces. While still a schoolboy he wrote to the Preservation Society in June 1969 asking it to do its best to save the Golden Lion, an ornate public house, and the nearby Ragg's chemist shop in Edmonton. These two 17th century buildings were ruthlessly demolished by Enfield Council to make way for the problematic and faceless Edmonton Green development, although they could well have been incorporated into the scheme to help give it some character, as urged by the EPS. Matthew Saunders subsequently joined the Society and he recalled: 'It was the Enfield Preservation Society and its historic buildings group that brought home to me, as a young member, the importance of informed public opinion in influencing the powers that be. I remember the battles fought and lost, as over the Old Bakery in Forty Hill, and those resoundingly won, as in the defeat of the inner relief road which threatened to plough its way through St Andrew's Churchyard.' Matthew Saunders added that the Preservation Society's growth in membership was still mentioned 'in hushed and envious

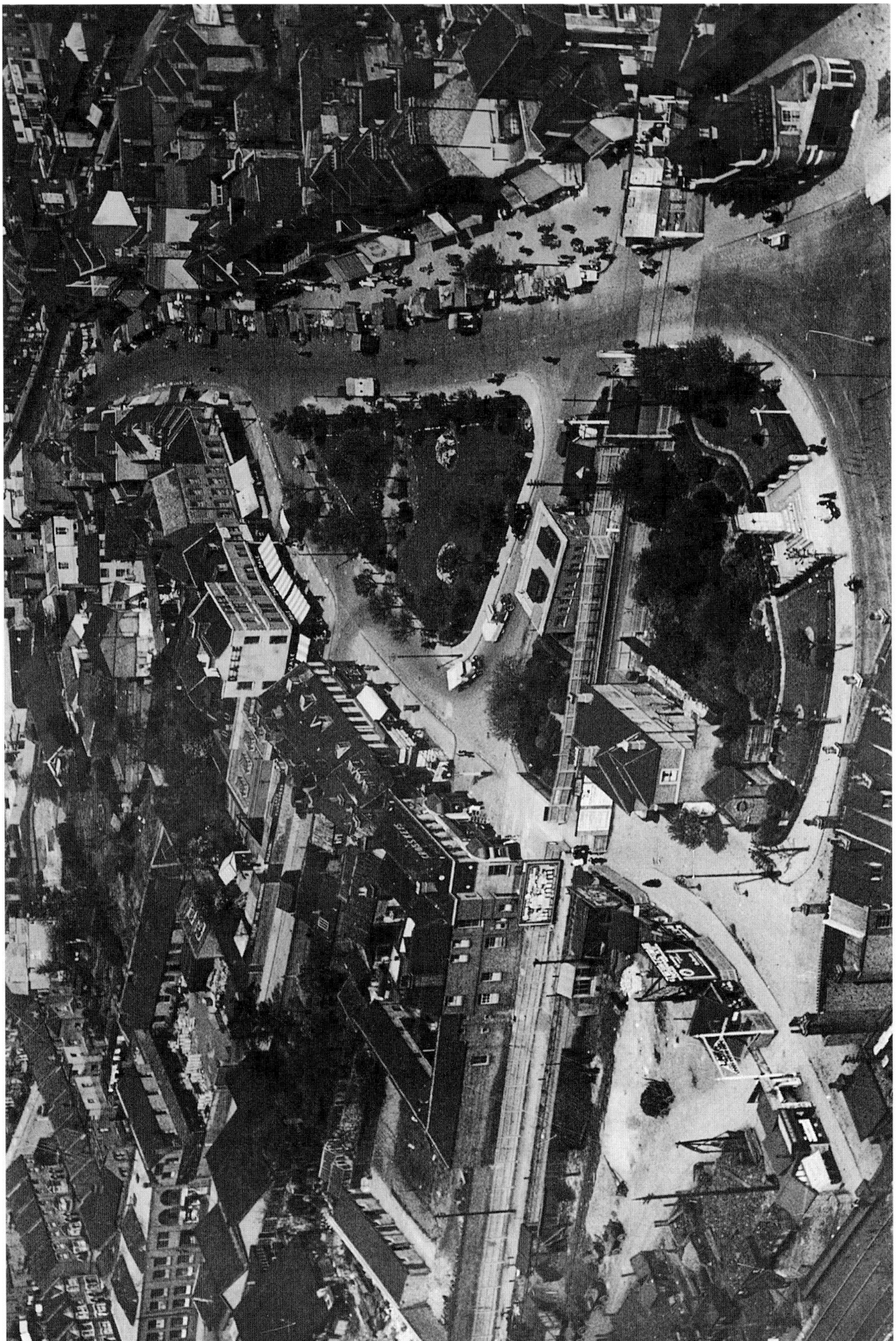

tones' by civic societies in much better-known historic towns where public support was noticeably less marked. His message concluded: 'For all those for whom Enfield is special, the EPS has been the voice and the very successful champion'.

Warm messages were received from the three local MPs, all of whom are EPS members. Tim Eggar thanked the Preservation Society for its work and said: 'I have particularly admired the measured, well-researched and responsible way in which you have argued your point of view.' A glowing testimonial from the Civic Trust, the organisation best placed to assess the work of amenity societies all over the country, revealed the high regard in which EPS is held nationally. Saskia Hallam, Civic Trust registrar, wrote: 'In 60 years the Enfield Preservation Society has done much sterling work to improve the quality of the environment. The saving of the Library Green and Chase Green, the campaign to save the New River, and the stalwart defence of the green belt are major achievements. Then one thinks of all the hundreds of trees that have been planted and the network of footpaths that has been cleared. Add to this the numerous guides and publications, photographic competitions and surveys: the Enfield Preservation Society has definitely left its mark on the area. The Civic Trust, only a stripling in comparison for it was founded in 1957, is fortunate to have under its umbrella such a resolute organisation with its heart in the right place — caring for Enfield.' Past differences between EPS and FERAA were ignored in a generous tribute from Harold Grant, joint general secretary of the federation. He had high praise for the Preservation Society's campaigns in defence of the green belt and said: 'There has been no other body in the borough which has applied itself so vigorously in the defence of our heritage'.

The support given by Enfield Preservation Society since 1942 to the Council for the Protection of Rural England was recalled in a grateful message from CPRE director Fiona Reynolds, who wrote: 'The results of your work are there for all to see but much of your achievement, like that of the CPRE, is very often what is not there. It is worth considering what Enfield would have been like had EPS not existed'. She added that the challenge now was to look forward to the next century and articulate a positive vision for our local environment.

Nearly every message stressed the need for the Preservation Society to remain strong, alert and active. It was instructive to see how well-wishers of various persuasions viewed the Society's future role. Councillor Jeff Rodin, leader of the Labour majority on Enfield Council, welcomed the EPS proposals for renovating the New River Loop and hoped the practical working partnership the project would involve would be symbolic of a deeper partnership between the council and the Preservation Society. He noted that EPS mem-

---

227 (opposite). Aerial view showing Edmonton Green in 1969, shortly before the area around the green was razed to the ground to make way for the problematic Edmonton Green shopping centre and tower blocks. Hertford Road curves away in the background; in the foreground the low level railway (built in 1849) cuts through the ancient green. Beyond the railway line, the row of shops facing the green on the left includes the Golden Lion public house and Ragg's chemist (two 17th century buildings the EPS vainly tried to save) and Dale's department store. The war memorial (centre foreground) was the only feature incorporated into the bleak Edmonton Green development; it now stands in the middle of a traffic roundabout. The EPS commented in 1974 that the high level of vandalism around the tower blocks showed they provided an inadequate environment for their inhabitants. In 1995 Enfield Council announced a £300,000 competition for developers to submit plans for revamping the shopping centre and tower blocks as part of an attempt to put new heart into the area.

228. Its cherubs holding aloft a new set of lights, the splendidly restored Victorian drinking fountain gives character to the pedestrian island in Enfield Town. The Preservation Society opposed more than one attempt to have the fountain removed. In 1959 the council suggested it should be replaced by a flower-bed, and ten years later council engineers had to be persuaded that the fountain would not interfere with the proposed one-way traffic system. Well-designed railings, seats and flower planters, installed by Enfield Council in 1994, have now made the island a focal point in the Town and should mean that the fountain is there to stay.

bers had long been regular observers at council and committee meetings and added: 'Stacks of reports stand testament to a substantial input from the Society on planning and environmental matters. We believe this is important because we are committed to open government. For open government to work it requires not only that those in power open their proceedings to the public, but that the public takes an interest in those proceedings'. Not surprisingly, Councillor John Jackson, twice Mayor of Enfield and for many years chairman of the planning sub-committee when the Tories held the majority, saw the scene from a different angle. 'The role of the Enfield Preservation Society is now more important than ever', he wrote, 'because in recent times we have witnessed some of the worst planning applications coming before Enfield Council that I have seen in over a quarter of a century as a member of the planning committee. It requires vigilance not only by residents, but through informed comments from societies such as the EPS, to make the planning committee aware of the feelings of the people of Enfield'.

Praise for the Preservation Society's staying power was contained in other messages. This quality had first been noted at the EPS annual dinner in 1971, when Arthur Percival of the Civic Trust said: 'We have the highest regard for all the admirable work done by the Enfield Preservation Society. We feel that perhaps one of your greatest achievements is simply sustaining such a vigorous level of activity over so long a period. From personal experience I know that this demands real stamina.' When he gave that tribute the EPS had been working at full throttle for just eleven years. Remarkably, its stamina has shown little sign of flagging. In a message congratulating the EPS on its Diamond Jubilee, Ronald Smith, chairman of the London Green Belt Council, wrote: 'Many societies aged 60 years (or less) tend to lose their verve as the years go by. Enfield Preservation Society has never done that. It well maintains the high standards of expertise and approach which have made it a most valued member of the London Green Belt Council. I am sure that its vigour will enable it to contribute much more to the protection of Enfield and its surroundings in the years to come.'

The message from borough planning officer Martin Jewell envisaged a future role for Enfield Preservation Society far wider than its existing remit. He also challenged the EPS on two contentious issues which, although both were exhaustively debated some 30 years ago, probably now deserve consideration by a new generation of members. 'Is the name

229. This little archway leading into a yard behind the Victorian shopfront of No.35 Silver Street probably dates from the 18th century. The picture was taken in 1979, when the premises were occupied by Leonard Fenn, optician. This varied group of shops in the ancient thoroughfare leading north out of Enfield Town has been eyed by developers for many years. Among past schemes (which happily came to nothing) was a proposal by the architect of Centre Point for a massive hotel on the corner of Southbury Road. In autumn 1995, plans were submitted to fill in the archway with a shop, and build high offices in place of some of the other shops. Both applications were opposed by EPS. So the struggle to preserve interesting survivals from Enfield's past goes on .....

of your Society still appropriate?' he asked. 'In these days of marketing hype, of an ethos when perception and image appear all important, does the Society really wish to have a name that in some minds can conjure up a certain degree of negativity?' A valid question. Activists within the EPS remain convinced that its record of innovative projects belies any suggestion that the Preservation Society is reactionary or resistant to change. But is that how it is seen by the general public? The Society's membership continues to grow. Would it attract more support and public sympathy if the name was changed, or would it merely forfeit some of the goodwill it has built up over 60 years?

Mr Jewell's second question was equally provocative: Should the Preservation Society expand its activities into other parts of the London Borough of Enfield? 'I recognise that there are other societies covering other parts of the borough' he said 'and yet I am conscious that not all of the borough is equally well served by guardians and improvers of the environment.' Following on from this pointed reference to the absence of an amenity society in Edmonton, Mr Jewell suggested the borough might be better served by a single society or a federation of societies, perhaps under the name of the 'Enfield Civic Society' which 'could not only take forward the valuable work of organisations such as the Preservation Society and the Southgate Civic Trust but would also balance the physical and environmental with the social and economic needs of the borough'. One can appreciate the logic of this concept — and its attraction for Enfield Council and other authorities, who would have only one organisation to deal with. But the risks of diluting the Preservation Society's influence within a larger organisation cannot be ignored. At present the borough's two leading amenity societies, though joining forces on matters of joint concern, remain fiercely independent, and each enjoys a sharper profile as a result. In Edmonton, an amenity society will flourish only if residents in that area are sufficiently motivated to form and support their own local group.

The aims of Enfield Preservation Society have remained virtually unchanged since its earliest days. Martin Jewell suggests the EPS should now consider whether a broader perspective would be valid, taking into account the social conditions of the borough, its economy as well as its environment. In the author's opinion it would be a sad day if Enfield Preservation Society allowed its single-minded defence of the environment and care for our heritage to be weakened by other considerations. There are plenty of eloquent vested interests who are eager to put forward economic and social arguments in the environmental debate. One hopes Enfield Preservation Society will continue to evolve and widen its scope. But though always ready to listen, it must continue to keep faith with its ideals, as it has for more than 60 years, by pursuing its aims and objects with wholehearted dedication.

The Society's diamond jubilee year ended in tragedy with the sudden death on 18 December 1996 of Irene Smith. Her unstinting loyalty to Enfield Preservation Society and the determination with which she promoted its aims during 27 years as its honorary secretary won widespread respect and admiration throughout the borough. Irene Smith's shining sincerity disarmed even the most adamant opposition and her warm, sympathetic personality endeared her to everyone who knew her. A suitable memorial will be planned, but the finest tribute to her memory is that, despite this grievous loss, the EPS is determined to maintain the high standards she set and will continue fighting for the future with undiminished zeal.

Appendix 1
Officers of the Enfield Preservation Society

Presidents

1961-67	Revd Ebenezer E. Rees
1967-78	Godfrey Groves JP
1979-88	Donald C. H. Potter
1988-94	Carinthia Arbuthnot Lane
1994-	Valerie Carter

Vice-Presidents

Sir Graham Rowlandson MBE (elected 1962)
Frank Vanderpump (1962)
Muriel Hollington (1962)
Revd Graham Buston (1962)
John Shewring (1962)
Robert Dugdale Sykes (1963)
Frances Perry MBE (1965)
Edward E. ('Spot') Ashton (1965)
Frank Bennett (1965)
Don Gresswell MBE (1965)
Donald C. H. Potter (1965)
William E. Palmer (1970)
Valerie Carter (1979)
Reginald T. Williams (1981)
Dr Christopher J. A. Jephcott (1981)
Alan J. Skilton (1986)
David O. Pam (1990)
Irene Smith MBE (1990)
Stanley R. Smith (1990)
Walter T. Woodfield (1990)
Priscilla Lowen (1991)
Denis Hoy (1994)
Lord Graham of Edmonton (1995)
John W. E. Jackson JP (1995)

Chairmen

1936-39	Revd Geoffrey W. Daisley
1939-61	Revd Ebenezer E. Rees
1961-63	Donald C. H. Potter
1963-65	Frederick C. Hymas
1965-68	Donald C. H. Potter
1968-72	Major Clayton Arbuthnot Lane TD
1972-73	Donald C. H. Potter
1973-76	Valerie Carter
1976-77	Gordon Macfarlane
1977-79	Valerie Carter
1979-82	Stuart D. A. Mills
1982-85	Alan J. Skilton
1985-87	Valerie Carter
1987-90	W. T. ('Wally') Woodfield
1990-93	Alan J. Skilton
1993-	Colin Pointer

Honorary Secretaries

1936-42	Stanley Adlard
1959-67	Carinthia Arbuthnot Lane
1967-68	Joyce Ball
1968-69	Pamela Mills
1969-96	Irene Smith MBE

Honorary Treasurers

1936-61	John P. Shewring
1961-63	Eve Price OBE
1963-67	Cecily Surplice
1967-68	Major Clayton Arbuthnot Lane TD
1968-74	Gertrude Maunder

Honorary Treasurers (continued)

1974-77	Donald Potter
1977-91	Priscilla Lowen
1991-93	Stanley R. Smith
1993-	Monica Smith

Other Office Holders 1936-1966

Membership Secretaries
Major C.A. Lane, Harold Ball, Frank O'Connolly, Don Grammer, Harold Howson, Maurice and Doris Connolly, Gordon and Mary Macfarlane, Denis and Joan Hoy, Brian Newton, Pat Atkins.

Minutes Secretaries
Peggy Sparkes, Sylvia Elmes, Hilda Dollery, Velma Byford, Beryl Dorrington.

Newsletter Editors
Carinthia Arbuthnot Lane, Valerie Carter.

Group Leaders & Committee Chairmen 1936-1996

Architecture & Planning Group
Robert Gowers, William Palmer, Alan Skilton, Christopher Jephcott.

*Anti-litter Group**
Beryl Dorrington.

Footpaths & Open Spaces Group
Don Gresswell, Jane Twitchett, Leslie Castle, Peter Woollett, Stuart Mills.

Historic Buildings Group
Carinthia Arbuthnot Lane, Peter Miln, Connie Eagles, Len Keeble, Caroline Carter.

Jubilee Hall Committee
Wally Woodfield, Alan Skilton.

Natural Environment Group
Beryl Dorrington and Frances Mussett (joint leaders).

Publicity Committee
Carinthia Arbuthnot Lane, Valerie Carter, Pamela Mills, Irene Smith.

Records & Research Group
Derrick Stone, Alan Skilton, David Fisher, Wilson Wyatt, Margaret Law, Stan Lowen.

Social Committee (now incorporated into Publicity Committee)
Velma Byford.

*Trees Group**
Christopher Jephcott, Harry Moore, John Hannah, Gordon and Mary Macfarlane, Wally Woodfield, Frances Mussett.

Junior EPS (disbanded 1992)
Prue Lambert

Council of management 1996/7
Pat Atkins, Caroline Carter, Beryl Dorrington, Christopher Jephcott, Tony Langston, Stuart Mills, Janet McQueen, Frances Mussett, Colin Pointer, Alan Skilton, Stanley Smith, Irene Smith (honorary secretary), Monica Smith (honorary treasurer).

* Incorporated into Natural Environment Group, 1994

Appendix 2
Enfield Preservation Society Publications

A History of Enfield by Cuthbert Whitaker (1911), reprinted by EPS 1965, 1969 and 1975

Enfield's Architectural Heritage — 1977

The Story of Enfield Chase by David Pam — 1984

Portrait of Gentleman's Row — 1986

A History of Enfield by David Pam:
Vol I A Parish near London — 1990
Vol II A Victorian Suburb — 1992
Vol III A Desirable Neighbourhood — 1994

Fighting for the Future by Valerie Carter — 1997

Heritage series:
Tree Trails round Enfield Town — 1981
A Guide to Enfield Street Names by Graham Dalling — 1982
Enfield Past and Present by Victor H. Allemandy (1914), reprinted by EPS 1984

Heritage walks:
Forty Hill & Bulls Cross — 1985, reprinted 1988 and 1995
Enfield Town — 1988, reprinted 1995

For young readers: *The Enfield Book* — 1992

Hand guide: *A Walk Around Enfield Town* — 1968

Footpath map: 1964, reprinted 1966, revised and enlarged colour editions 1973, 1980 and 1989

Colour view postcards: Series of 26 local views, the first card (White Lodge) published 1984

Christmas cards — A card showing a local view or reproduction of an old print has been produced nearly every year since 1963

Other items include local view notelets, limited edition prints, promotional goods, etc.

Acknowledgements

Numerous individuals have helped in the preparation of this book and I gladly acknowledge my debt to them all. This story of Enfield Preservation Society could not have been written without the minutes, correspondence and other documents so carefully compiled and preserved by successive EPS secretaries. Press cuttings collected by the EPS records group have provided lively contemporary comment on important events. Many of the illustrations come from the hundreds of slides and photographs donated to Enfield Preservation Society over the years, which the group has meticulously catalogued as part of the EPS archive.

I am particularly grateful to David Pam for his encouragement, wise advice, and practical help in many ways. Also to my son Paul, whose shrewd comments and professional expertise greatly improved the draft manuscript. It would have been physically impossible to complete the book without the unstinting help of Irene and Stanley Smith, whose enthusiasm never flagged and who devoted hours of their time to the project. Throughout the enterprise I have, as always, enjoyed the wholehearted support of my husband, Henry.

To the past and present officers of Enfield Council who patiently answered my questions and provided information, my sincere thanks. They include Norman Stonard, John Little, Bill Issitt, Martin Jewell, Andrew Cooke, Philip Sheail, Graham Dalling, Chris Mulvey, and Bernard Mould. I am obliged to Geoffrey Gillam for archaeological information, to Brian Warren for the excellent maps that enhance the text and to Stephen Sellick for making available so many pictures from his postcard collection.

I am grateful to the following for the loan of prints or permission to reproduce copyright photographs and plans.

British Library Reproductions: 15
Carleton Photographic Services: 96, 206
W. Carter-Lee: 106.
Paul Charters: 20, 94
Shirley Cotton: 115, 116, 118
Crown copyright: plans of Whitewebbs park, Brecon House area, and Enfield Town
Christine Fookes: 110, 111, 113, 192
Enfield Advertiser: 208
Enfield Gazette: frontispiece, 7, 28, 45, 64, 72, 74, 78, 97, 121, 130, 133, 153, 155, 180, 181, 186
Michael A. George: 177
Greater London Photograph Library: 89
Greater London Record Office: 185
Eddie Harris: 220
Ralph Hutchings: 162
Christopher Jephcott: 120, 210
Len Langride: 91
Leggat family scrapbook: 3
London Borough of Enfield: 4, 10, 23, 32, 191, 198, 227
Karen Plum: 176, 223
Sainsbury's Archives: 212, 213, 214, 215
Steven Sellick collection: 1, 9, 12, 14, 18, 24, 49, 50, 60, 67, 142, 143, 175, 194, 216
Philip Sheaill: 196, 197
Eric A. H. Smith: 62
Stanley R. Smith: 30, 31, 35, 51, 53, 54, 55, 66, 73, 76, 83, 90, 103, 104, 131, 138, 140, 141, 151, 156, 157, 158, 161, 163, 167, 169, 170, 171, 172, 173, 174, 183, 184, 187, 190, 193, 199, 201, 204, 205, 207, 224, 226, 228
Mary Soulsby: 178
M. Spinner: 165
Chris Wood: 222.

List of Subscribers

London Borough of Enfield
The Worshipful the Mayor of Enfield

Adamson, Mrs W. A.
Addington, Mr & Mrs E. W.
Alcock, June & Jack
Allbutt, Patricia
Allum, Mrs Norma
Andrews, Geoffrey L.
Artiss, Mr & Mrs E. F.
Atkins, Patricia
Badger, Mr John R.
Baker, Mrs June Mavis
Ball, Mr & Mrs H.
Bamforth, J. M.
Barnard, Chris & Joyce
Bayford, Mr Frank
Beaumont, Alan
Belson, Mrs M. G.
Benjamin, Jenny
Best, Anthony J. T.
Biggs, Mr A. J. A & Mrs M. J.
Billett, Virginia P.
Blake, Mr & Mrs J. H.
Bone, Mr & Mrs F.
Booker, Sylvia A. M.
Boote, David
Borner, Mr L. C. & Mrs J.
Bougnague, Mr Peter
Breton, Mr F. H.
Brown, Brenda
Browne, Adrian
Browne, Stephen
Bull, Graham & Lynn
Bull, Pamela M.
Bull, Patricia
Butler, Claire Dawn
Butler, Kirsty Joanne
Butler, Mrs Margaret L.
Byron, Derek & Pat
Capp, Alan
Carnaby, Miss L. G.
Carr, Mr & Mrs K. T.
Castle, Mr S. W.
Chamberlain, Helen and Andrew
Chamberlain, Robert Lamb and Julia
Chamberlain, Marian and Neville
Chaplin, Edgar
Chapman, Eric
Chase, Mr R.
Chipchase, Miss C. E.
Church, Roy
Clark, David
Clark, Victor E.
Clarke, Geoffrey T.
Clarke, Mr R. W.
Clarkson, Mrs R. M.
Claydon, Antony
Clifton, Mr J.
Cody, Valerie
Coldham, Mrs B.
Coles, Norman S.
Comyns, Mary C.
Corbett, Robin
Cordell, Mr J. R.
Cornell, Diane
Cotton, Albert and Shirley
Cox, Eileen
Cox, Mrs Helen M.
Coxshall, Mr R. A.

Cracknell, Mr M. E.
Cranfield, Miss I.
Crutchley, G. J. M.
Daley, Miss S.
Dane, Peter & Sheila
Day, Erik
Deamer, Mr & Mrs J. R.
Deering, Peter, JP
Dormer, Roger
Dorrington, Albert & Beryl
Doust, Mr & Mrs P.
Dowbiggin, Dr Stephen R.
Dumayne, Alan
Dunford, Janet
Ebbels, Mrs Daphne
Eccleston, Matthew
Eddington, Roger
Edmondson, Mr D. G.
Egan, C. & J.
Elkin, Roger
Elmes, Miss S. D.
Enfield County School
Errington, Robert
Evans, Mr & Mrs A.
Farmbrough, David M.
Farrell, Mr Michael
Featley, Mr Kenneth
Fisher, David, Paula, Zebaria and Samuel
Fisk, Peter
Flaherty, Frank J.
Fletcher, Mrs A. L.
Fletcher, Mr & Mrs K. E.
Flitter, Miss J. R.
Fogg, Mrs J.
Foo-Noble, Ye Wah
Ford, Mrs J.
Ford, Michael
Foster, Miss Edna
Frear, Brian
French, Mr Sidney W.
Fulbrook, Mrs Peggy
Ganderton, Mrs Margaret C.
Gelister, Jean
Gething, John and Jo
Gibbens, Colin
Gibbons, Mr & Mrs Paul
Gibbs, John G.
Gilburt, Stephen
Gillam, Geoffrey
Gleeson, Diki
Glenister, Miss A. G.
Gould, Mr & Mrs John
Gowers, Mr R., JP
Grammer, Don
Gravett, Constance
Hamilton, C. G.
Hannaford, Mr & Mrs J. L.
Harrington, Miss J.
Harris, Mr & Mrs H. J.
Harrison, Neil
Hastings, Mrs A. E.
Hebblewhite, B. G. V.
Hoad, P.
Holland, Mrs B. A.
Holland, Miss P.
Hoult, Constance
Hudson, Mr N. G.
Huggett, J. M.
Hughes, Mr & Mrs K. J.
Hughes, Walter and Mabel
Hugill, Andrew Robert
Hugill, Paul
Hunter, C. A.
Huntingford, Mr & Mrs Peter
Isaksson, Sadie
Issitt, Mr W. J.
Jackson, Cllr John
Jacob, Arthur & Edna
James, David and Joyce
Jephcott, Dr & Mrs C.
Johnstone, Kirsty
Jones, Ian K.
Jones, Ken
Jones, Peter and Jean
Keeble, Pat and Len
Kerridge, Mr J. F. & Mrs J. M.
King, Eileen
Knott, Ms Sandra
Knowles, Dr Wendy A.
Lambert, Prue
Lancucki, Mrs J. M.
Lane, Mrs Janet
Langston, Janet and Tony
Larrett, Mary
Law, Mr C. and Mrs H.
Layzell, D. E.

Leather, Mrs D. J.
Leighton, Mrs M. B. E.
Levy, Pamela
Lewis, Miss I. D.
Lewis, Mrs Valerie
Lister, Miss D. M. S.
Lister, Mr P. A.
Little, Mrs D.
Little, John E. H.
Lock, Miss W. P.
Londesborough, Stephen
Love, Philip
Lowen, Mr S. J. & Mrs P.
Macfarlane, Gordon
Malleson, Mr and Mrs Robert
Manders, R. I.
Manning, Mr E. S.
Martin, Mr R. W.
Maunder, Mrs Gertrude M.
May, Chris
McGrath, Mr J.
Miles, Ted & Mary
Mills, Stuart D. E. & Cope, Carol
Morham, Mrs Muriel
Mortimer, Mr A. T.
Mowbray, Warwick
Mussett, Mrs Frances
Needham, Christine and Derek
Negus, Pam & Den
Neville, Cllr & Mrs T., JP
Newstead, Mr & Mrs A. W.
Newton, Mr and Mrs Brian
Nicholls, Mr J. H.
Noble, Harold and Sheila
Norris, A. K. H.
Nyman, Mr Edgar
Oliver, Barry
Page, Mrs Barbara J.
Pain, Cherry & Tom
Palacio, Mrs Felicity
Pam, David
Parker, Mrs D. M.
Pavey, Mr & Mrs D. R.
Payne, Mrs Annette W.
Peach, John C.
Pearl, Mr & Mrs C. J.
Perkins, Mr Adrian
Perryman, Cllr Peter
Pidgeon, Janet & Colin
Plum, Karen
Pointer, Mr & Mrs C. L.
Porter, Mr & Mrs H. T.
Potter, Catherine
Potter, Cyrilla
Potter, Doreen E.
Prince, Mr & Mrs
Rackley, Mrs L. F.
Radden, Mrs E. B.
Ramsbotham, Leonard
Reader, Barbara and Glenn
Reed, Elizabeth
Reed, Mrs Janet K.
Reed, Mr & Mrs Nick J.
Reeve, Mr & Mrs Paul J.
Richardson, Stan & Joyce
Robertson, Mrs Marjorie
Roe, Mr & Mrs H. W.
Rogers, Edna
Rowbury, Mr & Mrs K. G.
Rowe, John A.
Rye, Mr Michael J.
Sargent, A. E.
Saunders, Mr & Mrs J. W.
Saunders, Matthew
Schofield, Miss Kathleen M.
Seeley, Mrs O. M.
Sellers, Mrs Marion
Sellick, Olive
Sellick, Stephen
Sharkey, Justine
Shirdel, Mrs Mary Anne
Simonsen, A. D.
Simpson, Mrs Phyllis R.
Skilton, Alan
Sluter, Mr & Mrs F. A.
Small, Miss Jean
Smith, Betty
Smith, Donald
Smith, Hildegard and Eric
Smith, Irene & Stanley
Smith, Margaret and Peter
Smith, Monica
Smith, Mr & Mrs R. L.
Smith, Mr R. N.
Smith, Mr & Mrs T. G.
Soulsby, Mary

Soutar, Mrs B.
South, Mr & Mrs N.
Speller, Faith
Spurgeon, Mrs Mary
Standbrook, Stan
Stares, Mr R. W.
Taylor, Dr A. R.
Thomas, Mrs Elsie
Thompson, Jacky
Thomson, I. J.
Tibbatts, Mr & Mrs K.
Tillbrook, Mr & Mrs C. J. C.
Tollady, Clifford A.
Triggs, Sue
Tuson, D. C.
Tuson, Jean & John
Tuxford, Paul
Vernon, Mr K. E.
Walby, Mrs J.
Walker, Pat & Brian
Ward, Trevor
Warren, Prof F. L.
Webb, Patrick A.
Wetherall, Emma J.
Whitaker, Mr & Mrs J.
White, Miss Joan L.
Wilkinson, Joan
Williams, Dr Molly
Wilson, Frank
Wing, Cecilia
Wolfson, L. R.
Wood, Mrs Gladys E.
Woodfield, Mr W. T.
Woods, Brian and Gillian
Woods, H. G.
Woods, Miss M. E.
Woollett, Peter
Woolveridge, H. T.
Wortley, Stephen
Wright, Cllr David
Wright, Mrs R.

Index

A 10. *See* Great Cambridge Road
Adlard, Stanley 11, 12, 18, 21, 23, 65
Agriculture, Ministry of 68
air-raid shelters 21, 22
Aire Valley 80
Albany Park 172
Albany School 187
Aldous, Tony105
Allan, Robert 258
Ambrose Fleming School 173
Amenity in Action 204
American Foundation for Temple Bar 44
Amwell 160, 170
Ancient Monuments Society 269, 273
Angel Road, Edmonton 255
Ansells Green 82
Applin, Col. R. V. K. 9, 10
Architectural Heritage Fund 230
Archway House 88-90
Archway Road 80
Arundel Tennis Club 192
Ashton, Ernest E. ('Spot') 12, 271
Atkins, Robert 169
Autumn Show 154, 273

B & Q DIY Store 213-214, 252
Baker, Kenneth 168
Baker Street 52, 82
Balmoral Road 184
Bane, Charles A. 44
Barclays Bank, Enfield Town 48, 116
Barnet 132, 251
Barnet Council 80
Barrett, house builders 234, 235
Beavan, Molly 122
Beech Hill 69
Bellamy, Dr David 168
Belling & Co 252
Bennett, Frank 23, 27
Berkeley Cap, developers 258
Betjemen, Sir John 43
Boots, chemists 95
Borgman, Trevor 73
Bossom, Bill 269
Botany Bay Farm 182
Bourne, The, Southgate 113
Bowles, Col. Sir Henry 9, 11, 12, 18, 19, 65, 171, 242
Bowles, Edward Augustus (Gussie) 12, 171, 172
Bowyer, Councillor John 112
Boys' Brigade 150
Bradford & Bingley Building Society 247
Bramley House 101
Brayshaw, Steve 154
Brecon House 117-122, 265
Bridgefield Nursery 49
Brimsdown 174
Brimsdown Avenue 150, 177
Britain in Bloom 202-203
British Horse Society 137
British Rail 176
British Telecom 199, 200
British Waterways 154
Brocket, Lord 46
Brooklyn, Private Road 101
Broomfield Historic Buildings Trust 229-231, 273
Broomfield House 117, 226-231, 239
Broomfield Park 117, 226
Broxbourne 160, 166, 168, 170
Broxbourne Council 43, 135, 137
Bruce Castle Museum 110
Bryn-y-Mawr Road 258
Buchanan, Sir Colin 92, 94, 95
Buckler, John Chessel 110
building preservation 29, 47-49, 101, 113-122, 238-241
Bull, Bartle, MP 12
Bull Lane, Edmonton 19, 21
Bulldog, The 209
Bulls Cross 7, 57, 82-84, 126, 174, 202
Bulls Cross Ride 79
Bullsmoor Lane 49, 81, 82, 83, 174, 209, 213
Bullsmoor Lane Nursery 49
Burnt Farm Ride 69, 135-137
Burtons menswear 247
Bury Green 139
Bury Road West 225
Bury Street 239
Bush Hill 63, 139, 162, 176
Bush Hill Park 60, 61, 192, 208, 271
Bush Hill Park Golf Club 139
Bush Hill Park Ratepayers' Association 61
Business Talk 223
Butler, Claire 156
Bycullah estate 46, 60
Bycullah Road 177
Byrne, Andrew 45

Cairo Nursery 49
Cambridge Preservation Society 10
Canada Life Assurance Company 204
Canada Life House, Potters Bar 204
Cannon Cinema 246, 255, 258
Canonbury Cottages 144
Canonbury Road 144
Capel estate 84
Capel House, now Capel Manor 101, 268
Capel Manor Centre 156, 213, 214, 240-244
Capel Manor stables 239-241
Carrs Basin 162
Carrs Lane 139
Carter, Valerie 51, 52, 80, 97, 168, 170, 206, 217, 227

Carterhatch Lane 82, 83, 146, 155, 192
casual wards 19, 21
Cat Hill, Southgate 231
Catholic Church, London Road 203
Cattlegate Road 69, 129, 179
Cavell Drive 115
Cecil Road 32, 36, 37, 90-92, 95, 115, 177, 199, 245, 246, 260-261
Chadwell Springs, Herts 160
Chapel of Rest 198
Chapel Street 88, 90, 198
Charter Day *24*
Chase Farm Home. See Chase Farm Hospital
Chase Farm Hospital 69, 173, 182, 231
Chase Green 7, 9, 10, 11, 17, *18*, 27, 57, 178, 179, 184, 275
Chase Green Avenue 9, 179
Chase Green Gardens 77
Chase Non-Ferrous Metals 49, 101
Chase Side 18, 21, 27, 57, 77, 90, 110, 122, 124
Chase Side House 15
Chase Side Place 18
Cheshunt 51, 131, 137, 160, 168, 247, 271
Cheshunt Council 43, 135
Chicken Shed 228
Chipperfield Press *93*
Christ Church, Chase Side 9, 23, 204
Church Lane 32, 97, 98
Church School of Industry 116
Church Street 15, 18, 23, 32, 36, 39, 77, 80, 90-92, 111, 112, 199, 202, 247, 248-251, 259-261
  EPS shops survey 124
Churchbury Lane 18, 32, 116, 144
Churchyards Handbook, The 97
City of London 42, 43
City of London Corporation 43
Civic Amenities Act, 1967 53, 63, 147
Civic Trust 26, 27, 41, 53, 79, 100, 114, 130, 143, 152, 170, 174, 198, 204, 275, 277
Clarke, T. H. M. 11
Clay Hill 71, 82, 101, 126, 191
Clock House, Forty Hill 18, 51
Collier, H. H. 12, 162
Colonel's Walk 104
Commons, Open Spaces and Footpaths Preservation Society 129
Connolly, Doris 208
Conservation Advisory Group 63, 177, 234, 273
Conservation Area Study Groups
  Bush Hill Park 61
  Eastern Enfield 61, 153, 273
  Enfield Town 57, 122, 273
  Forty Hill & Bulls Cross 57, 67, 83, 150, 213
  Gentleman's Row 53, 264
  Trent Park Conservation Group 60, 273
conservation areas 53, 98, 194, 251, 255
  Bush Hill Park 61
  Clay Hill 57
  Enfield Lock 61, 153
  Enfield Town 55, 57, 77, 87, 88, 111, 117, 162, 247, 249
  Forty Hill 57, 213
  Gentleman's Row 55
  Hadley Wood 193
  Highlands 231
  Ponders End 61
  Trent Park 59, 60
  Turkey Street 61
Conway, Councillor David 217, 220
Cook, Alderman Bill 109
Cooks Hole Road 150
Coopers Lane Road 129, 144, 146, 150
Coppermills Reservoir, Waltham Forest 168, 169
Cottage Place, Forty Hill *103, 104*
Cottenham, Councillor John *25*
Cotton, Albert 158
Council for the Protection of Rural England 23, 220, 275
Countryside Commission 187, 214
Course, Councillor Richard 222, 230, 236, 261
Crescent Road 193
Crews Hill 7, 49, 64, 71, 73, 129, 135
  green belt status 223-224
  garden centres 222-223
  nurseries 69-73
Crews Hill Golf Club 150
Crews Hill golf course 65, 66
Crews Hill Residents' Association 70, 71, 136, 190, 224
Crews Hill Station 72
Cricketers, The 18
Crofton Way 74
Crosland, Anthony 73
Crossman, Richard 38, 51
Crown & Horseshoes, The 18, 53, 55, 117
Crown Road 192
Cuffley 129, 131, 132
Cunneen, Councillor F. C. 126

D-Ring orbital road. *See* M25
Dabbs, S. J. 17, 22
Daily Telegraph 39, 44
Daisley, Revd Geoffrey 9, 10, 11, 12, 14, 15, 23
Daniell, Tim Tyndale 43, 44
Dartford tunnel 213
Data Connection 247
Daultry, Councillor Ron 38
Davies, Bryan, MP 88
Day, Wilfrid 91, 189
Defend Enfield's Green Belt Campaign 71-73, 109
Dell, The, Forty Hill 49, 50, 70, 75
Desirable Neighbourhood, A 207
Diocesan Advisory Committee 98
Dollery, Hilda 153, 154
Donald Insall Associates 229
Donaldsons planning consultants 259-261
Dorrington, Beryl 198, 250, 251
Dowbiggin, Dr Steven 241
Down your way programme 49
Duke of Abercorn, public house *94*
Duke of Lancaster Coffee Tavern 116
Dunraven Drive 74

Eagles, E. M. 12
East Lodge Lane 69, 150
Eaton Road 31
Edmonton, Borough of 86, 130, 182, 186, 278
Edmonton Borough Council 146
Edmonton Camera Club 102
Edmonton UDC 239
Edmonton Council of Churches 150
Edmonton Green 92, 273
Edmonton Hundred Historical Society 63, 159, 206, 217, 229, 271
Edmonton Military Hospital. *See* Grovelands House
Edmonton Town Hall 87, 116, 238, 239
Edmonton Vestry 238
EEC 79, 100
Eggar, Tim, MP 119, 123, 124, 157, 166, 189, 190, 217, 250, 251, 275
Elsynge House 243
Elvidge, Alderman Peter 102
Embroiderers' Guild 269
Emsden, Councillor Amy 179

Enfield & District Guides Association 150
Enfield & District Manufacturers' Association 172
Enfield & District Scouts Association *21*, 150
Enfield Advertiser 122, 160, 201, 218, 219, 220, 229, 230, 235, 239, 246, 248, 251, 255, 261
Enfield Archaeological Society 102, 217, 229
Enfield Book, The 209
Enfield Borough Council
  first meeting *25*
  presentation of Charter *25*
  Supplementary Town Map 31-40
Enfield Camera Club 102, 206
Enfield Chamber of Commerce 11, 14, 17, 29, 31, 247
Enfield Chase 9, 10, 64, 67, 69, 117, 181, 215
Enfield Chase railway yard 124
Enfield Chase, The Story of 206
Enfield Civic Centre 18, 72, 86, 95, 96, 104, 160, 161, 177, 263
  demonstration 217
  EPS meetings 159, 168, 209, 218, 221, 246
Enfield Collegiate School *26*
Enfield Community Care Trust 224, 225
Enfield Conservation Volunteers 187
Enfield Countryside Action Group 220, 222, 273
Enfield County School 250
Enfield Court. *See* Enfield Grammar (Lower) School
Enfield Crematorium 70, 75
Enfield District Health Authority 114, 122-124, 231, 233
Enfield District Manufacturers' Association 11
Enfield Gazette
  1935-1945 9, 14, 64, 82, 171, 172, 242
  1946-1976 26, 33, 34, 35, 39, 40, 43, 46, 49, 50, 55, 67, 69, 70, 72, 74, 77, 78, 80, 83, 86, 87, 90, 106, 109, 126, 129, 131, 139, 144, 146, 147, 174, 177, 178, 196
  1977-1996 45, 81, 91, 92, 95, 113, 115, 116, 124, 135, 157, 166, 168, 181, 183, 189, 190, 191, 204, 212, 216, 217, 220, 224, 227, 229, 230, 231, 247, 249, 251, 258, 261
Enfield Grammar (Lower) School 52
Enfield Grammar School 7, 32, 250, 268
Enfield Herald & Post 217
Enfield Highway 42
Enfield House. *See* St Michael's Hospital
Enfield in Bloom 201-203, 210, 273
Enfield Independent 112, 115, 119, 120, 181, 190, 198, 219, 220, 224, 227, 233, 236, 243, 255
Enfield Lock 81, 152-155, 176, 208, 236, 238
Enfield Lock Residents' Association 154, 176
Enfield Lock Village Clean-up Campaign 154
Enfield Lock Village Fair 273
Enfield, London Borough of
  Arts Council 273
  Borough Development Plan 69, 111, 245
  competitive tendering 185
  Enfield Town Action Area Plan 95, 96
  formation 86
  Inset Plan 245-247, 255, 260
  Local Agenda 21, 270, 273
  Unitary Development Plan 193, 194, 247, 252
Enfield Market 71, 179
Enfield Natural History Society 217
Enfield North Liberal Association 204
Enfield Observer 233
Enfield Palace 174
Enfield Park Ranger Service 140
Enfield Police Station 115
Enfield Preservation Society
  aims and objects 12, 14, 27, 263, 278
  annual dinner 46, 77, 80, 83, 91, 95, 105, 112, 276
  architecture and planning group 46
  anti-litter group 198
  charity registration 105
  exhibitions 102, 156, 268
  first council of management 12
  first postwar meeting 23
  footpaths group 46, 129
  footpath map 129
  formation 10-12
  groups, formation of 46, 124, 129
  historic buildings group 46
  membership numbers 18, 27, 29, 37, 46, 105, 204, 271
  membership subscription 12, 23, 26, 157, 271
  name 14, 55-57, 105-106, 277
  newsletter distribution 109, 208-209
  newsletter, first 46
    change of editor 52
  registration as a limited company 12
  trees group 46
  trees sub-committee 172
  Young EPS 209-210
Enfield Ratepayers' Associations 38
Enfield Residents' Association 15
Enfield Show. *See* Town Show
Enfield Society, The 27, 29
Enfield Sports Advisory Council 217
Enfield Town, A walk around 55, 122
Enfield Town Hall 9-10, 15-18, 33. *See also* Enfield Civic Centre
Enfield Town Station 176
Enfield Urban District Council 162
  green belt 64-66
  Town Plan 9, 18
Enfield (St Andrew's) Vicarage *77*
Enfield Weekly Herald 21, 29, 39, 49, 51, 53, 73, 75, 79, 83, 91, 95, 98, 110, 111, 112, 131, 139, 140, 147, 173, 178, 180, 198
Enfield-Southgate Conservative Association 109
Enfield's Architectural Heritage 102, 206
Englemann, Franklin 49
English Heritage 45, 192, 229, 230, 234, 236, 238, 242, 243
Environment Protection Act, 1992 201, 203
Errington, Bob 158
Essex Road 29, 57
European Architectural Heritage Year 100, 101
Eustance, Councillor Graham 217, 218, 219
Evans, Muriel 269
Eve, David Trustram 72
Evening News 50, 129
Evening Standard 39, 43, 230

Fairview Estates 74, 75, 238
Fairview Road 75

Fallow Buck, The 19
Family Leisure Ltd 251
Farmlands 75
Farringdon Street 43
Federation of Enfield Ratepayers' and Amenity Associations 107
Federation of Enfield Ratepayers' and Residents' Associations (FERRA) 49, 50, 77, 106, 107
Federation of Enfield Residents' and Allied Associations (FERAA) 61, 63, 70, 74, 92, 135, 190, 214, 217, 227, 228, 275
FERAA *See* Federation of Enfield Residents' and Allied Associations
Ferny Hill 214
FERRA *See* Federation of Enfield Ratepayers' and Residents' Associations
Fidler's Nursery 50
Fincken, A. C. 12
Finlay, James 143, 172
Fir Tree House 18, 96
Firs, The 101
First World War 125, 157, 238
Fisher, David 159
Flamstead End 51
Flash Lane 129, 137
footpaths 14, 46, 105, 125-141, 266, 275
Fore Street 116
Foresters Hall, Chase Side 90, 99
Forestry Commission 173
Forty Hall
  barns 239, 241-242
  estate 9, 11, 18, 126, 241, 242
  house and museum 101-2, 110, 124, 156, 208, 268
Forty Hall Farm 244
Forty Hall Park 57, 66-67, 69, 140, 143, 150, 173, 174, 176, 177, 216, 241, 243, 244
Forty Hall/Capel Manor Forum 273
Forty Hill 18, 27, 43, 51, 57, 75, 126, 130, 145, 168, 176
  traffic 82-84
Forty Hill Nursery 49
Forty Hill Primary School 187
Forty Hill Residents' Association 43
Forty Hill Vicarage 178
Friends of Enfield Museums 227
Friends of Theobalds 45
Frogmore Estates 255
Furncrafts 246
Further and Higher Education Act, 1992 241
Galliard Primary School 188
Gas Showrooms Lecture Hall 33
Gate Lodge Cottage *105*
Genn, Councillor Lionel 105
Genotin Road 32, 49, 90, 245, 246, 260
Gentleman's Row 26, 27, 42, 53, 88, 110, 117, 122, 194, 204, 208, 265
Gentleman's Row, Portrait of 122, 205-206
Gentleman's Row, River View and Holly Walk (GRH) Residents' Association 118, 120, 122
George, The 46, 80
Gilbert Street 50
Goat, The 126
Goffs Oak 132, 135
Goldsdown Road 174
Goldwater, Councillor Clive 227, 229
Gordon Hill 172, 191
Gough Park 43, 84, 126, 132, 139, 140, 150, 156, 162
Gough Park Cottage 176, 271
Government Row 61, 155
Gowers, Robert 23, 46, 271
Graham of Edmonton, Lord 38, 39, 40, 119, 130, 135, 166, 169, 181, 273
Grange Park 63, 125, 130
Grange Park Primary School 178
Grant, Harold 275
Great Cambridge Road (A10) 50, 70, 75, 80, 81, 82, 83, 84, 90, 111, 130, 74, 177, 213, 247, 251-254, 258
  A10 subways 210
Greater London Council 39, 50, 60, 68, 69, 77, 80, 81, 90, 111-113, 132, 133, 134, 139, 174, 180-181, 189, 190, 214, 215, 221, 231, 265
  abolition 113
  Land Agency 131
Greater London Development Plan 95
Greater London Industrial Archaeological Society 168
green belt 35, 49, 64-75, 78, 105, 111, 112, 126, 129, 130, 131, 147, 180, 189-191, 193, 194, 204, 212-225, 255, 275
  Green Belt Forum 273
  'right to buy' 214-215
Green Belt (London & Home Counties) Act 1938 214
Green Street 174
Greenwood, Anthony 39
Gresswell, Don 27, 46, 47, 49, 50, 78, 110, 124-133, 139, 142-144, 147, 148, 152-155, 157, 166, 196
Gresswell, Eileen 158
Greyhound, The 155
Groundforce 140, 271
Grovelands House 113, 114
Grovelands Park 63
Grovelands Priory Hospital. *See* Grovelands House
Groves, Godfrey 53, 94, 109, 110, 158
Guardian, The 50
Gummer, John 236
Gunpowder Factory 23
Guy Lodge Farm 220, 221

H. A. Hooper, mobile grocer 32
Hackney 160
Hackney Council 166, 168
Hadley Road 64, 74, 133, 148, 214, 224, 265
Hadley Wood 130, 132, 214
Halifax Building Society 92
Hallam, Saskia 275
Halliwick School 63
Hallside Road 83
Hamburger Halt 209
Hammond opticians 246
Hannah, John 67, 68, 150, 177
Haringey 169
Haringey Council 70, 73, 75, 166, 168
Harlow 212
Harrington, Illtyd 189
Harris of High Cross, Lord 212
Hatch , J. W., & Son *93*
Hay, Roy 202-203
Heavy Lorries (1970) 79
Henley, H. P. 139
Heritage Challenge Trophy 102
Heritage Lottery Fund 270
Hertford 132
Hertford Road 27, 50, 81, 173, 174, 177, 194
Hertfordshire Society 46
Heseltine, Michael 119, 120
High Oaks 178
Highlands Hospital 122, 124, 224, 225, 231-236, 237
Highlands Village 234, 235, 236
Highways Act, 1959 131
Hill, Mahala 49
Hills, Sydney 27, 42, 50, 92, 94, 106, 107, 135, 137
Hilly Fields Park 66-67, 131, 173, 184
Hinds, Kevin 122
Historic Buildings and Monuments Commission 44

History of Enfield (Cuthbert Whitaker) 47, 206
Hoddesdon 261
Hollington, A. J. 18
Holly Hill Farm 129, 133, 139, 189
Holly Walk 39
Hook, John 71
Hornsey 168
Hornsey reservoir 170
Horses and Ponies Protection Association 240-243
House of Commons 157, 168, 181, 251
Housing Acts, 1980, 1987 214
Howard, Sir Seymour *24*
Hoy, Denis 212-3
Humberts (Leisure) Estate Agency 217, 219, 220
Hundred Acres Charity 97, 98
Hymas, Frederick 139
Hymas, Sophie 173

Illustrated London News 105
Ingleborough, Cavell Drive 115
Inner Ring Road 32-40
  map 34
Institute of Economic Affairs 212
International Flavors and Fragrances 172
Inverness Avenue 145
Islington 168
Issitt, Bill 120, 124, 190, 231, 265-266

Jackson, Councillor John 191, 219, 221, 222, 238, 276
Jarvis, Councillor Fred 87
Jarvis, Rupert 48, 49
Jenkin, Patrick 214
Jephcott, Dr Christopher 46, 72, 73, 76, 79, 80, 84, 92, 94, 95, 96, 98, 104, 105, 111, 126, 143, 172, 174, 177, 178, 182, 189, 192-194, 196, 198, 224, 231-236, 238, 240, 246, 247, 249, 252, 255, 258, 259-261, 265, 266
Jesus Church, Forty Hill 18
Jesus Church Scouts 101
Jewell, Martin 61, 222, 237, 246, 266, 277-278
Johns, R. Harvey 42
Jolly Farmers, The 147
Joseph, Sir Keith 49
Jubilee Footpath 139
Jubilee Hall 125, 184
  meetings 158-9, 217, 222, 271
  refurbishment 125, 157-8

Keeble, Len 44, 113, 116, 120, 157, 158, 228, 229, 230, 236, 239
Keep Britain Tidy Group 155, 198
Keep Enfield Tidy Group 198, 273
Keighley, Dennis 95
Kenilworth Crescent 145
Kennet, Lord 33
Kenny, Bob 173
King & Tinker, The 140
King George V Playing Field 258
Kingswood Nursery 213
Koch, Revd E. H. A. 12, 18

Ladly, Frank 38, 77, 132, 150
Ladysmith Road 46, 183
Laings Garage *93*
Lambert, Prue 198, 209
Lancaster, Duchy of 64, 65
Lane, Carinthia Arbuthnot 23, 26, 33, 36, 39, 40, 46, 49, 106, 271
Lane, Major Clayton (Tony) Arbuthnot 26, 49, 67, 71, 72, 83, 107, 108
Langham Playing Field 192
Lanscroon, Gerard 226
Latymer School 150, 210
Laurels, The 117
Lavender Hill 51, 150, 172
Lea, River 23
Lea Valley 50, 130
Lee Enfield rifle 236
Lee Valley Park 130
Lee Valley Regional Park Authority 43, 155
Legal & General Assurance Society 43
Legal & General Insurance Society 91
Leggatt, Dudley 9, 10, 12
Lennox, Audrey 106, 168
Lewis, Councillor Barry 66, 67
Library Green 7, 15, 17, 18, 21, 29, 31, 92, 94, 95, 111, 199, 202, 260, 275
Lindsay, Alderman John 90
listed building plaques 49, 101, 122, 271
litter clearance 46, 99, 125, 142-155, 203, 210, 266, 271
Little Gate 210
Little, John 264, 266
Little Park Gardens 32, 90
Little Park, Gentleman's Row 9, 10, 110
Little Pipers, Clay Hill 48
Livingstone, Ken 112

Local Government (Access to Information) Act, 1985 263
Local Government Act, 1974 263
London and Middlesex Archaeological Society 48
London Forum 273
London Green Belt Council 212-213, 214, 273, 277
London Planning Advisory Council 215
London Road 31, 90, 91, 115, 178, 203, 246
London Road & District Residents' Association 250
London Topographical Society Newsletter, The 207
London Tree Forum 187
London Weather Centre 178
London Wildlife Trust 217
lorry routes, designated 80
Lowen, Priscilla 267
Lowen, Stan 124, 166
Lynch, Roger 247

M11 213
M25 81, 84, 111, 132, 155, 189, 213, 235
MacDonald, Brian 162
Mackenzie, Alderman Ernest 173
Mackie, John, MP 130, 131
Mackmurdo, A. H. 101
Maidens Bridge 57, 75, 82-85, 130, 140, 168
Maidens Bridge schoolroom 101
Mandeville Gate 252
Market Place 11, 27, 36,39, 247, 271
Marks & Spencer 29, 95, 247
Mason, Councillor David 220
Mason, John 219
Matthey, Johnson 174
Maunder, Gertrude (Trudy) 71, 267
McAndrew, Brian 216
McBreaty, Councillor 81
Medcalf, Colonel Sydney 12, 240
Meridian Way. *See* North/South Road
Merryhills School 178
Metropolitan Water Board 148, 162, 166
Meux, Sir Hedworth 43
Meux, Sir Henry Bruce 43
Meux Trust 44
Middle Temple Lane 44
Middlesex County Council 11, 17, 19, 21, 33, 35, 64, 65, 130, 132, 174, 194
Middlesex University 229, 230, 231

Mile-and-a-Quarter Alley 132, 140
Millennium Commission 45
Millfield House 114, 238
Mills, Stuart 69, 133, 135, 137, 192
Ministry of Agriculture 147
Mollison Avenue. *See* North/ South Road
Moore Stephens 268
Morgan, Revd Peter 97
Muldoon, W. J. 11
Museum Steering Group 273
Muspratt, Horace 12
Mussett, Frances 168, 170, 186-188
Myddelton Avenue 82, 144
Myddelton House 162, 171
Myddelton House Gardens Advisory Group 273
Myddelton, Sir Hugh 160

Nags Head Road 80
Nairn, Ian 39
Napley, Sir David 36, 39
Nash, John 114
Nathan, Ronald 258
Nature Conservancy Council 215
Naybur Garden Centre 204
Naylor, Robert 123
Nazeing 131
Nellis, Councillor Frank 124, 246
Neville, Councillor Terence 220, 221, 251
New River 7, 63, 117, 126, 160, 162, 204, 275
New River Action Group 152, 160, 168, 273
New River Company 162
New River Head 162
New River Loop 18, 32, 55, 77, 150, 160-170, 171, 247, 275
EPS survey 162-166
renovation project 269-270
New River Path 170
Nicholas, A. C., Ltd 74, 75, 118-122
Nicholas, Andrew 120
North Circular Road 80, 81, 238
North Enfield Ratepayers' Association 37, 70, 83, 145
North Middlesex Hospital 19, 21
North, Sir George 251
North/South Road 81, 82
Northaw 131, 132
Northern Hospital 233
Norwich Union Insurance Group 91, 258

Oak Avenue 178
Oaks, The 224, 225
Oakthorpe Junior School 210
Oakwood 132
Observer Weekend Review 39
Oddfellows Hall 9, 12
Old Bakery, Forty Hill 273
Old Park Avenue 9, 31, 77, 139, 177
Old Park Ridings 139
Old Vestry Offices 23
Orchard Road 180
Ordnance Road 82
Oscar, Henry 46

Palace Gardens shopping precinct 32, 33, 90-96, 210, 247, 258
Palace Mews *93*
Palmer, William 36, 37, 46, 55, 76
Palmers Green 117, 226
Pam, David 158, 206-207, 212
Parish near London, A 207
Parker Bowles family 126
Parkinson, Cecil, MP 43
Parkside Coach House 214
Parkside Farm 133, 135
Parkside House 214
Parsonage Gardens 18
Parsonage Lane 52, 125, 184, 187
Paternoster Square. *See* St Paul's Cathedral
Payne, Councillor John 134
Peachey, Ronald 172
Peacock Cottage *113*
Peake, H. Deryck 31, 32, 34, 36, 78
Pearsons Ltd 91, 174
Pembroke Avenue 184
Pennine Way 132
Percival, Arthur 276
Perry, Frances 172, 202
Perryman, Councillor Peter 91, 206
Phillips of London 110
Pickfords 252
Pika Print *93*
Platten, Cyril 27
Plenicar, Dusan *93*
Plough, The, Crews Hill 69
Pluckett, Charles 44
Pointer, Colin 170, 230, 222, 224, 241, 269, 270
Ponders End 176, 180, 208, 255
Ponders End Ratepayers' Association 146
Ponders End Residents' Association 179
Portcullis Lodge 52, 87, 88
Portillo, Michael, MP 168, 222, 235, 251
Potter, Daphne 204
Potter, Donald 27, 33, 41, 77, 118, 120, 121, 122, 125, 172, 177, 204-205
Potter, Kathleen 204
Potters Bar 81, 111, 131
Potters Bar Society 129, 136
Potter's Wood 205
Powell, Ken 227
Pride in Place 156
Private Road 101, 177
Public Health Act, 1931 215
public inquiries 17, 34, 36, 37, 38, 39, 42, 44, 49, 51, 52, 71-73, 74, 75, 79, 81, 90, 92, 111, 118, 120, 121, 124, 137, 192, 204, 213, 214, 224, 250, 258
Public Offices (now the Register Office) 194

Quakers Walk 177
Queen Anne's Gardens 192
Queen Mother 86
Queens Road 193

Radcliffe Road 192
Radio London 79
RAGE. *See* Residents Against Gaming in Enfield.
Ragg's chemist, Edmonton 273
Raleigh Road 57, 245
Ramblers' Association 129, 132, 136, 137, 217
Rank Leisure 248-251
Rayment, Councillor Ernest *28*
Rectory Farm 131, 182, 216, 218, 220
Redlingtons 101
Redmond Mullin Ltd 230
Reed, Councillor John 156
Rees, Revd Ebenezer 9, 10, 12, 23, 26, 41, 109, 173
Rendelsham Viaduct 131
Repton, Humphry 59, 60
Requisitioned Land and War Work Act 1945 147
Residents Against Gambling in Golders Green 251
Residents Against Gaming in Enfield. 250
Reynolds, Fiona 275
Richie, Revd, vicar of St James's 42
Ride, The, Ponders End 178
Ridge, Dr Eric 37, 105
Ridgeway Farm 22
Ridgeway, The 68, 80, 115, 129, 133, 178, 182, 204, 224
developments on 104

golf course 216, 220
green belt 64-66, 71, 74-75
militia camp, 22
traffic 111
tree felling 67, 68, 177, 178, 265
Ridley, Nicholas 212, 214
Ringway 3. *See* M25
Ripaults 192
Rippon, Geoffrey 70, 74
River View 53
Road Haulage Association 79
roads and traffic
Enfield Town 29-40, 76, 77
Enfield Town bus lane 111-112
Forty Hill 82-84
lorry routes 79-81
Windmill Hill 31, 76, 78
Rochford Nursery 49, 50
Rodin, Councillor Jeff 222, 230, 275
Rosewood 73
Rosewood Drive 69
Rotary Club of Enfield 10, 11, 242
Rowlandson, Sir Graham 77
Royal Fine Arts Commission 118
Royal Ordnance plc 237
Royal Scottish Museum, Edinburgh 239
Royal Small Arms Factory 23, 152, 236-238
Royal Small Arms Tavern 152
RSPB 72
Ruberoid Ltd 192

Sadlers Mill Stream 165
Sadler's Wells 162
Sadler's Wells Theatre 168
Safeway Superstore 252, 255
Sainsbury, J. 192, 251, 255
Sainsbury, J. Waring 39
Salisbury House 239, 268
Sandys, Duncan, MP 26, 53
Sarnesfield Road 92, 94
Sassoon family 132
Sassoon, Sir Philip 12
Saunders, Matthew 269, 273
Save Britain's Heritage 227
Save Enfield Campaign 35-40, 42, 46, 47, 96, 109, 264, 271
Save Temple Bar Campaign 45
Save Whitewebbs Campaign 217-220, 263
Schlumberger factory 251
Scott, W. Gilbee 116
Sealed Knot 243
Second World War 29, 129, 142, 226
preparations 21-23
Shewring, John P. 12, 23
Silver Street, Edmonton 238
Silver Street, Enfield Town 18, 33, 77, 86, 101, 109, 115, 116
Silver Studio Collection 229, 231
Silverdale,Silver Street 18
Sketty Road 182
Skilton, Alan 38, 102, 112, 126 157, 206, 268
Slades Hill 77, 150
anti-aircraft gun site 147
Smith, Chris, MP 169
Smith, Denis 168
Smith, Eric 158
Smith, Irene 97, 98, 99, 121, 122, 156, 157, 188, 206, 214, 217, 219, 243, 248, 250, 266-267, 278
Smith, Ronald 277
Smith, Stanley 156, 158, 188, 208, 263
Smith's Nursery 50
Smythe, Councillor Rita 87
Smythe, Councillor Eric 235
Society for the Protection of Ancient Buildings 44, 47, 63, 273
Somerset, Sir Alfred 52
South East Study,1961-1981, The, 49
South Lodge Hospital 231, 235
Southbury Road 80, 90, 91, 111, 162, 166, 172, 177, 193, 246, 252, 255
Southbury Road swimming pool 258
Southbury Station 176
Southgate Borough Council 146, 264
Southgate, Borough of 86, 182, 247
Southgate Civic Trust 63, 114, 168, 229, 231, 234, 278
Southgate District Civic Trust 106
Southgate Photographic Society 102
Southgate Town Hall 87, 227
Southgate Urban District Council 226
St Andrew's Church 7, 11, 32, 39, 99, 109, 198
St Andrew's Churchyard 36, 7, 129, 200, 273
removal of tombs 96-99
St Andrew's Churchyard committee 97-98
St Andrew's Parish Centre 99, 109
St Andrew's PCC 97-99
St Andrew's Road 32, 163
St Andrew's Vicarage 18, 77, 101
St Faith's Cottage, Brigadier Hill 48
St James's Vicarage, Enfield Highway 42, 177
St John's Church, Clay Hill 18, 57, 71, 72
St Michael's Green 122-124, 225
St Michael's Hospital 21, 122, 225
St Paul's Cathedral 43, 44, 45
St Paul's Church, Enfield 247
Stacey, Councillor Richard 198
Stacey, Douglas 178, 182
Standard Life Assurance Company 258
Stansted Airport 213
Stockingswater Lane 174
Stoke Newington 168
Stoke Newington reservoir, Green Lanes 162, 170
Stonard, Norman 38, 57, 63, 69, 70, 72, 96, 118, 120, 264, 265, 266
Stratton Avenue 57
Strayfield Road 150
Sunley plc 220
Swan & Pike pool 153, 154
Sydney Road 33, 57, 90-92, 245, 246, 260
Sykes, Robert Dugdale 29, 176, 271

Tansley, Kenneth 12
Temple Bar 42-46
Temple Bar Trust 44
Tesco 91, 247, 255, 258
Thacker, Councillor Audrey 250, 251
Thames Water Authority, now Thames Water plc 160, 165, 166-170, 190, 270
Thames Water News 169
Theobalds House 45, 240, 241
Theobalds Park 43, 44, 45, 126, 241
Theobalds Park College. *See* Theobalds House
Theobalds Park Estate 135
Theobalds Park Road 137, 222, 223
Thorn Electrical Industries 174
Thorn EMI 252
Times, The 50, 132
Tingey's Tops Pond, Crews Hill 150
Toop, Dr B. M. 12, 23
Tottenham Church 110
Tottenham Hale 81

Tottenham Hotspur Football Club 110
Town and Country Amenities Act 1974 63
Town Park 15, 29, 110, 160, 162, 163, 166, 172, 184, 246, 273
Town Show 109, 129, 173, 217. *See also* Autumn Show
Townhouse, The 203, 246
Trafalgar House plc 238
trees
  loss of 46, 59, 67, 172, 174, 176-188, 231
  planting 46, 150, 154, 200, 266, 275
Trent Park 7, 60, 69, 75, 132, 133, 147, 189, 208, 214, 268
Trent Park College 59
Trent Park Show 217, 273
Treweek, Donald 87, 196, 198
Trinity College Cambridge 64, 65
Trustee Savings Bank 246
Tudor Room 10, 27, 110, 172
Turkey Brook 50, 143, 150, 154
Turkey Street 49, 61, 83, 130
Turkey, The 61
Turnford 72
Twells, Phillip, MP 15
Twinn, Dr Ian, MP 251
Tyme, John 80

Upper Edmonton Shopping Centre 255
Uvedale, Dr 174

vagrants 19, 21
Vanderpump & Sykes 23, 271
Vanderpump, Frank 11, 12, 23, 271
Venning, Philip 273
Vicarage Farm 22, 220
Victorian fountain, Enfield Town 42, 112
Victorian Suburb, A 207
Village Road 177

Waggon Road 224
Waldegrave, William 214
Waltham Abbey 271
Waltham Cottage 51
Waltham Cross 72, 92, 247, 261
War Memorial Hospital 122, 225
War Weapons Week 23
Ware 130, 168
Warwick Field 176
Wates, builders 69-73
Watts, Sir Roy 166, 168
Waverley Road 193
Webster, Anthony 120, 122
Webster, Susan 122
Wellington Road 177
Westmacott, Kathleen 117, 118
Westwood Cottage 110
Wheathampstead 204
Whitaker, Cuthbert 47
Whitbread plc 220, 231
White Lodge, Silver Street 18, 49, 208
Whitewebbs Golf Club 217, 218
Whitewebbs golf course 215-220
Whitewebbs House 48, 215, 216, 217, 219, 220
Whitewebbs Lane 78, 130, 140, 150, 190, 215, 220
Whitewebbs Park 66-67, 69, 126, 132, 140, 143, 162, 173, 184, 217, 218
Whitewebbs Road 78, 179, 216, 223
Whitewebbs (Wilkinson's) Wood 132, 215
Whitman, Michael 135
Wildlife and Countryside Bill 135, 181
Wildwoods 129
Wilkinson, Dr Abraham 215
Williams, Reginald 205-206
Willow estate 7
Willow Residents' Association 83
Willow Road 83, 255
Winchmore Hill 192, 204, 236
Windmill Hill 18, 77, 80, 177, 261
Windmill Theatre 46
Winnington Road 130
Wiseman, Ambrose 12, 162, 171, 172
Woldens Nursery 69
Wolverton 224, 225
Women's Institute 72, 101
Wontner, Sir Hugh 44
Wood Green 92, 126, 170
Wood Green Crown Court 250
Wood, Kingsley 17
Wood Well 137
Woodfield, Stanley 11
Woodfield, Walter (Wally) 81, 158, 182, 184, 189, 212, 266
Woollett, Peter 132
Woolworth's Ltd 90, 245
Wortley, Councillor Stephen 222
Wright, Councillor Charles 49
Wright's Flour Mill 61

Yates, Councillor John 222, 224
York Terrace 176
Young, Councillor Alan 86
Young, Sir George 220
Youth Opportunities Programme 140, 143

Zucker, Judge Kenneth, QC 250

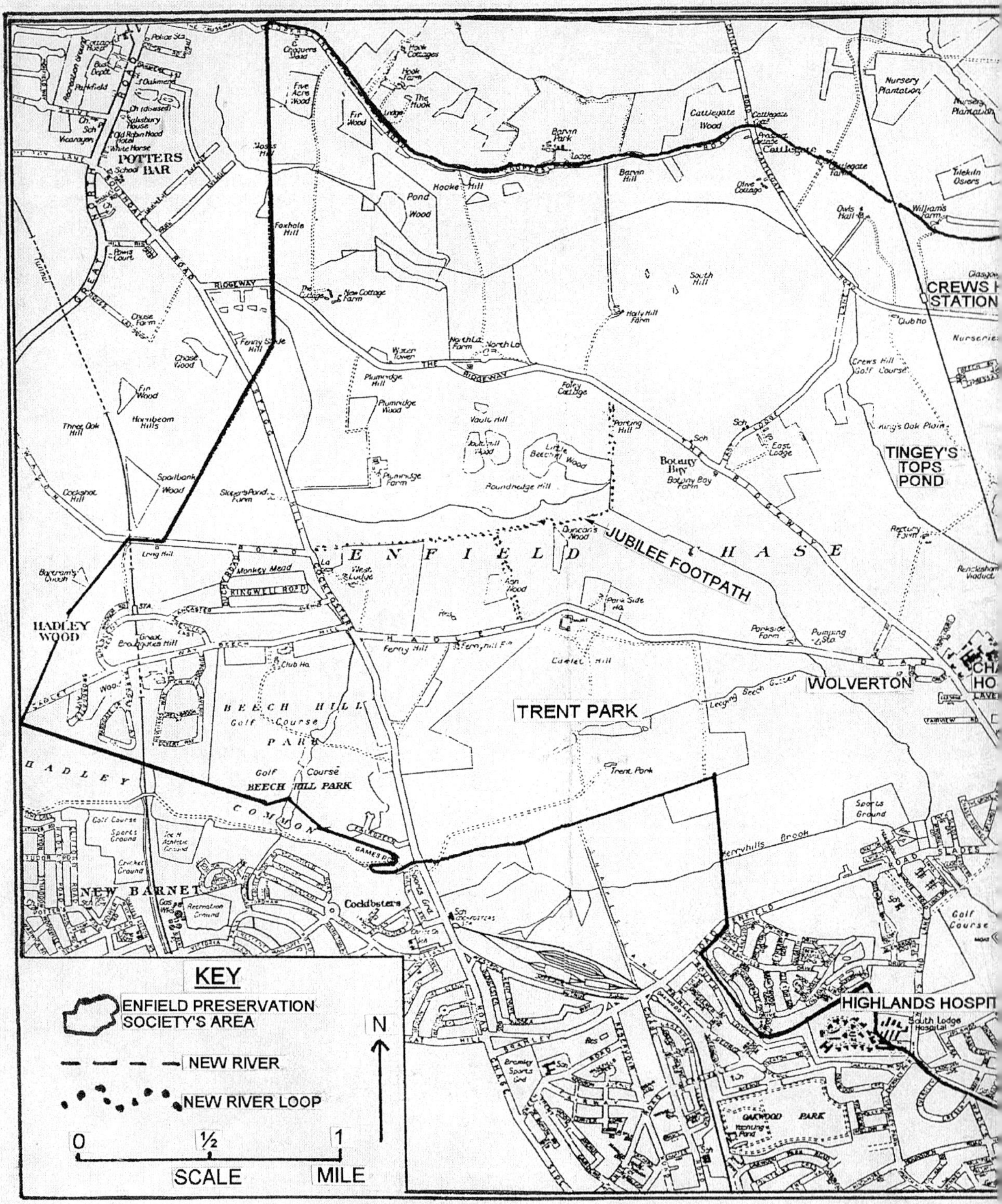
KEY
ENFIELD PRESERVATION SOCIETY'S AREA
NEW RIVER
NEW RIVER LOOP
N
0
½
1
SCALE
MILE
POTTERS BAR
HADLEY WOOD
NEW BARNET
ENFIELD CHASE
JUBILEE FOOTPATH
TRENT PARK
WOLVERTON
TINGEY'S TOPS POND
HIGHLANDS HOSPIT
BEECH HILL PARK
HADLEY COMMON
OAKWOOD PARK
Cattlegate
Cockfosters
THE RIDGEWAY
Botany Bay